MILITANT

RESURRECTING AUTHENTIC CATHOLICISM

Michael Voris, S.T.B.

St. Michael's Media Publishing

For permission requests, write to:

St. Michael's Media Publishing
2840 Hilton Road
Ferndale, MI 48220

www.ChurchMilitant.com

Printed in the United States of America

ISBN 978-0-9969150-0-7

First Edition

15 / 1

Today the phrase ecclesia militans *["Church Militant"] is somewhat out of fashion, but in fact we can understand ever more so that it is true, that it contains within it the truth. We see how evil wishes to dominate in the world and that it is necessary to fight against evil.* ~Pope Benedict, 2012

This work is dedicated to my two mothers: my biological mother, Anne Josephine, who prayed her son back into the Faith, and my Heavenly Mother, to whom my mom would always say: "Wrap your mantle around him, Blessed Mother."

Contents

ACKNOWLEDGMENTS   i

PROLOGUE   v

INTRODUCTION   xiii

1   THE CHURCH MILITANT:
The Barque of Peter   1

2   THE UNIQUE CRISIS:
Unrecognized Disaster   13

3   THE STORM BREAKS:
The 1960s   19

4   WHAT HAPPENED?
Martin Luther Plants the Seed   25

5   THE AMERICAN PETRI DISH:
Luther's Liberty   31

6   FEMINIST MEN:
The Church of Nice Is Born   43

7   BORROWING FROM THE CULTURE:
Father Theodore Hesburgh   59

8   THE BERNARDIN MACHINE:
Plowing the Faith Under   65

9   AMERICAN BISHOPS FOR AN AMERICAN CHURCH:
Four Types   75

10 THE FEMINIZED HIERARCHY:
Masculinity Abandoned   105

11 THE MUSTARD SEED:
Unless a Grain of Wheat Falls into the Earth   109

12 THE CHURCH OF NICE:
Never Giving Offense   117

13 REASONABLE HOPE THAT ALL MEN ARE SAVED:
Not!   125

14 CATHOLIC MORALITY ABANDONED:
The Consequences   149

15 REVOLUTION:
The War over Catholic Identity   155

16 THE NEW EVANGELIZATION:
Without the Evangelizing   175

17 THE PROBLEM OF CATHOLIC IDENTITY:
A Thoroughly Catholic Solution   181

18 THE CHURCH OF NICE:
Nice vs. Charitable   187

19 THE CHURCH OF NICE:
Satanic   189

20 THE CHURCH OF NICE:
It Brings Damnation   201

21 A CHOSEN PEOPLE, A HOLY NATION:
Our Manifest Destiny   207

ACKNOWLEDGMENTS

In my time away from the Church, my father and mother prayed for me incessantly to return to the faith of my early childhood. Eventually my mother sacrificed her life for this singular goal, praying in near desperation one day after years of what she saw as unanswered prayers, "Jesus, I don't care what you do to me. Do whatever you have to do, but spare the eternal lives of my two sons." A couple of weeks later she was diagnosed with stomach cancer, which had been discovered by accident. She would die of that cancer after three years of great suffering.

This was the beginning of the apostolate, although it was not clear to me at all at that time. Eighteen months after my mother's death, with the strong encouragement and blessing of my father, I invested my life's savings (approximately $750,000) and went into an additional debt of another $100,000—a loan on which I had to default and was only able to pay back after seven years—to create St. Michael's Media. The goal was to create programming based on Catholic teaching to help show people the glory and necessity of the Catholic religion.

Other people have made substantial financial sacrifices to keep this apostolate able to function in the material world, and I wish to acknowledge them and their sacrifices, although I suspect they would prefer not to be acknowledged. In 2008, the Marc Brammer family in South Bend, Indiana took out a mortgage on their home for $250,000 to help establish what has come to be known as ChurchMilitant.com (formerly RealCatholicTV.com).

In 2012, John Carroll and his wife in Dallas, Texas gave us a donation of $200,000 so we could purchase what is right now our current studio facility in Ferndale, Michigan when the former space we were leasing was sold and we were threatened with displacement. Prior to 2012, they had made various smaller donations totaling close to an additional $70,000 over the course of two years.

Not a few people who have expressed the desire to remain anonymous have made singular donations of more than $10,000, and one individual a considerable deal more. These donations have been used to further expand our operations and keep up with the high-technology, high-cost tools needed to continue our daily work.

We must also acknowledge the many generous people who always respond to our various specific appeals each year for things like our PAUSE Program, our *All Things New Campaign*, our *Synod Coverage Appeal*, and the like.

And then, over the years, there are the numerous other benefactors from all over the world whose donations have totaled over half a million dollars. All the donations we have received always come with no strings attached, trusting we will be good stewards of their money as they have placed their confidence in us and the work we do here. There are the multiple people all over the world (over a dozen countries) who work very hard to arrange talks and conferences where we appear so that people local to them can find solace in their current spiritual sufferings.

Then there are, of course, the many thousands and thousands of subscribers we have who trust us and believe what we are doing here is God's work, as we believe it to be. We are daily indebted to them.

All of this is added to by the daily sacrifice of those who work here because they, too, accept the mission and the associated work. Almost forty people here, many of them aged thirty or younger, make manifold sacrifices in terms of days they make themselves available, long travel, late hours, and so forth. They do all this for low pay, no benefits, and no insurance because they are committed to the mission.

Besides the material-world contributions, of course, are the spiritual benefactors we have—religious brothers and sisters and priests, diocesan priests and, yes, even bishops and cardinals, who pray for our work here daily. We have hundreds of priests and seminarians from all over the world who keep our work in their daily prayers and Masses, and for this we are eternally in debt.

ChurchMilitant.com/St. Michael's Media began as one man's effort to try and do something to fight evil in the culture and the Church. It quickly became a spiritual team effort joined by thousands and thousands of souls all over the world daily who unite with us in this work through prayer, time, finances, and resolve to engage in spiritual warfare. Regardless of how it began, ChurchMilitant.com/St. Michael's Media now belongs to the Church.

We take very seriously our obligation to ensure that everything entrusted to us is not dispensed with lightly. That also places a responsibility on me personally as the head of the apostolate to ensure that all matters are handled in the most just and charitable fashion possible. You have my continuing pledge that that is, and will continue to be, the case. From the deepest recesses of my soul, I wish to express my gratitude to everyone who has helped us and continues to help us in our mission of advancing the glory of the Holy Catholic Church, in an effort to save souls and beat back the forces of confusion that have infected so many of Her members.

Even though it must be fought in part in the temporal world with the tools of the temporal world—which in the case of TV/Internet production are extraordinarily expensive—ultimately this is spiritual warfare waged on a spiritual level, and each Catholic worth his weight in salt must live this reality every day and conquer the ancient Enemy every day until our last breath. Thank you for trusting us, helping us, and encouraging us in our mission. God love you.

Michael Voris

PROLOGUE

I reverted to the Catholic faith of my childhood in 2004 following the death of my mother Anne (June 15, 2004) from an almost three-year battle with stomach cancer. Born in 1961, I was among the first generation of Catholics raised in what I've termed the "Church of Nice." From 1968–78, I was an altar boy and saw the various assaults against the Faith materialize, although obviously at the time I had no realization of what was going on inside the Church. I was, as were many Catholics of the time, a first-hand witness to the abuses being introduced into the liturgy—Holy Communion in the hand, for example, and guitar music (I was in a folk group when not serving).

Like so many others, I had no idea what was happening, but the clergy kept instructing *this* new thing had to be done and *that* novelty was happening next week and so forth. I recall with great clarity when the black-and-white surplice (standard altar boy garb) was replaced with the long, hooded albs with a rope around the waist. Next to go was the Communion patens, which no longer had a purpose since everyone was now receiving in their hands. The music changed from religious to secular, a sign of much greater things to happen in the decades to follow. The 1970s were pivotal years in the Church because they greatly affected the Catholic identity of so many. Great destruction was wrought in those years, replacing much of what had come before.

Likewise, my parents' generation was completely caught off guard. The customary means of transmitting the Faith had been first at home, then in Catholic schools with nuns, and of course the Mass. Once a child reached school age, parents were accustomed to their children learning more advanced topics of the Faith from religious sisters and brothers as well as from lay faculty. The flood that swept through the Church simultaneously in the areas of parish life and Catholic education in America in the 1970s was a spiritual tsunami. It was brought about by an increasingly liberal clergy anxious to deform the Catholic

Church. They pointed to the "Spirit of Vatican II" (a myth that continues to this day) as their motivation. What had been a storehouse of Catholic identity markers was gone practically overnight: statues, Catholic songs/hymns, altar boy apparel, religious habits (followed by the religious who wore them), authentic Catholic education—you name it, it was wiped away.

It was in this "Church" that I and my generation came of age, and it is this "Church" that has pretty much taken over and rules the roost today, a combination of emotion-driven compromise with the world aimed at never offending anyone—except God. In the process, Catholic identity was swept out, an intentional outcome.

Many leaders of the Church, so anxious to make compromise with the prevailing trends of the day, left faithful Catholics abandoned as they went out into that world. It did not take long for many of them to be plowed under by the developing culture of death. It's important to remember it was this generation that first saw contraception become a constitutional right, followed quickly by the enshrinement of abortion as a worldly sacrament. The prevailing morality changed at a surprising speed. Movies, music, the entire entertainment industry now glorified sex. The Sexual Revolution had exploded onto the world at the precise time leaders in the Church were embracing the world. And no one in the Church really said that much about any of it.

Like so many in my generation, I fell prey to all this and took up a life of promiscuity. By the time the 1990s came around, the Sexual Revolution had "matured" into the hookup culture, and so-called one-night stands were commonplace. I knew, somewhere back in the recesses of my Catholic mind formed by my parents when I was a child, that all this was wrong and sinful. Yet I fell out of regular practice of my faith life, attending Mass intermittently out of a vague sense of obligation.

I was a successful TV journalist with multiple awards and accolades, respected by my fellow professionals, and I had a degree from the University of Notre Dame (1983). On the outside, it would seem all was fine. On the inside, I was troubled in conscience, but not enough to do anything about it; it was just a distant troubling. The promiscuity continued, and the occasional accompanying pangs of guilt followed; and so the cycle continued year after year.

It was that early childhood Catholic knowledge planted in my soul by my parents that kept "nagging" me in my young adult years. I was never tempted to go seek out a "less judgmental" religion because I knew they were all wrong. I knew Jesus Christ is God. I knew Jesus Christ established the Catholic Church. I just ignored it all to continue in my sin—whistling past the graveyard, you could say.

My parents, of course, had known all along I wasn't living my faith life, and it was greatly disturbing to them. They prayed incessantly, constantly begging God to do something to reel me back in. My older brother Marshall had also wandered into the Church of Nice and set up home. While he was not as openly negligent of the Faith as I was, he was, nonetheless, a total convert to the Church of Nice and likewise a great concern to my parents. So their prayers dragged on for years, seemingly to no avail. One day in 2001, my mother, having lost virtually all hope that her prayers would ever be heard, uttered the following cry to Our Lord in total frustration: "Jesus, I don't care what you have to do to me; do whatever you have to, but spare the eternal lives of my two sons."

She had no idea of the speed with which that prayer would be answered as she cried out from the depths of her soul.

Within weeks, during a routine checkup for acid reflux, she was diagnosed with the beginning stages of stomach cancer. It was so early in its progress that it had actually been discovered by accident, so to speak, during an endoscopy. This was October of 2001. Doctors wanted to waste no time in performing surgery, and it was done within a week of the discovery. The conclusion was that the surgery had been successful and they had gotten all of it.

The conclusion turned out to be wrong. She never really recovered to what could be termed full health. There were various lingering issues and pains. About seven months later during a follow-up visit the next summer, her doctor delivered the shocking diagnosis that the cancer was not only back but had progressed to stage four. He added the paralyzing news that she only had two to three months to live. The doctor said the cancer had metastasized to the liver, and other vital organs would soon fall victim. That was July 15, 2002.

My parents and I decided it would be best for them to immediately move out of New York's Westchester County to Detroit, Michigan, where I live, so I could be involved with my father in looking after my mother. Being the loving husband, my dad arranged everything in New York while I prepared all that needed to be done in advance on my end, and my parents arrived in Detroit two weeks later on July 30, 2002.

And so started the deathwatch. Families in these situations have that quiet clock always running in the back of their minds, and this case was no different. Questions swirled around like "Will she be here for Christmas?" According to what the doctor had said, she likely would not be around for that season of Notre Dame football, which I shared each year with my parents as avidly as possible, even from long distance.

But something strange happened. My mom's condition reached a plateau. She was clearly sick, but the progress of the illness had been arrested. The deathwatch had been temporarily put on hold.

Fall and Notre Dame football season came and went. Thanksgiving arrived, and so, too, Christmas and the New Year, her 69th birthday at the end of March 2003, and then Mother's Day. Her condition didn't change. She had a perpetual cross to carry that showed neither improvement nor decline. All the while during my visits, she was telling me that I needed to get back to the Faith and start living for God. While I knew what she was saying was right, it was too easy to ignore her based on sinful habits I had developed all those years before.

On August 2, 2003, while I was in Denver on business, I received a call from my sister-in-law that my older brother Marshall had just died of a heart attack at the age of 48. By all appearances, Marshall was in excellent physical condition. An avid swimmer, he used to get up almost daily and swim laps for a considerable distance in the Gulf of Mexico near their Corpus Christi home one block from the beach. The news that he was dead was stunning. In one of the more difficult things I've had to do, I called my mother and told her, as she was dying, that her firstborn son had just died. Her immediate response: "Jesus, how many more crosses can You give me?"

My parents could not go to their eldest boy's funeral because of my mom's weakened condition. The day before the funeral, I went into the mortuary to say my private goodbyes. None of it seemed to be processing. It couldn't be true. It didn't make sense. I ran my hand through my brother's blond hair, partly from affection, partly for proof that what I was seeing was actually real. As it began to sink in that what lay before me was my brother's lifeless body, I grabbed my cell phone and called my mother.

"Mom, I'm standing with Marshall's body right now. Is there anything you want me to say or do?"

She responded, "Give him a kiss for me; tell him I love him and that I will see him soon."

That was the moment the conversion process began. In a funeral home in Corpus Christi, Texas, standing over my brother's dead body, talking on a cell phone with my dying mother, I began to recall all those simple truths I had learned as a small boy about death and Heaven and Hell that my parents and my second- and third-grade teacher-nuns had taught me about my Catholic faith before my first Holy Communion and training to be an altar boy.

I returned to Detroit, and the conversations with my mom changed. People die. They will be judged. This life comes to an end. It was all real—not just in the mind, but in reality. By the time 2004 dawned, her condition started to slowly decline. By the time May came, she had to be admitted into the hospice care center. I drove her while my dad followed behind. It was an extremely difficult, emotional struggle for her to step across that threshold knowing this was the last place she would see on earth. It was distressing for her, and I saw it all up close.

A couple of days before going into the hospice, she said the most charitable thing she could have ever said to me as a mother: "Michael, I don't want to be in Heaven knowing you're in Hell."

She sensed perhaps that her time to do what she could to save my soul was running out. The end was approaching; there was no more time for saying things politely. During those six weeks in her hospice room, amid her cancer pains she described as little shards of glass churning around inside her, her first concern was my salvation. One day she said, "I think that Jesus has something special planned for you. I don't know what it is, but I just feel it." I passed over her remarks without much thought.

On the afternoon of June 14, 2004, I sat by my mother's bedside and shared my last hour together with her on this earth. She had suffered during her lifetime from bipolar depression, as well as a severe case of obsessive-compulsive disorder. These conditions had caused no end of grief during my and my brother's youth, and much of our childhood had been adversely impacted. This last hour provided a final moment for her to shed her tears for all the difficulties that had arisen between us all those many years ago owing to her mental illnesses, as well as a chance for me to repeat to her that all was forgiven.

Around five in the evening, her sufferings increased enough for a pain reliever to be administered. My mother and I exchanged our last expressions of love as she nodded off to a comfortable sleep. I looked up at my father and said, "She's going to die tonight, Dad. Maybe I should stay in the room with her since your hearing is so bad." He agreed.

About 4:30 a.m., I awoke (or was awakened) and stepped toward my mother's bed. She was breathing in a gasping fashion, and her feet had turned cold. When people are approaching death, they often don't like things on them or around their neck owing to their incredibly increased sensitivity. A couple of weeks earlier, she had asked for her brown scapular to be removed because it hurt her skin. Now as she lay drawing her last breaths, I found it and put it on her so she would not be without it as she entered into eternity. It was slightly after five o'clock in the morning on June 15, 2004—the eve of the Feast of the Sacred Heart, to which she had always had such a strong devotion.

The next day, in the funeral home, I knelt down at the side of my mother's coffin and placed my hand on her womb and said, "Mom, what you went through for me, you will not have gone through in vain. I'm a changed man."

For the next year and half, I studied the Faith with abandon. I read thousands of pages about Catholicism and all aspects of it—devotional, spiritual, intellectual. The Faith of my childhood came roaring back to life. I experienced an odd mix of remorse, repentance, exhilaration, and thirst to know even more. I wanted to do something for the Church, for Our Blessed Lord Who had, despite all my sins, answered the prayers of my mother and brought me back to the Church—her dying wish.

It was at that time the book *The DaVinci Code* by Dan Brown was released and was all the rage. Its story was that Jesus and Mary Magdalene were romantically involved, and their heirs were the guardians of the Holy Grail. That book, and the subsequent film, was what brought things into focus for me. With my expansive knowledge of TV production, I decided to take part of my inheritance and retirement fund and produce a thirty- or sixty-minute documentary on the errors of that book, so indignant that anyone could speak of our great loving Lord in those blasphemous terms—the same loving Lord Who had rescued me from the power of death through the prayers of my mother.

The next day, as I was drawing up the outline for the documentary, it occurred to me that by the time I would have written, shot, produced, edited, and aired this, the book would've been long forgotten and no one would care about it anymore. I concluded that the reason such a book could gain the traction it did, even among Catholics, was that they didn't know the Faith—just like I had never known it well enough.

So I resolved to work to change that. I took all the money I had and founded St. Michael's Media around Thanksgiving of 2005 and into early 2006. I bought all the cameras, lights, audio, everything necessary, and had a studio constructed in the spring. Construction began at precisely 11:10 a.m. on March 10, 2005 and was completed, engineered, wired, and ready for lights, camera, and action on May 8, 2006, when the very first taping of the show *The One True Faith* took place. It was the Feast of St. Michael of Gargano, and the entire apostolate was dedicated to the honor of the Prince of the Heavenly Host and consecrated to the Immaculate Heart of Mary.

As part of the work, I successfully completed studies for my ecclesiastical degree awarded from the Pontifical University of St. Thomas Aquinas in April of 2009, graduating *summa cum laude*. The university, located in Rome, is also known as the Angelicum, after St. Thomas, the Angelic Doctor.

The apostolate has since spilled over into the work of ChurchMilitant.com (formerly RealCatholicTV.com) and strives to alert Catholics to the desperate need to recover their Catholic identity. The effort of this apostolate has been met with severe opposition from inside the establishment Church. We talk about things they don't want talked about. It upsets the status quo. We ask questions they don't want asked. We explore problems and issues they don't want explored. As a result, we have been lied about, maligned, attacked, and so forth.

The Church finds Herself at a crossroads. She may not as yet have encountered what Pope St. John Paul II termed a "global apostasy." In such times, it is the duty of every Catholic who loves Our Blessed Lord to do whatever he or she can to commit to a restoration, a resurrection of authentic Catholicism, to realize what Pope Leo XIII in the nineteenth century stressed: that Catholics "are born for combat." What leaders in the Church have done for the past fifty years has failed on an epic level to save the world and bring souls to Christ. The more honest and self-reflective among them know this, but are paralyzed from also having been raised in the same conditions. What is needed is a whole new approach, not where the world is accommodated, but where it is challenged and confronted—as the Apostles did. The world needs to hear "We don't want to be in Heaven knowing you're in Hell." It's time for a change.

INTRODUCTION

The Church in the West is in shambles. Perhaps never more in 2,000 years of sacred history has She witnessed such destruction within Her own walls. Even during the persecutions of the Caesars She was flourishing, enough to eventually win the day and convert the empire. But the devastation She has undergone in just fifty years is beyond words. Apostasy, schism, heresy, dissent—every form of neglect, abuse, and treachery the mind could imagine has all occurred in these almost three generations.

But did this all happen in the course of just fifty years? In reality, no. It has all become visible in these past five decades, but truth be told, this has been in preparation for centuries, stretching back to the beginnings of the Protestant heresy of the sixteenth century and earlier. It has been a century-long gathering storm that each generation of Catholic leaders and laity has contributed to in its own manner.

There certainly were many saints, popes, clergy, holy men and women, mystics, visionaries who saw the storm gathering on the horizon, but perhaps none of them could have conceived of the immensity of the falling away from the Faith that would occur in our own day. Various storm systems crashed into the Church at the same moment in the 1960s and continued uprooting nearly all vestiges of faith up to even our present time.

The Church established by Our Blessed Lord on St. Peter currently resembles from the outside very little of Her glorious inner self. With the exception of small pockets here and there, She has virtually vanished. For someone to be a believing Catholic, faithful to Heaven, he must accept everything the Church teaches—everything. Today, that could not even be said with certainty of even half Her clergy, much less Her laity. Within the Church there has been such a demolition of the Faith, an eradication of supernatural faith, that it requires some effort to simply identify Her in Her fullness.

There have been periods of setback and storms in Her past, true, but very little even beginning to approach this degree of intensity. We will save the in-depth statistics for later in this book, but suffice it to say when one understands what is meant by the phrase "faithful Catholic," something less than ten percent of the baptized would qualify. In America, seventy-five percent do not even go to Mass every Sunday, leaving only a pool of *possible* faithful Catholics of just twenty-five percent. In other parts of the Western world, it is even fewer—far fewer. In the United States, a majority of that twenty-five percent who do attend Mass regularly do not regularly go to confession, they accept the evil of contraception, and they reject that human souls go to Hell owing to a great distortion of the understanding of the mercy of God and the horror of sin, all taught to them by the clergy—and they believe that a Catholic can disagree with one or more dogmas of the Church while still being a good Catholic. These people's children, when they grow into adults, do not marry in the Church and abandon the practice of the Faith themselves.

And even more sobering is when one considers that of the twenty-five percent who do still attend Mass, the lion's share are much older. In ten to fifteen years, they will be mostly if not entirely dead, and there will be very, very few to replace them. In roughly this next decade, current trends show the Church in America will experience a hemorrhaging of believers and a shrinking of size that will make today's disaster seem like nothing.

The hierarchy of the Catholic Church has largely abandoned the sheep these past fifty years by refusing to confront the evils of modern man, failing to boldly teach the truths of Jesus Christ or arm the faithful for spiritual warfare, laying down its weapons in the face of diabolical fury directed at the people of God. Can it then be surprising that after being abandoned by the shepherds, the sheep in their turn would abandon them?

This is what we now witness playing out during these last moments of visible Christianity in the West. What will now follow, because there is no other alternative or scenario, is persecution on a grand scale. The refusal of leaders to teach, govern, and rule has prepared the way for the mass apostasy that now must be addressed by Heaven directly. Whenever the hand of the State is raised against the Church, it does not happen without the express will of God. This time will be no different. In a mysterious mix of divine justice and divine mercy, God Himself will have the final say over the current crisis of faith.

What we must now concern ourselves with is not how to reestablish a way of living the Faith from the so-called golden era of the Church in 1950s America. For the foreseeable future, all that is long dead and gone. Back then, the Church was at least somewhat in step with the culture, or better said, the culture was more or less in step with the Church, at least morally speaking—but no longer.

As leaders betrayed Christ and His Church through infidelity, cowardice, and sexual sins, the culture surrendered Catholic morality and set the stage for the current reality. Today, any mention of truth with regard to morality, especially sexual morality, is met with a barrage of charges of homophobia, bigotry, and hate.

The quiet acceptance on the part of Church leaders of homosexual sins—in too many cases even participation in those same sins—has resulted in a paralysis among today's leaders in confronting this grand evil. The homosexual priest sex abuse scandal and the refusal to acknowledge it and deal with it has sucked the life out of the moral authority of Church leaders to speak on anything of relevance.

They are reduced to having to score cheap political points by railing on about immigration, poverty, gun control, climate change, and religious liberty. Having been stripped by their own actions of any spiritual voice, they must now pander to any political audience that pretends to give them a hearing. What a sad state of affairs indeed.

They cannot even authentically address the *real* evil of the Obamacare contraception mandate, which is of course the intrinsic evil of contraception itself. They have to hide behind the issue of religious liberty and appeal to the courts.

As the country was dissolving morally, the bishops of the day in the 1960s, 70s, and 80s refused to defend the truth. Their up-and-coming replacements were tutored by them in how not to rock the boat, how to appease everyone who can be appeased, and how to keep silent in the face of monstrous evils. The bishops of the 1990s, 2000s, and today learned well. With a few notable exceptions, they have all fallen into lock step with the decline of the Church and now find themselves on the precipice of near-total extinction.

Great observers of Church history have commented on the fact that if the Church anywhere in the world loses three generations in a row, then She loses that nation completely. We now have five years left of the third generation, and nothing is changing with enough intensity to hold back the inevitable. For those few intrepid souls remaining who meet the actual definition of "faithful Catholic," be you laity or clergy, it will be up to you to keep the fires burning, reestablish and maintain a Catholic identity, and *be* the Church Militant, no matter the odds, no matter the degree of persecution.

Chapter 1

THE CHURCH MILITANT:
The Barque of Peter

The use of the word "militant" today conjures up images of wild-eyed fanatics brandishing swords and machine guns, destroying everything in the path to their ultimate goal.

We should hold on to that image—or rather what it symbolizes—for a moment as we examine what it means for Christianity, and specifically for Catholicism. The Catholic Church has three aspects or dynamics: the Church Triumphant, the Church Suffering, and the Church Militant.

The Church is not isolated to a merely earthly existence; indeed, the earthly existence She enjoys in the temporal order is passing away. In the end, all that will be left is the Church Triumphant. In Her nature, the Church *is* triumphant. She is the Bride of Christ, and as such, is completely one flesh with Him. As He is Triumphant, so is She.

The Triumphant Church refers to the dynamic of Her life where the saints currently enjoy the Beatific Vision. They behold God in the face; they are forever now bound up in the eternal rhapsody of bliss, and of this "kingdom there will be no end" (Luke i: 33). They are in Heaven. Hence, it is triumphant for the elect, those who have persevered to the end. And in a beautiful twist, having persevered to the end, there no longer is any end for them. They are saved; they have attained the goal of earthly existence. They now enjoy what the fallen angels will never know from experience.

The Church Suffering refers to the dynamic of Her life where the saints who have persevered to the end have been escorted before the throne of Jesus Christ and found to be in a state of grace—an interior communion with the Divine Majesty, the Holy Trinity, so as to merit

1

Heaven, but insufficiently prepared to endure the glory of the Divine Radiance. While being in a state of grace, they have not yet attained the necessary perfection demanded of them to be admitted to the Beatific Vision, so they are in need of enduring some final purgation of their appetites for sin. In the course of events, they too shall be united to the elect and brought into the celestial realms out of reach of the fallen angels.

The souls that comprise the Church Triumphant and the Church Suffering are saved; they either do or will behold the Face of God. "[H]e will wipe away every tear from their eyes, and death shall be no more, neither shall there be mourning nor crying nor pain anymore, for the former things have passed away" (Rev. xxi : 4).

Ah, but for the Church Militant, the old order is in fact the present order. The Church Militant refers to the dynamic of the Catholic Church's life where the struggle is still going on—where the fight of perseverance is played out. Members of the Church Militant—we individual Catholics—are still very much in reach of the fallen angels, and even if we are in a state of grace, we are still capable of being ensnared by them and their leader Satan, who "prowls around like a roaring lion, seeking someone to devour" (1 Pet. v : 8). Unlike our compatriots in the Church Triumphant and Church Suffering, we are very much engaged in the fight, and nothing is assured until it is over— nothing. It is why St. Paul strictly warns all of us to "work out your own salvation in fear and trembling" (Phil. ii : 12).

They were once where we stand today—fighting, slaying dragons, being set upon by the legions of Hell. And while the battle rages on, we should take great comfort and hope that not only did they attain to perfection, and so might we, but they are allies in this fight.

The Church Triumphant and the Church Suffering are totally and completely aligned with the will of the Holy Trinity, and the Holy Trinity wills that we be saved and be united to the Divine Majesty for eternity. So we have not only the assistance of God Himself but of his own legions, both angelic beings and human beings who stand at the ready to assist us.

But we should not take a presumptuous attitude in this regard. The reason they are at the ready is, simply put, because we *need* them to be at the ready—because for us it is impossible to do battle against demons. The least significant demon has far more power and intelligence than the most brilliant man ever to have lived, if that man is unassisted by grace.

So we Catholics need to comprehend correctly the situation that lies before us. We are in a titanic struggle for our souls, each one of us. Nothing is guaranteed in this regard. No matter how holy or pious a person may be, we must never forget that at this moment there are souls in Hell who were, at one point in their lives, far holier than we are now and who had access to incredible storehouses of grace. Judas Iscariot comes to mind, for starters. He performed miracles and drove out demons in Jesus' name—yet he is now those same demons' slave. In fact, St. Alphonsus Ligouri reminds us that Judas raised people from the dead but lost his own soul!

To put it in the starkest terms, imagine a soul, after having battled demons and successfully vanquishing them at various moments in his life, only ultimately to fall prey to them through their cunning and be consigned to Hellfire with them now as his masters. What vengeance do you suppose those same individual demons would exact on that poor soul who did not persevere to the end? That human who had brought them an increase in humiliation, as they were subject to him, and who increased their pain, would now be subject to their tortures, and there will be no end of it for that wretched soul who was once on the trajectory to salvation.

So when the Church speaks of Herself in terms of *militant*, She speaks the truth, for militancy is what is required. As noted above, we should hold on to the symbolism of wild-eyed fanatics brandishing weapons and destroying all that prevents us from reaching our goal. It is useful imagery, even if it is borrowed from the chapters of earthbound violence and bloodshed.

A Catholic, a true Catholic, understands that this is the only proper attitude with which one can approach spiritual warfare—the attitude of complete destruction of the enemy, Satan. The infernal enemy, he who was cast out, must be utterly conquered by us in our own souls and cast out again. Satan makes war on the people of God, on the Bride of Christ, and so the Bride of Christ, collectively and in Her individual members, must make war in return. As Ven. Pope Pius XII said:

> We belong to the Church militant; and She is militant
> because on earth the powers of darkness are ever restless
> to encompass Her destruction. Not only in the far-off cen-

turies of the early Church, but down through the ages and in this our day, the enemies of God and Christian civilization make bold to attack the Creator's supreme dominion and sacrosanct human rights. (Pontifical North American College, Rome, October 14, 1953)

So there we have it. From the first Pope, St. Peter, down to our own day and age, up to and including not only Ven. Pius XII but also his successors, including Pope Francis, we have direct warnings from the mouths of the Vicars of Christ that Satan is roaming about seeking to tear us to pieces. We have this imagery in Scripture, the writings of the Fathers, the Doctors, innumerable saints, mystics, holy men and women, not to mention from the mouth of Our Blessed Lord Himself: "He was a murderer from the beginning, and has nothing to do with the truth, because there is no truth in him" (John viii : 44).

He is, in no short order, a destroyer, a deceiver, a killer of beauty in souls, the one who has deceived the nations. He is the bearer of chaos, the sower of discord and malice. He is the one cast down by St. Michael from Heaven to crash on the earth, and the Holy Spirit warns mankind through the Beloved Disciple: "But woe to you, O earth and sea, for the devil has come down to you in great wrath, because he knows that his time is short!" (Rev. xii : 12).

And what is the aim of the diabolical? It is a question that all ardent Catholics must concern themselves with daily. It is to attack God through His sons here on earth. Evil has not only a certain cold logic to it; it also has a kind of insanity about it. Like God, Satan acts according to his nature, and his nature is infernal envy—born of pride certainly, but that pride is expressed in such hate-filled envy of God's creation that he *is* murder itself. His pride is fueled by envy, envy of any being that could still possess what he himself had to surrender.

We must recall that before their fall, Lucifer and his legions had not beheld the Face of God. They were no more admitted into the Beatific Vision than we are here today. They experienced God in His Glory but not in the Face. But just the glory of God was so overwhelming to them, so majestic, so profound, that their imaginations, which are housed in great intellects, could speculate on what awaited them if they were admitted to the Beatific Vision.

But it was never to be—for the announcement to them that, in all their glory, they were not to be the highest order of creation was more than they could bear, and they rebelled. And so pride entered the created order, and they were cast out and into Hell. And at the creation of man, their pride found new life in their envy—envy of the ensouled material being that might one day be escorted into the Vision that they would be forever denied.

And what is key to remember is this one point: Satan no more sees mankind as a collective than does God. Of course there is a corporate aspect to us, a human nature in which we all share and participate, but at day's end, we are individuals, and we will all be rewarded or damned as individuals. Only after salvation or damnation do we proceed into the larger society of the elect or the society of the damned.

The envy with which the infernal beholds man is the fuel that keeps the flames of Hell so intense. The envy of man is in reality a hatred of God, and so the diabolical nature is simply to hate, kill, destroy. It gets no pleasure or satisfaction from hating, killing, or destroying. It simply *does* these things, much like the sun gets no pleasure from shining, for it shines by its very nature.

But unlike the sun, Satan has intelligence and knows that his time is limited, that one day the curtain will draw down on history and his ability to exercise his nature in the created order will come to an end, and he will be forever and eternally frustrated, knowing that with all his powers, he will no longer be able to kill and destroy further, for those will have passed away.

But that is for the new order. For now, we need to look to the present state of affairs. From the moment of Adam's creation, the dragon has concerned himself with creating various crises, both individually and collectively, to throw man off from the end God desires for him. In a master stroke, he created a crisis of beauty Eve was unable to escape. And following the lead of his wife, Adam fell, unable to endure his own crisis of truth. And creation fell, losing its primordial goodness.

And this event, the Fall, has been the pacesetter for all of our sad history: the attempt to reclaim beauty and truth and goodness; to be reconciled to our original design and moreover elevated to even greater heights, absorbed into Truth and Goodness and Beauty Itself.

At every age and era, in every heart and mind polluted by original sin, Satan is there with crisis after crisis creating no end of misery for the objects of his envy: us. Every crisis of the collective is first born from a crisis of the individual. And the crisis of the collective, be it political or economic or militaristic, has the very real potential of folding back onto individuals and creating even further crises in individual souls.

Consider, for example, in our own day the crisis of the family, broken by infidelity. Born ultimately out of lust in the mind of an individual, it moves beyond the individual and out onto the greater stage, joined by others with a similar personal crisis. The many individual crises then join to form a collective, and that collective crisis then folds back onto individuals—the displaced children—and creates individual crises for them. And so it goes.

The role, therefore, of the Church Militant is to militate against the diabolical, to be the military force invading enemy territory, using the power of the Cross and Him crucified to liberate individual men from the yoke of Hell's oppression. No small matter, that. Indeed, it is *all* that matters.

What we shall explore, then, from here on out, is the pitched battle being waged between the Church Militant and kingdom of Satan. We shall pay close attention to the weapons the enemy employs, for they have proven extremely effective against many individual soldiers and officers in the Church Militant these past decades.

That the powers of the diabolical were stepping up their attacks after centuries of careful preparation was hardly news to Pope St. Pius X, who wrote in his landmark encyclical *Pascendi Dominici Gregis* in 1907:

> Still it must be confessed that the number of enemies of the Cross of Christ has in these last days increased exceedingly, who are striving, by arts, entirely new and full of subtlety, to destroy the vital energy of the Church, and if they can, to overthrow utterly Christ's kingdom itself.

While he was still not yet pope, Cdl. Karol Wojtyła, taking note of the spiritual carnage following Pope St. Pius X's warning, noted nearly a century later:

We are now facing the final confrontation between the Church and the anti-Church, of the Gospel versus the anti-Gospel. This confrontation lies within the plans of divine Providence; it is a trial which the whole Church, and the Polish Church in particular, must take up. It is a trial of not only our nation and the Church, but in a sense a test of 2,000 years of culture and Christian civilization, with all of its consequences for human dignity, individual rights, human rights and the rights of nations. (Eucharistic Congress, Philadelphia, PA, August 13, 1976)

And in a stark summation of the state of spiritual affairs, Pope Benedict XVI, comparing the fall of Ancient Rome to contemporary humanity, said:

The sun was setting over an entire world. Frequent natural disasters further increased this sense of insecurity. There was no power in sight that could put a stop to this decline. All the more insistent, then, was the invocation of the power of God: the plea that He might come and protect His people from all these threats.

Excita, Domine, potentiam tuam, et veni. Today, too, we have many reasons to associate ourselves with this Advent prayer of the Church. For all its new hopes and possibilities, our world is at the same time troubled by the sense that moral consensus is collapsing, consensus without which juridical and political structures cannot function. Consequently the forces mobilized for the defense of such structures seem doomed to failure. (Christmas Address to Roman Curia, December 20, 2010)

When one examines the qualities, therefore, of the Church Militant, one immediately encounters a spirit of confrontation, an active seeking out of the enemy, a desire to search him out and destroy him. This approach rings foreign in the ears of the contemporary Catholic, raised for the last fifty years on the syrup of the Modernist heresy—a heresy that exalts indifferentism and tepidity toward the sacred, that promotes the horrible sin of being lukewarm.

While it may be a shocking thing to introduce into the contemporary conversation regarding salvation, not that much of a conversation is even had today owing to the sin of presumption on the part of so many.

There is one thing God hates (and yes, God does hate—He placed hatred between the serpent and "the Woman"): He detests even more than mortal sin the lukewarm soul. We read the words that issued forth from His own mouth in St. John's Apocalypse: "So, because you are lukewarm, and neither cold nor hot, I will spew you out of my mouth" (Rev. iii : 16).

Being indifferent to things of God is more insulting to God than actually working actively against them. The lukewarm soul is despicable to Almighty God and has the terrible distinction of being the one the Divine Majesty is most displeased with, so much so that He will vomit such a soul from his mouth.

The primary sin of the contemporary Catholic is that of being lukewarm. And it is this sin the Church Militant must attack with greatest energy. One may rest assured that if this is *the* sin most despised by the Almighty, then it is the one *most cultivated* by the infernal regions of the diabolical.

We see the evidence all around us. Catholics are bored with the Faith. The overwhelming majority do not attend Mass, not because they out-and-out reject God but because "they get nothing out of it." It is boring to them. On one hand, such a stance is somewhat easy to understand. The celebration of the Mass has become so trivialized, so emptied of its meaning to the eye and ear that what is left in many parishes is little else than what appears to be a social get-together with next to nothing of the transcendent. If someone were to step into the average Mass in the average parish these days, the idea of battling evil, of calling on the powers of Heaven to save souls from eternal damnation, of standing contemplatively at the foot of the Cross and absorbing the great mercy of God into our souls so that we are transformed into ferocious warriors—"born for combat," as Pope Leo XIII correctly observed—such notions would never even enter into the person's mind. How could they? Virtually every access to such thoughts or stirrings of the intellect have all been cut off owing to a multitude of abuses.

People have grown indifferent to and bored with the Real Presence of Jesus Christ on the altar because Satan has manipulated affairs in the Church so as to obscure the truth of the Blessed Sacrament. Using great cultural trends, he has brought under his influence leaders and laity alike to so water down the Faith and restyle it into being about man and nature and not about God and the supernatural that the only result possible could be lukewarm souls.

It is this—the whole evil proposition—that the Church Militant must militate against. It must confront this evil, call it out, go in search of it, and destroy it before it destroys more souls and rains down more supernatural terror on the people of God. Since so much of the evil is already institutionalized and has been absorbed into the daily life of the Church, the institution itself must be challenged and called out, for the evil is great in the midst of the Church: a paralyzed leadership, a lukewarm world of the baptized—in short, a global apostasy.

> We must be prepared to undergo great trials in the not-too-distant future, trials that will require us to be ready to give up even our lives, and a total gift of self to Christ and for Christ. Through your prayers and mine, it is possible to alleviate this tribulation, but it is no longer possible to avert it, because it is only in this way that the Church can be effectively renewed. How many times, indeed, has the renewal of the Church been effected in blood? This time, again, it will not be otherwise. We must be strong, we must prepare ourselves, we must entrust ourselves to Christ and to His Mother, and we must be attentive, very attentive, to the prayer of the Rosary. (Pope St. John Paul II, Fulda, Germany, November 1980)

That such disaster could befall the Church so readily and with such seeming ease is a terrifying reality to behold because it means the same could happen to each individual soul. If Satan can bring about world events to achieve the present reality, how much easier is it for him to work such diabolical doings within the soul of just one person? As he does in the individual, he has set up a series of events that have caused the world to first doubt, then begin searching anew, but from a different perspective. Satan cannot create; he can only pervert and destroy. What he has at his disposal are the goods of the created world. So he uses the gifts God has granted man to destroy man. He twists man's intellect. He accelerates man's passions. He capitalizes on the resultant chaos and creates even more chaos.

The state of constant chaos brings about a first crisis, which in turn brings about even more crises, each one feeding off the other and constantly begetting ever new ones. Man is kept always off-balance, always in search of some stability—that is our nature—but stumbling and being tossed about in the hunt for it, much like passengers on a ship in the midst of a violent storm. They desire safe harbor, they seek it out, but they are unable to find it. They set sail toward what appears to be a lighthouse, only to discover it is a mirage of the ocean. No sooner do they lose sight of that one, and another illusory one appears, and they turn course for that. Meanwhile, the ship is breaking apart, unable to sustain the constant battering.

While this is an apt analogy for the current crisis, what is curious is why there can be, at the same time, so much indifference, so much lukewarmness. Why is there no sense of alarm? If we return for a moment to our analogy, imagine the passengers and crew on the ship are extremely intoxicated. They have been drinking down below deck for almost the entirety of the journey. As conditions on the sea worsened, they were anesthetized to the effects of the storm because their state of willful drunkenness made it appear to them all was normal. Using this analogy, the Scripture verse "[b]e sober, be watchful" is perhaps better understood (1 Pet. v : 8).

If one could assign to the storm a personality behind it, an author, a great and evil Poseidon—and further assign to Poseidon the plan that he remain hidden from the knowledge of the ship's passengers so he could bring about even more destruction, you would have a good analogy for the diabolical. Satan's plan, from the Garden onwards, has been to bring about crisis upon crisis but remain deeply hidden, unidentified, so much out of view that no one gives him any thought beyond fanciful mariners' tales of the high seas.

He wants no talk of a ships' graveyard or of Davy Jones' Locker, or of ships traversing these seas, being smashed to pieces on the rocks, and the passengers all drowning. Those are tales to frighten children and amuse the storyteller. They are not based on reality—so goes the mind deceived by the diabolical. How truly St. Paul warned the baptized that they had "made shipwreck of their faith" (1 Tim. i : 19).

The Church Militant, to extend the analogy, is the great warship with the duty to rescue the ships that cannot prevent their own destruction. It has sufficient armor and construction to withstand the storm. It has a crew well trained in emergency rescue. Its only duty is to pull alongside the battered hulks and drag aboard as many passengers as possible. But its job is made all the more difficult in that with the passage of time, the passengers on these vessels destined for destruction have become so drunk, so inebriated, that they don't recognize their own danger, the frightful peril to which they're exposed.

Moreover, Poseidon, grown weary of having his plans thwarted by the Church Militant warship, has turned his attacks toward it—a special plan of attack, because if he can cripple and sink the warship, then he wins it all, for there is no other ship that can save. The Builder of the warship knew in advance of the severity of the storms and the great hatred of Poseidon, so He engineered the ship accordingly, ensuring it would be unsinkable. It might certainly feel the effects of the storms and be tossed and bashed around, but it would never sink. It was built of a different material from all the rest. And the crew knew that all the lighthouses were Poseidon-inspired illusions, that the only hope of rescue was being on deck. One day the storm would cease—but for now, the battle had to be engaged.

So while whipping up storms and squalls to smash the weaker ships, Poseidon put into action a special plan of attack against the warship. It was not a new plan, since he had tried it before and had some degree of success. But the captain had always discovered the plan and countered it effectively. So he developed a new twist: Get the crew drunk, like the passengers they were attempting to rescue—especially the senior officers and senior crew. If they could be softened up, the whole rescue operation could come to a grinding halt. He might never sink the ship, but he could sure as hell cause it to drop anchor and abandon its mission by crippling it through convincing as many crew and senior officers as possible to jump overboard. It would take quite a series of events, of crises, eventually becoming onboard crises, and even mutiny, to bring such a reality into existence—but this was his singular purpose.

Certainly from the perspective of more than a century of popes, it was no secret that the diabolical had been successful in setting the world stage for a current crisis by employing various crises stretching back more than five centuries. If one ever wonders about the condition of the Church, one need look no further than the condition of the world. If it is in shambles, it is because her champion, the Catholic Church, is in shambles and unable to come to its assistance.

No other institution in all of human history has been empowered to battle and defeat the diabolical other than the Holy Catholic Church.

It is Her sole purpose for existence, and She carries the promise from Her Divine Founder and Groom that "the powers of death shall not prevail" against Her (Matt. xvi : 18).

This, of course, presupposes that She is ready for battle, that She has been vigilant and awake and sober, suspicious of all that might be a threat to salvation. In crisis after crisis in Her sacred history, She has stood vigilant and emerged victorious, however scarred from the tempest of battle. The flag of the Cross still whipped from Her mast. But as Pope St. Pius X, Pope St. John Paul II, and Pope Benedict XVI each duly noted, something was far different in our day: Satan has created a crisis never before encountered in the Church, a perfect storm.

Chapter 2

THE UNIQUE CRISIS:
Unrecognized Disaster

A crisis usually brings with it opportunity, a chance to become something greater. Contained within each crisis, by the very definition of the word "crisis," are the seeds of destruction of a former way, be it a civilization, a culture, or an attitude.

Far from the opportunity being recognized and seized, a crisis more often than not results in the aforementioned destruction—the near if not total annihilation of what formerly existed. Such is the nature of a crisis.

Many people in history have recognized the time of crisis and chosen up sides, so to speak, have perceived correctly that a moment to transform has arrived, and they seized it. Some clung to the former way and tried mightily to reinforce it, to give it new life. Others sensed the moment had arrived to overthrow the former way and spent their energies to wipe it away.

One need only imagine the thoughts, for example, in the minds of King George on one side of the Atlantic and the American colonists on the other, on the verge of the War of Independence; or the musings and ponderings of the French monarchy against the agitations of the revolutionaries in 1789.

The record of civilization provides large numbers of cases to consider: the moment of crisis that enveloped the Roman Empire as the barbarians breached the walls in the third and fourth centuries; the crisis that enveloped the Catholic Church and the nascent countries of Europe as the Mohammedan swarms ran roughshod over North Africa and jumped the Mediterranean into Iberia in the seventh and eighth centuries; the moment of crisis for all of Europe as the Vikings attacked via the continental waterways and laid waste to much of a land just being re-civilized after the Fall of Rome.

All of these crises, be they military or otherwise, bear one thing in common: They were all recognized for what they were—a fork in the road where the old would vanish and be replaced by the new, or the old would conquer and grow stronger than was formerly the case.

But there currently exists a crisis in the West that bears the hallmark of being the most unique in all of human history: *the unrecognized crisis*—a crisis so great in proportion as to hurtle former Western civilization far backward in terms of spirituality, and resultantly, morality, and yet at the same time so unappreciated for its scope it boggles the mind.

It's as if a giant earthquake of 9.0 magnitude were splitting the earth open and the affected neighborhoods were populated with the descendants of Rip Van Winkle, fast asleep and undisturbed, even as their walls and ceilings were crashing down around them.

To understand *why* this is the case today, it's necessary first to understand the nature of the crisis, then its scope, then proceed backwards and identify various historical markers that serve as both symptoms and causes, and then most importantly, to understand why so little is being done about it and why it is so unrecognized.

While the unrecognized feature of the crisis is the standout component of it in relation to past historical crises, it shares many things in common with past crises. A crisis by its nature is always spiritual, rooted in the transcendent. The very action of a crisis' coming about is always connected to a lack of spiritual contentment, a dissatisfaction with prevailing conditions; so to appreciate any crisis, one must first understand that all the *preconditions* for a crisis are present in every man.

This is why a given crisis is not restricted to the large and epochal, but can be had on the lowliest of planes: the individual person. In fact, every world-upheaving crisis always begins as an individual personal crisis. For example, the crisis of the Protestant Revolution in the sixteenth century, which destroyed the unity of Christianity, took definite shape as the result of one man's individual, personal crisis.

Father Martin Luther's individual, personal crisis happened to coincide with the individual and personal crises of many others at the same time, thus elevating his own crisis to that of a "multi-crisis," or a collective crisis, where many individual crises join together to unite into a broad crisis, which has the effect of dominoes falling into one another and causing even more dominoes to tumble, until what once was is no longer. What replaces the former can sometimes take a while to come into focus.

We see the same impact in the crisis that toppled Tsar Nicholas II of Russia in the Bolshevik Revolution. How many at the time really understood the number of dominoes that would fall (needless to mention the heads that would roll) as the Bolsheviks rampaged over the monarchy? The thoughts of one or a few, given the right conditions and times, can and do remake, refashion, reconstitute history.

In fact, this *is* history: the unfolding of events whose nature is rooted in spiritual warfare, both personal and collective. Without understanding history in this manner, it appears to be little else than a random set of circumstances, which bang up against one another with random results. But that view could not be more erroneous. Human history unfolds in a manner determined and predicated on the very real truth that we are spiritual beings in search of truth, goodness, and beauty.

A crisis in history occurs when one wave, with a certain interpretation of truth, goodness, and beauty, crashes up against another wave with a different interpretation. In that moment, one is going to give way to the other, will be assumed into the other.

The entire human race today is at such a moment, made more real and tangible by the technology of media, which can so precisely highlight all the different undulations present in each wave. What is so remarkable about this world crisis is that so many *in* the world do not see it. They have been anesthetized to the crisis, to the great moment, the precipice on which the entire race now stands.

How this came to be is a topic that also needs exploring. Why is it that so many former crises were easily recognized, while this one remains hidden from so many? Could it be that what many of the others had in common was that there was a risk to life and limb, to the material order—the overrunning of towns and villages by barbarians, Moslems, Vikings, or revolutionaries?

When the material order is threatened, it seems easier for people to rouse themselves to sufficient awareness that a crisis is at hand. But what about when the *spiritual order* is threatened? Is the connection between the material and spiritual not easily understood and therefore the spiritual crisis goes unrecognized? Can a people not see that a spiritual threat carries the potential to be even more devastating than rampaging armies?

In the case of material devastation, order of some sort must be restored for the conquerors to exploit their conquest. And as time passes, as history bears out, the vanquished—or at least their descendants—are restored to some normalcy and regain the ability to enjoy on some level the new material order, however harshly it may have been brought about.

But spiritual devastation bears with it the unique hallmark of being able to keep the conquered and his descendants forever in chains, always enslaved. A conquered body is one thing; a conquered soul is something of a different magnitude altogether. A body is of the natural order and so dies; a soul is of the supernatural order and lives forever.

Nature has placed limits on a body's suffering; supernature has employed no such limits on a soul's sufferings. And given that each crisis, which eventually erupts onto the material stage of human history, first erupts onto the supernatural stage of the soul, it stands to reason that *this* modern crisis, so spiritual in its origins, so unrecognized on a temporal level, is the greatest ever facing humanity.

What is being refashioned is much more than just the material order, as in past crises. It is the soul itself, the nature of man as understood by man, that is now the last domino to fall. Man either understands himself as a solely material being, with all that implies, or he correctly comprehends himself as an amalgam of material and immaterial (body and soul) with all *that* implies.

Man is either connected to God or there is no God and man is self-determining. It is a crisis of anthropology.

The two great waves of the modern crisis are now laid out before us, and they have been crashing into each other for quite some time—two utterly opposite comprehensions of the reality of man. All other crises that have gone before have been little else than a prelude to this, a final clash, a crisis never before seen in the annals of history.

So why do so few see it plainly?

Chapter 3

THE STORM BREAKS:
The 1960s

In the past fifty years, Western society has undergone a transformation of devastating speed never before witnessed in history. Consider: The *potential* of bearing children was once viewed with excitement, indeed as a blessing, but is now viewed as a problem. Having too many or unplanned children is seen by huge numbers of humanity—individuals and governments—as a problem in need of a solution. The solution has boiled down to a two-pronged approach: prevention and, failing that, elimination (contraception and abortion).

No one is suggesting that previous times did not have people who also clung to this view, but it was never accepted as the unchallenged orthodoxy of a society. Contraception, the first component of the "solution," is in fact so accepted that many who abhor abortion do not so much as blink an eye when it comes to actively preventing new life from being conceived.

It is one of the great ironies and tragedies of the anti-abortion movement, which has restyled itself the pro-life movement, that it really is in fact what abortion supporters have long labeled it: anti-abortion. For in being opposed to abortion but in support of contraception, members have made themselves not really pro-life, but merely *pro-birth*. Their respect for life only comes into play in the actual, not the potential. In this regard, even many avid pro-lifers share common ground with those they march against.

The question could and should be asked of pro-lifers: Do you disagree with Planned Parenthood across the board, or just on the issue of abortion? Do you have no issue with their distribution of condoms, for example?

19

And as is the case with any question that goes to the heart of one's self-understanding, many other questions follow. Do pro-contraception, anti-abortion (PCAA) pro-lifers oppose premarital sexual relations between a couple the night before the couple is to be married? Do they oppose the action occurring, say, the week before? How about the month before?

How about the question of cohabitation? Do PCAAs oppose a couple "trying it out" for a few months before getting married just to make sure they are compatible? What could be wrong with that?

And what about overall promiscuity of a general nature? If one or both of the couple were absolutely certain they would not get pregnant and bring into question the potentiality of an abortion, would PCAAs object to a sexually rambunctious lifestyle? Imagine, for example, that each partner had been "fixed" (a term that in itself implies a problem has been overcome) so that what we had in reality was a couple with each partner sterilized, where the chances of conception are totally non-existent; would a PCAA find anything in this case to which he could object?

This little questioning exercise is not to pick on a segment of the self-styled pro-life movement, but to point out that contraception is king in the new moral order—so much so that even supposedly rational people, who can see so clearly on the question of child murder, have become blind to the question of child prevention.

Another aspect in which society has undergone a massive refashioning in the past fifty years is the relationship of the individual to the society. This has borne itself out and made itself present in the constant battle between rights and responsibilities. It is, in fact, the continual battle we see played out every night and day in various media reports covering issues like immigration, welfare, "reproductive rights" cases, healthcare, and so forth.

These battles, waged in legislatures and courts, are not at their heart about the individual questions at hand, but go more to the question of how we see ourselves—either as people with a claim on one another and who have corresponding duties to meet those claims, or as an individual with a claim on everyone else, but with no resulting claim on himself.

Is the Obama supporter *owed* his Obama phone, or should the Obama phone holder go get a job? Does the taxpayer have the obligation to ensure to his best ability that the culture is perfectly equitable so everyone can get a job, or is it incumbent on the downtrodden man to get off his rear end and break the habit of living off hand-outs financed by the taxpayer?

These questions, these struggles, of course develop quite healthy legs of their own in the political world, as men and women jockey for votes and power by testing the winds of any particular voting constituent and try to manipulate the winds of war to their advantage. Politicians, instead of being leaders of men trying to establish a correct understanding of what it is to be human, are very often little else than parasites, maggots feeding on the nearly decomposing corpse of a fetid society—a society that has decided it's more advantageous for a man to look out for number one than to sacrifice for the common good.

While there has always been the native instinct to look out for number one, it is hard to recall a time in the history of the West when such an outlook was so enshrined in culture as to nearly obliterate the countering view of the common good.

What has emerged in the past fifty years or so is such a distorted self-view of man that what follows from this view can only bring about misery, both on the individual and collective level—a misery that many continually try to escape but only sink more deeply into because they fail to realize the cause of their misery is their view of themselves—a view they have both been given and have handed on to others. They have accepted it, and accepted it willingly.

So what misery is commonplace? For starters, the notion of marriage— a lifelong commitment to the other with the expectation of sharing the love between the two with children—now seems almost quaint. Marriage, divorce, remarriage is now the cycle. And *this* is a monumental change of the past fifty years, whose impact has barely begun to be felt.

The entire material order has been turned on its head because contemporary man now sees himself disconnected from any real material world obligations. Man's self-view now consists of a being with rights that others must support, the chief of which is to be able to copulate, without outside limits imposed on him and with no consequences as long as it's "consensual."

This self-view subordinates all other aspects of man. The cry of contemporary man is simply: "I have a right to an orgasm with whomever, whenever, however often I want." It has become the centerpiece of every issue that comes up—political, social, media, familial, and even theological.

An entire political party (the Democrats) has based itself on this "freedom." An entire society, the whole nation, has accepted and practices this "freedom" with its near-unanimous support of contraception. Being able to have consensual sex with whomever you want is a mainstay of the entire media and entertainment colossus, and families are routinely fashioned around the notion that sex is king. (Is it not often the case that the reason so many children are shuttled between parents is because those same parents wanted to have sex with someone other than that child's true mother or father?)

As we look out on the vast changes that society has undergone these past fifty years or so, the issue of homosexuality is the last domino to fall. And it stands to reason that if a culture says sex is recreational and geared to the individual and brings along with it no real responsibilities to the collective, then why can't men have sex with men? Why can't a woman legally marry another woman? For that matter, why can't two lesbians marry a third?

Logic dictates that if the primary end of sex is pleasure (which contemporary man has decided in his self-view that it is), then by what distortion of logic can someone maintain that sexual pleasure is restricted only to so-called heterosexuals? This was a major underpinning of the US Supreme Court's ruling on June 26, 2015 in *Obergefell v. Hodges*. The Court had already ruled years before in *Lawrence v. Texas* on the constitutional right to engage in consensual homosexual sex. So how could it not in short order rule that the constitutionally protected right to engage in sodomy also permits a constitutional right to engage in sodomy within a marriage? That is precisely what it did rule.

The answer to the question why so few see plainly the crisis as it unfolds before us is simple: The crisis has already occurred and is past. Most have been swept up in it and are now paying the price, or soon will be, for such a transformation.

The crisis has come and gone. One wave has completely overwhelmed the other. What remains now is the aftermath of the crisis. And as in the case of any aftermath, there is always blood—and lots of it. One side has won, and now it must assert its victory so there is no misunderstanding on the part of the vanquished that they are, in fact, vanquished.

But remember, this is a spiritual crisis, as in fact they all are. This has been one of such intensity, however, not to mention speed, that its aftermath will also be intense. The aftermath will be so intense, in fact, that it will be felt by every person, in each man's soul, and in many, many men's bodies as well. The mindset that has conquered is the fruit of much action, but also of inaction, of much intense advancement, but also of pitiful opposition.

Consider: In the space of fifty years, an entire civilization, bound together in self-understanding and morality, a civilization that developed and lasted more than a thousand years, has been almost completely refashioned, paying little more than lip service to its storied past—oftentimes even rewriting that past to conform to the new reality, which is a crash of such magnitude that the aftermath can only be of an equal magnitude.

And standing alone in the rubble is one remaining vestige, what many see as little else than an artifact: the Catholic Church.

A distinction of enormous import, however, needs to be made at this point between the Catholic Church as She exists in Herself—which is the indefectible, immaculate Bride of Christ—and the Catholic Church as She is lived in Her individual, sinful members.

Here is a paralyzing thought: If the world were to end at this moment and all the inhabitants of earth would fail to be joined to the Church Triumphant, She would still be triumphant, even without us. That even one human being scaled the heights of Heaven, ascending even beyond the realm of angels, is a monumental defeat for Hell and a victory for the Church—hence the term Church Triumphant.

So no Catholic on earth should ever feel as though he has a place waiting for him and that without him the victory is somehow diminished. The victory is already secured. Whether we as individuals are participants in that victory or among those over whom the victory is won is entirely of our own choosing. The presence of just one human assumed into the Divine means Hell lost the war. So no one is guaranteed anything.

It is vital always to remember this: We need Heaven, but Heaven does not need us. God is not diminished by our absence from the Divine Majesty—but we *are*, to our everlasting shame. So there is no room for an attitude of certainty, or near certainty, when it comes to the question of salvation. Indeed, as most of the saints and Doctors and Fathers of the Church warn about again and again, most men are damned—Catholics included.

The Church Triumphant is already in existence, but it is a certainty that individual members of the Church Militant shall not ascend to the heights of victory but will join their master down below in the society of the damned. And this should come not as a surprise but as a terrible call to holiness, a frightful call to arms in the Church Militant. From the very beginning, the Church Militant has had traitors among its ranks. Judas would be the first; he would not, sadly, be the last.

As the holy and esteemed Fr. John Hardon astutely observed, any soul in a state of mortal sin is a tool of the devil. There are today within the ranks of the Church Militant many who are operatives of the diabolical—wittingly or unwittingly, it makes no difference. Treachery, whether intended or not, has the same devastating result.

Chapter 4

WHAT HAPPENED?
Martin Luther Plants the Seed

Father Martin Luther was not the first traitor among the ranks of the priestly class; Judas owns that dishonor. But he was among the more significant, owing in no small part to the fact that the demon he loosed on the Church in the sixteenth century is still seething and raging against the body of Christ. What history terms the Protestant Reformation is more fittingly called the Protestant Revolt, for it was a revolution, not a reform. The Church is always re-forming in each successive generation. She is never in a state of revolution, but many of Her individual sons are.

Martin Luther was one such son. In his own mind, so unsteady and uncertain, a crisis had arisen: He needed a guarantee that he was saved, assurance that he would not be damned. Here is the jumping-off point for the cataclysm in which modern man finds himself today, 500 years after Luther's revolution.

He asked a question and sought an answer that cannot be known this side of eternity. As long as we live and breathe, Heaven can be won or lost in the next moment. From Judas to Dismas hanging on the Cross next to Our Blessed Lord, salvation is at our fingertips; all we need do is grasp it, or let go of it.

It was Luther's psychological drama of needing assurance that drove him to his eventual theological absurdities. He was one of the leading Scripture scholars of Europe, yet a man devoid of supernatural hope, or trust. He stormed the gates of Heaven demanding an answer and convinced himself that Heaven had responded in the affirmative.

He developed an entire doctrine around his ramblings, and his ramblings became doctrinaire. His process for ending theological unity across the continent was brilliant in its simplicity.

The Scripture scholar claimed that since man was justified by faith *alone* (an entirely anti-scriptural notion), there was ultimately no need of a Church with its sacraments and priesthood and sacrificial Masses and saints and hierarchy and Pope. Man could simply open the Bible and use it as *the* authority—*Sola Scriptura.* What he did not reckon with was other revolutionaries arriving at differing interpretations from his as to the meaning of this or that particular Scripture passage.

But the damage was done. In his attempt to overthrow the authority of the Church in matters of salvation, he had merely *transferred* the authority, not abolished it. Every individual man now became his own individual pope, deciding right or wrong and attributing his personal peccadilloes to a right reading of Scripture. It does not matter if others disagree with him. It is right *for him.* The individual now became the sole arbiter of right and wrong.

What Luther unleashed in the world of the theological would soon travel across the common boundary shared with the philosophical. Once self-styled intellectual elites got hold of the notion that truth was something determined by the individual and not an objective reality in itself, Satan had the world right where he wanted it.

An individual crisis in the mind of a psychologically disturbed German cleric was about to become a collective crisis, the repercussions of which are still being felt in great sonic booms even today.

The old order would pass away soon enough. The idea of authority had been laid waste; all that would follow would be the necessary revolutions and wars and realignments of the political and societal spheres. Sure, it would take a couple of centuries for this to play out, but the devil saw his moment and played it for all it was worth. Mankind was hurtling toward a total dismantling of self-understanding. Ever since the very beginning, no matter what civilization or empire, men had never seen themselves as autonomous, as unconnected to the divine— whatever their idea of the divine may have been.

From Anatolia to Assyria to Persia to Egypt to Greece to Rome, throughout all the Eastern regions, from Judaism to Catholicism to

Islam, man had always seen himself as subordinate to God or the gods—but no longer. In the new philosophy, we could no longer determine even what reality is, much less what is true about it.

Philosopher after philosopher emerged onto the scene, each one tearing away at the world of objective truth more than his predecessors had done. They cut great swaths through logic and thought, which laid waste to an entire civilization—the same civilization that had taught them to read, and had provided books and manuscripts. That civilization had done all this and more, guided by the star of objective truth, and that objective truth not only existed but was knowable.

Now the ungrateful sons of that civilization would not only deny objective truth and that it was knowable, they would come to deny that anything is knowable in itself, that there is in the end no truth, that everything is knowable only in relation to everything else.

It would take a few generations for all this to be wholly absorbed and played out, but before it was all over, monarchies would be toppled and new nations would emerge complete with their new gods of individualism and the rights of man, built on the philosophically flimsy apparatus of simply being declared true on man's say-so. They could be attributed for expediency to some kind of universal sovereign to shore up any cracks in the foundation, but it was little else than a counterfeit understanding of man, bereft of any true self-examination.

For example, why would a Creator grant any inherent rights to man? Who had the authority, in the new world of no authority, to declare what is in the mind and the intention of the Creator? Since the Creator was so circumspect as simply to allow fallible man to stumble across these "self-evident truths," who was to say the Creator could not simply reverse course the next day and provide a whole new set of "self-evident truths"? After all, if they were so self-evident, how could they have been missed by all of human history up to the eighteenth century? Doesn't "self-evident" imply there is a degree of evidence?

To base an entire national life on certain truths being self-evident while ignoring the reality that no one up to this point in all of humanity had noticed these truths could be easily seen as mere philosophical caprice. Nonetheless, the Great American Experiment was underway. The break from the past was now complete, and a new nation was born.

But was the break from the past so complete? Not as much as trumpeted. It may have been complete from a governing standpoint, but a self-governed people would only be able to succeed in self-government if there were agreed-on rules and protocols and so forth. Despite the fact that the North American continent's first European arrivals in the sixteenth century were Catholic—from Florida and the Caribbean to Quebec and the St. Lawrence Seaway—it was Protestantism that ultimately prevailed from the Finger Lakes of New York to the Bayou of Louisiana.

But it was a Protestantism that shared one major aspect with its despised Catholic enemy: morality. Despite the fomenting over theological claims, Protestantism still clung, nearly ferociously, to Catholic morality, and most especially to sexual morality. It will be one of the ultimate conundrums of history that a religion that began as a clarion call for the rights of the individual to determine truth would cling so tenaciously to the demand that everyone give up that self-determination in the realm of sexual morality. There would be no deviation tolerated—at least, not yet.

From the perspective of the new America, the perfect society had been formed, a nation beholden to no state Church, yet vigorously accepting of and enforcing the moral code of a Church their forebears had thrown off. It was having their cake and eating it, too. America was a Christian nation, without any of the messiness of deciding which brand of Christianity—so long as it was not Catholic.

Yet the whole edifice was a giant sham, a practical theology with no philosophical underpinnings. Nothing had been thought out or thought through. In the rush to throw off King George's government, no one had realized that King George's religion (or at the very least, King George's religious system) had been kept, and no one knew why or even noticed. *This is the way everyone has always worshipped, right? We all believe in God, right? So let's move on.* An unofficial state religion *did* exist in America, but it was precisely because it was unofficial that the stage was set for its collapse.

If there had been a religious war in the States, perhaps some things would have been made clearer. At least a great religious debate might have provided some clarity. All these religions couldn't all be correct; they each taught different things, but they had *enough* in common to skate by, for a while. When Methodists would talk about the Bible,

Presbyterians thought they understood. When Baptists spoke of Jesus, the Lutherans recognized the name. It was all Christian, after all, and everyone seemed to believe the same *essential* things. For the time being, all appeared quite placid and workable.

Even when the upstart Catholic immigrants started crowding into US cities in the nineteenth and early twentieth centuries, they could be reasonably tolerated—up to a point. At least they shared the same sexual morality, despite charges by the Know-Nothings that Catholics were rapists, among other things.

Even when the Ku Klux Klan unsuccessfully marched on the University of Notre Dame in the 1920s to burn it down, it was from the imagined threat that the Vatican wanted to overthrow the government and establish a Catholic province; it was not because Catholics and Protestants saw things differently with regard to the moral code.

The same claim inspired anti-Catholic backlash when John Kennedy ran for president in 1960. No one was claiming that Catholics would ruin the morals of a nation, only that the Vatican had secret plans to take control of the government and make the United States a puppet state, a theocracy. The great concern that Protestant America had toward Catholics in America was confined to a fear of outside control by the Pope, not the forsaking of a shared moral code.

So impressive, in fact, was this Catholic morality that, despite Martin Luther's despoiling of Catholic Europe nearly 500 years earlier, the moral code was still very much intact throughout not only Catholic lands but formerly Catholic lands, as well as new nations like America. It appeared that the theological differences didn't amount to that big a difference after all. And that is exactly what Satan wanted everyone to believe as the 1960s dawned.

Chapter 5

THE AMERICAN PETRI DISH:
Luther's Liberty

It was all well and good for people to accept the same sexual morality, for it had major societal advantages. As well, it had built-in biological checks and balances, courtesy of Mother Nature. Too much promiscuity and consequences would stare a society in the face: unintended pregnancy. In fact, it could be argued that the acceptance of the sexual moral code was more owing to this than theological principle; people had merely come to accept that if you had sex outside of marriage, the results would be "bad."

But recall that Americanism was built on an individualism inherited from a philosophical system born from Martin Luther's rejection of authority in the theological realm. If nothing else, Americans are pragmatic. When the consequences of a certain behavior are too severe, most people won't engage in it. If their non-engagement in the behavior just happens to coincide with the prevailing moral code, then all the better.

But what would happen if the American individualism suddenly encountered a situation that was consequence-free? Would that individualism continue to restrict itself to a moral code that had never really been hashed out and debated and understood beyond its mere practical application? Since America had never had the great religious debate, had never engaged in the discussion of which religion is right, none of the moral tenets had ever been explored from a theological perspective.

Is sex outside of marriage wrong because it is a sin, or just because some poor unfortunate most likely would become pregnant? The first possibility had never been debated because an entire antecedent dis-

31

cussion would have to have happened on what is sin, according to whom, by what authority, and so forth. The country would have been hurled right back to 1517 Germany.

Besides, it was easy to sidestep such prickly issues because, regardless of whether it's a sin or not, it was a given that sex outside of marriage almost certainly meant a baby—if not the first time, then certainly shortly thereafter. It wasn't worth the risk in most cases. But if the threat of risk were to be removed, then a whole new dynamic could emerge.

The same year Catholic John Kennedy was apologizing for being Catholic to a group of Protestant ministers in Houston during his presidential run, another Catholic was putting the finishing touches to his research that would produce the birth control pill. Doctor John Rock was the natural heir of Martin Luther. More than 400 years after the barons of Germany gave cover to Luther for his heresy, the rulers of the United States gave cover to the result of his heresy: The US Food and Drug Administration gave approval to the birth control pill.

The crisis had at last emerged, had come into full bloom, and almost no one recognized it for what it was. Satan had capitalized on the crisis of thought in the mind of Martin Luther and set in motion the idea that man is his own authority. Once that belief was in place—indeed, was enshrined as a governing principle—all he had to do was look for a way to exploit it. Sex would be his weapon.

There are two powers that even angels do not possess that man does: One is the ability to receive the actual Body and Blood of Jesus Christ in Holy Communion, and the other is to unite with God in the act of creation. I will for the moment leave aside exploration of the first and examine the second.

Recall the envy Satan holds toward humans. Not only might any individual man ascend to heights greater than the devil once occupied in his celestial glory, but man can also enjoy an intimacy with God in the act of creation. If this act could be perverted, ripped from its original purpose and subordinated to the merely carnal, then the intimacy man shares with God could be destroyed and man reduced to his more base instincts, and consequently, denied the Beatific Vision. Satan had set the stage for man to be his own master over everything to this point; so, too, even his sexuality man would now rule over.

It was the Garden all over again. Shorn from its relation to God, sex would be the instrument by which Satan would say once again to mankind: "you will be like god" (Gen. iii : 5).

The first instruction that God gave the first human family was to "[b]e fruitful and multiply" (Gen. i : 28). How fitting then that the death-dealing devil would take such aim at this highest physical power of man, a power he himself does not possess. So strong and innate in our human nature—in fact, in all of nature—is the inclination to reproduce that it would require a near-herculean effort on the part of the diabolical and the patience of his old nemesis Job to accomplish an overthrow of the established order.

Basic, fundamental understandings of human nature itself, sexuality, "gender" roles, and psychology would each have to be completely wiped away. Empirical evidence would have to be trotted out to present to man's intellect the idea that reproduction is a bad instead of a good. The entire order of life would have to be turned on its head. The value of life itself would have to be so completely lost and disfig-ured that anything would become possible.

Even for Hell, this would appear a near impossibility—the complete perversion of good into bad while tricking mankind into thinking it was a good. Sex would have to be uncoupled from procreation on such a scale that the very walls of Hell itself would shake. Satan set about his work in a very patient manner, for "the serpent was more subtle than any other wild creature that the Lord God had made" (Gen. iii : 1).

It is always instructive to glance backward to more clearly see the trajectory of certain things. The crisis begun in Luther's mind, which resulted in a crisis of theological authority, prepared the way for a crisis of philosophy, which itself exploded into a crisis of political order, which brought about the ascendancy of man as the determiner of his own rights. Man was supreme. Over the course of roughly two to three centuries, authority had been taken from God and delivered into the hands of man. *Liberty* was the catchword of a newly minted people.

Of course, at the dawn of the nineteenth century this may not have been entirely clear. All seemed well on the surface; new governments were emerging, new nations and former nations realigning themselves into a new civilization. There was widespread acceptance of the idea of a Supreme Being who ordered our days and lives. Morality was widely viewed as being the system by which lives were lived appropriately so as to maintain the common good.

It was healthy for the citizenry that women would be mothers, fathers would be the head of the household and earn a living for the brood (most of which were large), and that society would keep in place legal and moral codes to foster this atmosphere. It was the duty of religion to remind the nation that we lived by an established moral order for maintaining the common good so that we could "secure the blessings of liberty to ourselves and our posterity."

America's Founding Fathers all recognized the need, the requirement, that a nation not have multiple gods or moral codes. They spoke often of religion and its necessity for binding a nation together. And when they spoke of religion, and when their audience heard them speak of religion, what was understood was the *Christian religion*, in whatever form or denomination it may have taken. But what they did not contemplate was that a religion, a man-made religion, could just as easily be replaced with another man-made religion with a completely different set of moral codes and an entirely new morality.

It was precisely because the attitude exhibited toward religion was so rooted in liberty that the prevailing religion of the United States would eventually give way to a different religion, also rooted in liberty—a personal, autonomous liberty without respect to anyone but the individual.

In some ways, the lack of morality we have in the United States today is the logical outcome of that *laissez-faire* approach to religion, a model of pragmatism seeking to use religion simply as a means to an end. Having never had the debate over which religion was right (and one religion certainly is, which necessarily means the others are false) meant that no religion ever became enshrined; therefore, the moral code, the nation's morality, was always in a state of being "up for grabs." It was settled only because we agreed it was settled—which, of course, had the real-world effect of setting the stage for its being settled—until it was not.

In the nineteenth century, as some families were busy securing the blessings of liberty to themselves and their posterity by amassing unimaginable personal fortunes, there arose an attitude of superiority, one that gave way to exploration of the idea that some races were inferior and should be dealt with as such.

This was hardly a novel idea. Practically every major civilization up to this point had some undercurrents of this, if not actual policy. What is slavery if not the politicized belief that someone is the master and someone else the slave, a superior and inferior? Slavery had been present throughout nearly all of history and had almost always come about as a result of military conquest. But what made the new approach to the question of inferiority of some peoples so unique in the nineteenth century was the air of respectability it assumed under the mantle of the Rockefellers, a truly American family if there ever was one.

It was John Rockefeller, Jr. who first brought the subject of eugenics into the family. In the late nineteenth century, the "science" of eugenics was described by its proponents as "the self-determination of human evolution." Once again, the notion of self-determination, of the autonomous man, was at work.

While studying at Brown University in 1894, the young Rockefeller wrote a paper called "The Dangers to America Arising from Unrestricted Immigration" in which he denounced immigrants as "the scum of foreign cities; the vagabond, the tramp, the pauper, and the indolent . . . ignorant and hardly better than beasts."

He sought to rid the planet of these "scum" through the science of genetics. Rockefeller did this by giving money away to organizations that supported and advanced his views. The Rockefellers' initial foray into the field was the establishment of the Eugenics Record Office at Cold Spring Harbor, New York in 1910, furthering the Rockefellers' support of eugenics research and John's racist convictions.

Three years later, the crown jewel of the Rockefeller family was established; the Rockefeller Foundation was founded in 1913 when the New York State Legislature passed an act on April 24 incorporating the Foundation. The Foundation would evolve into an organization that would infiltrate some of the most important structures of American Catholicism, but more on that later.

For the present, the Foundation became the conduit for financing various efforts to control populations and manipulate population growth. It was the method the Rockefeller family used to funnel huge sums of money to numerous projects whose chief aim was in harmony with theirs: controlling populations.

The Rockefeller Foundation statement of purpose read: "To promote the well-being of mankind throughout the world" (an ambiguous purpose if there ever was one, since the question of actually who determined what "well-being" means was left open). Once the Foundation was incorporated, the seventy-five-year-old John D. Rockefeller, Sr., the organization's founding father, made gifts to the Foundation totaling $35 million, followed a year later by $65 million. Adjusted for inflation, $100 million in 1913 would be the equivalent in today's dollars—a century later—of $2.5 billion. Clearly, the Rockefellers were serious about moving the needle.

The secretary of the Foundation at its beginning in 1913, Jerome D. Greene, said in a memorandum describing the Foundation's principles and policies that the Foundation's work is to "go to the root of individual or social ill-being and misery." This established a rough framework for the Foundation moving forward.

At a first meeting of the board, a longtime advisor to John, Sr. by the name of Frederick Gates argued that "disease is the supreme ill in human life" (placing bodily, material needs over that of spiritual needs). The general concept of "health" became established as a Foundation priority and would be the basis for later designs on world government through population control and climate change initiatives.

In June of 1913, the Rockefeller board paid out its first grants in the sum of $25,000 to create the International Health Commission, which launched the Foundation into the area of health on a global scale. "Health," in fact, came to have a very broad meaning, as the Foundation also helped establish the American Social Hygiene Association to direct the scientific study of biological and social factors that influence human sexual conduct. These early years set the course of the Rockefeller Foundation to the present day.

"Health" became the cover under which the entire population control movement would maneuver. Today, if you peruse any of the notable foundations dedicated to population control, you will find the cover word "health" on prominent display, not the least of which is the Bill and Melinda Gates Foundation. The Foundation established by the Gates makes the Rockefellers appear to be rank amateurs in comparison. While John, Sr. poured in the equivalent of close to $3 billion, the Gates Foundation is sitting atop $40 billion in assets. The Bill and Melinda Gates Foundation has assumed the mantle from the Rockefeller Foundation in the arena of population control.

While the Rockefeller Foundation does not use the term "eugenics" as it so freely did in its earlier days, it is still very heavily involved in "social research." This interest was revealed by the Foundation's financial support for the Bureau of Social Hygiene for some twenty years. The mission of the Bureau was to research and study social ills like prostitution as well as provide "education" in birth control, maternal health, and sex education. The Bureau finally shut its doors in 1940, as the family set its sights on other venues for "social enrichment," such as population control.

In 1952, the Population Council was founded by John D. Rockefeller III, grandson of the robber baron and son of John, Jr., who had become the eugenics enthusiast. In an effort to separate the Council from the negative connotations of eugenics in a post-World War II world still reeling from the horrors of Nazi death camps, the word "eugenics" was dropped and replaced with the euphemism "population control."

The Council also fostered the development of contraceptives and the study of the social sciences in order to increase the use of contraceptives among the general public. Some common contraceptives available today were developed by Rockefeller's Population Council. These include the Copper-T IUD, Norplant, Jadelle (Norplant II), and the Mirena IUD.

Heresy Come Full Circle

However, the focus on the Rockefeller's mid-century work is getting a little ahead of the game. The real success that paved the way for the Rockefellers came not at the hands of any government, but via the world of religion. It was the Anglican Communion—the Church of England—at its 1930 Lambeth Conference that opened the floodgates to seeing contraception as morally permissible.

After a series of rejections in previous years, contraception was approved following pressure from well-financed eugenics groups tracing their ideologies back to Rockefeller. For the first time in nearly

2,000 years of Christian history, what had formerly been considered a grievous sin was now scrubbed from the list, first by the Anglicans and eventually by every major Protestant denomination, and many minor ones as well.

The heresy of Protestantism was now coming full circle. Having broken from its moorings in Catholic truth, having advanced through universities and palaces and governments for nearly four centuries, it was now coming back into the churches. The heresy had marshaled its forces in every conceivable arena—political, academic, legal—and was now ready to explode onto a nation's morality.

What happened to cause the Church of England to reverse course after previously rejecting contraception as immoral? The difference was the organization and funding of the global forces seeking to legitimize contraception, namely, the Rockefeller Foundation.

Only one lone voice rang out against the evil. Just as Pope St. Pius X had warned twenty years earlier of the gathering storm seeking to overthrow the kingdom of Christ, now his successor, Pope Pius XI, issued his encyclical *Casti Connubii*, in which he decried birth control as a moral evil and answered Lambeth with authentic Catholic moral teaching that refuses to compromise with modernity. He reaffirmed the age-old teaching on abortion and contraception, clearly calling them moral evils to be avoided within civil society, the family and marriage:

> [Those who contracept] commit a deed which is shameful and intrinsically vicious. . . . [T]hose who indulge in such contraceptive acts are branded with the guilt of grave sin. . . . Priests and pastors must teach about contraception or they will be lost as well. . . . [In marriage, men and women] will reap that which they have sown in childhood.

Much of the Rockefeller Foundation money went to the Planned Parenthood Federation of America, known as the American Birth Control League in the early days of the birth control movement and driven by personalities such as Margaret Sanger. One by one, as various Protestant groups throughout America began accepting contraception, it became clear that Protestant America posed no significant opposition to the contraceptive culture that was quickly emerging.

And really, how could it? The consensus morality that had governed the United States since its inception was not rooted in authentic theology and correct philosophy, but in a socially accepted contract to bind together the nation for the good of the nation's simply being bound—"to secure the blessings of liberty to ourselves and our posterity." Once it was presented as an alternative good to actually limit the number of that posterity, contraception would be accepted wholesale. Those presentations were not far in coming.

In 1960, the birth control pill appeared following FDA approval. In 1965, the US Supreme Court ruled in *Griswold v. Connecticut* that married couples have a constitutional right to use birth control. Prior to *Griswold*, the sale or distribution of contraception was actually against the law. It's hard to imagine by twenty-first-century standards that contraception was actually once *prohibited* by law. The law overthrown by *Griswold* was known as the federal Comstock Law, established in 1873, which banned the sale or distribution of contraception and other items deemed immoral.

In 1968, a book appeared on the scene titled *The Population Bomb*, written by Stanford University's Paul Ehrlich, predicting the starvation and deaths of hundreds of millions of people in the 1970s and 80s. It was an instant bestseller and a game-changer. Its obvious inaccuracies and woefully incorrect predictions didn't matter; the seed had been planted among the general population that there were too many people on the planet. Even to this day, the common man still sees the world as overpopulated.

It was enough to set the stage for the final victory for the contraceptive mentality—that not only is it theologically acceptable to uncouple sex from its procreative reality, it's good for humanity. Imagine: all the sexual pleasure and license a person could wish to engage in while actually helping to improve the human condition.

As Satan had so skillfully done in centuries past, he manipulated fallen man to act in defiance of his true end. He played pride and power like the proverbial violin and set the stage for contraception to become the norm—which by the 1970s it had become. But why stop there? Despite his loathing for mankind fueled by his envy, his real target has always been the Bride of Christ, the Catholic Church.

Whether even the demonic mind could foresee the opportunity that would be presented to lay waste the Church Militant through the collapse of sexual morality is something we cannot know with certitude. But if Satan had not anticipated it with sufficient clarity, he certainly saw the opportunity as it unfolded. Not only could he reorient the highest gift of creation given to man, he could use the consequence of that reorientation to attack the Catholic Church directly and in a devastating manner.

Contraception was affording men the opportunity to lay aside their authentic masculinity—aimed at protecting and preserving through self-sacrifice—and instead encouraging a return to self-absorbed, inward-turned adolescence. But it was also giving women, future mothers, a whole new self-conception, a never-before-known self-understanding. The moment was imminently exploitable. Satan would use it to strike at the very heart of the Church.

The heresy of Martin Luther, which can neatly be summed up as "I am my own authority," had come full circle by the dawn of the 1960s. Thirty years later it would even be pronounced as such by none other than the US Supreme Court when Justice Anthony Kennedy (a Catholic) would declare, writing for the majority: "At the heart of liberty is the right to define one's own concept of existence, of meaning, of the universe, and of the mystery of human life" (*Planned Parenthood v. Casey*, 1992).

Radical Feminism

The radical feminism of the 1960s through the 80s launched in the popular consciousness of Americans was beyond revolutionary. Women had been seen up to this point as wives and mothers, a kind of "biology is destiny" mantra. Since they were the ones who conceived and carried to term the next generation, they stayed at home, raised the children, got pregnant, and raised even more children.

It was the man who left the house to provide for the family's material needs. Leaders of the Women's Liberation movement saw this as a great injustice in need of righting. If men could be liberated from the burden of fatherhood and enjoy sex with no consequences, then why should women also not be able to enjoy the fruits of liberation?

They no longer had to be mothers. They, too, could have careers and money and self-determination. They could be freed from the shackles of dependency on men and at long last pull up alongside them as equals—and all thanks to the birth control pill.

The invention of the washing machine a few years earlier had already freed up much of their time otherwise taken up doing various household chores. Now they could run a house *and* have a career. So they poured into the workforce, a trend that had already begun a generation earlier during World War II. They began filling up college classrooms, in search of the needed education and degrees to compete for jobs and launch careers of their own.

The entire self-understanding of womanhood, of the feminine, was altered in one generation. The Helen Reddy blockbuster hit "I Am Woman" said it all. It became the anthem for the entire Women's Lib movement. In an interview years later Reddy said she felt the song had supernatural inspiration.

> I remember lying in bed one night and the words "I am strong, I am invincible, I am woman" kept going over and over in my head. That part I consider to be divinely inspired. I had been chosen to get a message across.

Pressed on who had chosen her, she replied, "The universe."

In the same year feminist icon Gloria Steinem launched her *Ms. Magazine*, the song quickly captured the imagination of the nascent women's movement. In a 1973 interview, National Organization for Women (NOW) founder Betty Friedan conveyed that the song had been played to close out that year's NOW convention in Washington, DC.

> Suddenly, women got out of their seats and started dancing around the hotel ballroom and joining hands in a circle that got larger and larger until maybe a thousand of us were dancing and singing "I am strong, I am invincible, I am woman." It was a spontaneous, beautiful expression of the exhilaration we all felt in those years, women really moving as women.

In that same year Betty Friedan was giving her interview about women dancing enthusiastically at their gala dinner in DC to rhythms celebrating their new empowerment, the US Supreme Court just across town had delivered them the biggest empowerment they could imagine—the power to legally kill their own children in the womb.

41

Satan had engineered women to become murderers. They had indeed pulled up right along beside men. They had exchanged nurturing for death. But the diabolical was just beginning. The assault on the Church Militant was about to be fully launched.

Chapter 6

FEMINIST MEN:
The Church of Nice Is Born

One of the enduring effects of the Women's Lib movement is not only did it make women more like men, it also had the impact of making men more like women. To be masculine, to exhibit what were traditionally considered masculine traits, was greatly frowned on. After all, it was those same masculine traits from which women were liberating themselves. To be a masculine man was seen to be on the losing side.

So it should come as no great surprise that the homosexual rights movement also found its footing during this same time period. The 1969 Stonewall Riots in New York's Greenwich Village did for homosexualists what the bra-burning displays accomplished for the Women's Lib movement on the opposite coast. It was a message only a dead man could miss—the masculine was out, the feminine was in. Anything associated with the masculine had to be done away with and consigned to history's ash heap. Now the plan of the diabolical was coming into sharp and clear focus.

In the great rush to expunge their consciences of treating women as sexual objects, hordes of men quickly boarded the Women's Lib bandwagon. How convenient! Men wanted to have sex; along came a technology that allowed almost wanton promiscuity, and women were happy participants for their own reasons. And if it failed, backup abortions were at the ready.

Numerous men convinced themselves that the ideology of the Women's Lib movement was perfectly reasonable and should be supported and advanced. As more and more women threw off the old moral clothing and engaged in anonymous sex as much as men did, why would men complain about that? After all, birth control was a good for humanity—at least, that's what the social scientists backed by wealthy foundations were saying. Everyone knew it. It was in the news every day. Books were published about it. College professors were teaching it. It was a given, an unquestioned orthodoxy.

In the ensuing years, Mother Earth worship would emerge from the shadows, Gaia worship would receive its share of attention, and college courses and entire degrees would be awarded for so-called feminist studies. The entire culture was being drowned in the feminine, including the masculine. And while the Church Militant has always had an air of the masculine, that masculine was now being eradicated in the culture, and it would only be a matter of time before it was attacked in the Church as well.

Recall that while all this became visible to the common man in the 1960s, the forces behind the scenes had been at work for decades earlier, preparing the culture to accept the radical changes. Young men entering the seminary in these days were coming from families that had already been experiencing subtle attacks for at least one generation, and in some cases two or more.

In the United States, the notions of liberty and self-determination and independence were simply part of the national DNA. Prior to the 1950s, the identity of Catholic Americans was still much more Catholic than American. But the post-World War II era began to change all that. Catholics who had fought alongside their Protestant countrymen in Tripoli and Normandy and the Pacific Islands in the 1940s were no longer viewed with as much suspicion and hostility. They were becoming more accepted than in previous generations.

As the 1950s dawned, it felt good to be American if you were Catholic. America was, after all, the unchallenged moral superpower, the unspoken master race. While the religion was still not Catholic, the morality was. As long as the morality remained, we could work on the religion issue. But as the culture began a tectonic shift in morality, owing largely to those forces patiently at work behind the scenes, it would be Americanism that would invisibly come to predominate in Catholic homes—and Americanism was pronouncing that a new moral order was being established.

Many young men who entered the seminary from this point on would come from homes more American than Catholic and would introduce into the Church an American view of humanity corrupted by the same ingredients that would give birth to radical feminism and inauthentic masculinity. Over the next forty years, these young men would change the face and heart of the Church in America from the Church Militant to the Church of Nice—a Church with an exaggerated sense of the feminine and no sense of the masculine.

It would parallel exactly the culture, which itself had been hyper-feminized and castrated, and it would follow that from this crop of young men would come the eventual leaders of the Church in the coming decades. The one thing not foreseen was this: The feminized culture was itself militant, while the Church of Nice had laid aside all such notions.

It rivals the greatest displays of naïveté in the history of the Church and perhaps the world. The Council Fathers, in their exuberance over the changing times, forgot about or failed to account sufficiently for the effects of original sin. They got swept up in a kind euphoria that offered the possibility that man was moving beyond the horrors of his past, that man was much more in control of his passions than in former times. A whole new world was dawning, and man had somehow mysteriously evolved into a more sophisticated, aware, intellectual being than in previous epochs.

The countries of the world had gotten together after all and united in common purpose to form the United Nations. There was a much greater understanding of our shared existence on every level—socially, politically, culturally, economically, environmentally, and even theologically. The belief was evident that man had embarked on a whole new era in human history. Humanity was going to reach the stars, land on the moon, erase racism, eradicate poverty, do away with discrimination. There was even a Catholic in the White House.

The new worldview was evidenced in spades at the Second Vatican Council, as a kind of naïve euphoria seemed to dominate in view of the new humanity. Mankind had survived a world war, a holocaust, entered into a peaceful if still fragile state of affairs in the nuclear age. What could go wrong? The Council Fathers, who consecrated bishops when the Church understood She had to be militant, were now ever so happy to put down their weapons and embrace the world. They had not taken into account the extent to which the Old Adversary, the Enemy, completely understood human nature and the means by which he could exploit it. He was content, for the moment, to let the world speak in terms of peace and prosperity.

Much is made of how Vatican II is to blame for all the evils that have beset the Church, with a strong emphasis placed on the abandonment of the Traditional Latin Mass. What this complaint overlooks is that every single bishop—more than 2,000, who were the Fathers of the Council—grew up in, went to catechism classes in, were ordained in, and were made bishops in the Old Rite. While the Tridentine Mass was the norm, the Church was already falling apart. It was not the new liturgy that brought about the collapse—although a strong case could be made that it has greatly accelerated it.

No, the collapse occurred on the watch of those who offered the Traditional Latin Mass. All the pieces were already in place, put there by bishops, priests, and theologians long before anyone ever heard the phrase *Novus Ordo Missae* ("New Order of the Mass"). What brought about the collapse is what brings about every downward spiral in the life of the Ancient Church—a lack of holiness brought into being by a lack of faith and knowledge. Most Catholics went to Mass every Sunday before Vatican II; yet these very same Catholics rushed to embrace contraception like youngsters in a candy parlor. Likewise, with a few notable exceptions, their bishops and clergy in country after country said very little, and in some cases such as Canada, actually egged on rejection of the Faith.

In the first handful of years immediately following the Second Vatican Council, the Church would be pushed to and prepared for even further collapse by these same men who celebrated the Old Rite, as they accepted weaker, more feminized men into their seminaries, appointed them to important posts, even looked the other way as an atmosphere of homosexuality began to establish itself among these less manly men. Elements of this new homosexual clergy would give rise to a scandal so shocking that more than a dozen US dioceses would go bankrupt, the spiritual lives of victims almost obliterated, the faith of millions shaken, and the image of the Church so completely tarnished that whatever the next generation of leaders would say in the moral realm (which would prove to be next to nothing) would be mocked and discounted.

But even more devastating than the widespread acceptance of weak men as well as homosexuals into the ranks of the ordained would be the earthquake-like devastation inflicted on souls in the day-to-day life of the average Catholic. In the space of just two generations, Catholic identity was destroyed and assimilated into the American mainstream—and it was accomplished on the watch and with the assistance of the clergy who tossed aside their own masculinity in favor of going along and getting along with the culture, a culture that had long since abandoned any semblance of Catholic morality.

Just at the precise moment when the Church needed men to do battle, the men who showed up were cowardly, feminized, and homosexual, who had no more care for the truths of Our Blessed Lord than they did for any sense of the authentic masculine.

The Masculine

The masculine is not superior to the feminine, any more than the feminine is superior to the masculine. They are complementary, not adversarial. But each has a dark side in direct opposition to its nature.

The masculine is geared toward sacrifice for the good of the community. Exercised in its perfection, it is protector. It must fight against the dangers that threaten the community, whether that community is family, city, faith, country, what have you. The masculine stands as a sentinel and repels all destructive forces. To perform its duty, the masculine needs to be strong, stubborn, immovable, unyielding. It needs to be aware of the outside world and its looming threats. These are the masculine powers.

The dark side of the masculine, however, can overwhelm a person and pervert his true end. That strength can easily be turned on weaker opponents. It can be used to ravish families, assault wives, frighten children, destroy faith. It must be tempered always by the overriding notion of sacrifice. The reality must set in that the awesome powers of the masculine are not for the privilege of the one who possesses them but for the community. They may reside in a man, but they are *for* the community.

When a man uses his powers for himself, for his own gain, he becomes little else than a beast. He can overpower the weaker, use his strength to rape, rob, kill, and destroy. This can happen in violent acts, and it can happen in non-violent but still aggressive actions in various relationships, including in the life of religion.

A man can become possessed by sex, power, fame, or fortune. He can feed his appetites with all his masculine energies and become a horror internally, however socially polite and unassuming he appears on the outside.

This is the polar opposite of what a true man is. A true man is gentle, as in a *gentleman*. He knows the great power that resides in his being, and he employs it only as needed, like a sentinel who carries his great sword at the ready but rarely draws it from its sheath.

He is willing to die to protect the life of the other, both in the physical order as well as in the spiritual and psychological order. A gentleman gives up something for the good of the other, dying to himself a little in the process. He burns down like a candle, sacrificing his own being in order to provide light for those in need.

This is the true meaning of the masculine. It is why the Second Person of the Holy Trinity took on the flesh of a male—not because men are superior to women, but because the natural role of the masculine is to die to save others.

This does not mean that the masculine doesn't also have qualities of nurturing and warmth and kindness associated with the feminine— only that the primary qualities of the masculine are of sacrifice for the community. It's the reason men are so stirred by images of US servicemen crashing ashore on the beaches of Normandy on D-Day, for example. Those images speak to the primordial masculine present in every male.

The Feminine-Masculine Error

The feminine, on the other hand, is related to nurturing and rearing, comforting and community. The feminine shapes the community, makes the home, so to speak, that the masculine stands watch over. The feminine provides soft love, while the masculine provides tough love.

The feminine needs protecting, not because it is unable to defend itself, but because its primary duty is nurturing, not defending. The feminine brings forth the masculine, gives birth to a son—a son who will have to be ripped away from the comfort of the community and undergo pain and sacrifice in order to become the masculine that will return to the community to protect it. A coddled, babied male will never grow to manhood. A male's natural disposition is to remain being coddled and comforted, something the feminine is disposed to do.

The distinction between the feminine and the masculine is rooted in biology and psychology. Early in infancy and into the toddler stage, both boys and girls feel connected to Mommy, almost a part of her. There is no significant separation in their little minds between themselves and Mommy.

Eventually, however, a certain maturation occurs whereby both little boys and girls realize they are, in fact, distinct, that Mommy is Mommy, and I am not a part of her. However traumatizing this might be at first, it is a natural part of maturing, and soon gotten over. For the little girl, that's it. There is no other significant identity issue. She soon discovers that while she is not a part of Mommy, she is *like* her; they share a sameness, a commonness. The little girl recognizes her femininity, even though she does not have the ability to articulate it yet.

But for the little boy, there is a double circumstance to deal with. Like his sister, he has come to realize he is not a part of Mommy, that there is a separation of identities. But here is the rub: He cannot look at Mommy and recognize something of himself there. Not only is he not a part of her, he does *not* share a sameness with her, a commonness like his sister does.

What the young boy knows at this stage is only a *negative*. He knows what he is *not*; he does not know what he *is*. So he looks beyond Mommy in search of something he intuitively, instinctively knows he *is* like. The little girl resides in the feminine, secure in her *type* of identity. She is in community. The little boy is not in community in his psyche. He is in search. He separates himself from the community in order to find himself, to discover his identity.

It is for this reason that various studies show that women are much more communicative than men, saying more than six times the number of words a man says in a given day. Men as a rule are more inwardly turned and don't "share" as freely as women because they developed that way. Of course, we are speaking in very broad terms here and not every male or female undergoes this precise process, nor each to the same degree; but in general terms, this is the course of events.

So from nearly the outset, the masculine is about separation while the feminine is about unity. This is why a mature man can stand alone on a position and be unmoved by various appeals. (An immature man can as well, but for all the wrong reasons.) Making emotionally based appeals to a mature man aimed at hurting his feelings or mocking his position usually won't have any favorable impact. Having to be separated from the community is nothing new to him. He may not like it, but he will live with it.

But studies show a completely different reaction in females. High school girls cut off from the "in crowd" or rejected by a clique of former friends suffer greatly and on a deeper level than boys. It may be the first time in their lives they have not been in "community." However unpleasant for the boy it may be, it is not his first rodeo. Even if he has no clear memory of it, his psyche has already absorbed some of this and has readied him for separation more so than the girl.

All of this is to say that there is a difference between the masculine and the feminine, between boys and girls and men and women. Even the popular culture recognizes this in such bestselling books as *Men Are from Mars, Women Are from Venus.*

But the popular culture has a dichotomy at work within it. It has fused the idea of equality with the idea of sameness. Both sexes are of course equal, but they are not the same. The value of four can be represented numerically by 2+2 or by 2×2. Both equal four, but the arithmetical expressions are completely different; they are not the same. This equality-sameness conflation has found rich soil in which to grow in various other areas of society as well. And the error has had catastrophic consequences in the areas of education, healthcare, politics, and most especially theology—but that is for another time.

For now what is important is to recognize that this error has caused a great diminution of both sexes. It was perhaps best expressed on the popular level in the famous tennis match between Bobby Riggs and Billie Jean King, where the mantra was a woman could beat a guy at anything. What was left somewhat unspoken was the underlying assumption that men and women are the same—and in this case, women are actually superior.

As the 1960s and 70s played out, it became clear that the new orthodoxy was not just that men and women are equal but that women are actually superior in many ways. In the 1970s, for example, one of the most watched TV shows was the *Battle of the Sexes*, a set of athletic competitions between B-level TV celebrities, divided into teams of men and women. The gender war was in full swing.

As the entertainment media chimed in, the intensity increased. Back in the 1950s, TV favorites like *Leave It to Beaver* and *Father Knows Best* showed calm, reasonable men in control and the clear heads of their respective households. By the time the feminists got done with their work, the head of the household was reduced to a bumbling, lazy moron. Whatever dispute arose in a sitcom, it was almost always the woman who solved it. The American sitcom world went from *Leave it to Beaver* to *Married with Children.*

Women were and are portrayed as smarter, more mature, better leaders, and more competent than their husbands. Smash hits like *All in the Family, The Jeffersons, Maude,* and so forth all portrayed men as stupid oafs, barely in touch with reality, while the female characters were, simply put, "with it." Within a generation, the big screen had followed suit, showing 100-pound women unrealistically body-slamming and kickboxing male assassins like they were slicing through butter. Even TV commercials portray the male as a hapless nincompoop in need of the superior woman to guide him safely through his little thirty-second disaster and purchase the correct cell phone, detergent, or insurance plan.

The vocabulary changed as well on the road to sameness. There were no longer actors and actresses, just "actors." The formal designation of "Mr." versus "Miss" or "Mrs." was also eliminated. Women wanted to be like men and not be distinguished by their marital state. "Miss" and "Mrs." were out; "Ms." was in. A magazine even debuted with that title. "Waitress" disappeared in favor of the more equitable "server," and up in the air, "stewardess" went the way of the Dodo Bird; they were all now simply "flight attendants." "Chairmen" became "chairpersons."

In this flurry and rush to make the sexes the same, Congress passed legislation called Title IX, which required, in part, colleges to spend as much money on women's athletics as on men's. (This is still the law today, and is enforced to the letter.) Nevermind that it was men's sports that generated the vast majority of revenue; the dollars spent by the universities fielding varsity-level teams had to be equal based on the ratio of male-to-female student enrollment numbers. While large, big-name institutions were able to absorb this financial tsunami, many smaller colleges couldn't. So they simply eliminated various men's varsity sports to avoid running afoul of the new law.

"Sex integration" it was called. Even the US military academies—Army, Navy, and Air Force—were brought into compliance. Every former bastion of masculinity was being overrun by the feminine, from the family, to the athletic field, to the media, to the military. At least the Church was still safe. But was it?

The Feminized Church

Many of the leaders in the Roman Catholic Church in the United States, today's bishops, came of age in this highly charged atmosphere of intense feminism. While they were still young seminarians in the 1960s and 70s, feminism was banging on the door of the parishes and chanceries. Women religious were throwing off their habits as a sign of revolt against the male-dominated, patriarchal Church. Clamoring for women's ordination was reaching a crescendo, and staying there. Feminist theology courses were appearing on Catholic college campuses and in seminaries.

Feminist instructors, be they male or female, became teachers of future priests. In an embrace of the feminine dynamic of community, seminarians were instructed that the Mass was about the people and the community. The former emphasis on sacrifice and a Father God who sent His Son to be a sacrifice to save the community was insignificant in the new theology.

Scripture began using inclusive language, and textbooks and commentaries and lectures emphasized the feminine in God. Words like "he," "him," and "his" were seen as offensive and not community-supporting. All were not embraced when the language was so gender specific. While not much could be done to skirt around the reality of the *Son* of God, use of the term was kept to a minimum.

As the young men who sat through these classes and brainwashing exercises gradually began filling up the ranks of the ordained, they were more easily conditioned to accept aberrations like altar girls, a horde of female "eucharistic ministers" (it's worth noting the incorrect nomenclature: The actual term is "Extraordinary Ministers of Holy Communion"; only an ordained man can be called a eucharistic minister), and women running the day-to-day life of the parish in the areas of religious education.

The priesthood quickly lost its appeal among young, masculine men as effeminate and homosexual men flocked to the seminaries, oftentimes recruited by other homosexual men in charge of fostering vocations. Many homosexual men, or at least those extremely sympathetic to homosexuality owing to their seminary friendships, went on to become bishops and further advanced homosexuality in the clerical ranks. What began as something of a trickle in the 1960s had become a flood by the 1980s and moving forward. Even famed *New York Times* columnist Maureen Dowd could not avoid pointing out that the Catholic priesthood in America had largely become a haven for gays.

Between poorly catechized women taking charge on the parish level and homosexual men running the show in chanceries, chancery departments, and seminaries, the Catholic Church in the United States didn't stand a chance against the onslaught of the highly charged feminized culture.

The feminized radicals and all the tools of the diabolical used to attack and destroy the Church kept the drum pounding for women's ordination. Sister Theresa Kane confronted Pope John Paul II during his visit to the National Shrine in Washington, D.C. on October 7, 1979, saying:

> We have heard the powerful message of our Church addressing the dignity and reverence of all persons. As women, we have pondered these words. [The Church] must respond by providing the possibility of women as persons being included in all ministries.

The Pope sat in silence as applause thundered throughout the cathedral. Women's Lib had come to the Throne of St. Peter.

There was a specific cigarette at the time marketed to women: Virginia Slims. The ad slogan was "You've come a long way, baby." They certainly had. Twenty years earlier, many of these women were in habits and quietly laboring in schools teaching children their catechism. Now they were confronting the Pope to his face, demanding to be made priests, in their smart pant suits with a small cross pin on the lapel—a long way, indeed.

But while standout events like Sr. Kane's challenge to the Pope garnered all the headlines, the real work of destruction was being carried out in less glamorous but much more effective ways. The Church of Tradition—that male-dominated, misogynistic patriarchy—had to be brought down, dismantled brick by brick, if necessary. And that is precisely what the radical feminists set about doing, radical feminist men as well as radical feminist women.

Many people often ask: If they hated the Church so much, why didn't they just leave it like Martin Luther, John Calvin, and so many others? To understand why they stayed and worked to destroy it, one has to understand the temper of the times. This wasn't about theology, although that would be the battlefield on which this war would be fought. It was about sexual license. It wasn't enough to just pervert the moral law; the perversion had to be given the blessing of the Church to make it valid. Otherwise, the social-sexual revolutionaries would still have their consciences to deal with.

The scourge of their consciences, the voice of God as it emanated from the Catholic Church, had to be overrun and defeated. Many in the halcyon days of the Sexual Revolution understood this. Most did not. But those who did made it their life's work.

The priesthood would have to be feminized and all traces of the masculine eradicated. The push for women's ordination could never be abandoned. The acceptance and advancement of homosexual men in all areas of Church life, but especially the priesthood and episcopacy, had to be accelerated. The laity had to be dumbed down even further, confused and made complicit in the destruction—and on this score, the revolutionaries found a pleasant surprise.

The laity willingly threw off the Church's teaching on contraception and so became indistinguishable from the rest of the culture, fornicating, committing adultery, and cohabiting with just as much gusto as their Protestant friends and neighbors. Still, many clung to the Church of their parents with a sentimental attachment, but as the decades went by, they either left slowly or died, and their children, suffering from no false sentiment since they had not been raised in the Faith, stopped going altogether.

The goal of the Catholic sexual revolutionaries was never to leave and set up a counter-Church in opposition to the Church. No, it was to take over the existing Church and get it to proclaim the acceptability of women priests, contraception, divorce and remarriage, abortion (however regrettable), and homosexuality. It is a much smarter tactic to simply usurp as opposed to confront and openly challenge—and usurp is precisely what the revolutionaries did.

"Not If They Go to Hell"

This is precisely what was placed in evidence at the Extraordinary Synod on the Family held in Rome in October of 2014. Prelates, many of them very powerful indeed, insisted that Catholic couples who were divorced and civilly remarried be admitted to Holy Communion. The German bishops led the way in the person of Cdl. Walter Kasper, a cultural icon to the feminist ideology-minded clergy throughout the world. He was joined by the president of the German Bishops' Conference, Cdl. Reinhard Marx, as well as various others from all over Europe.

These adulterous relationships underwent a vocabulary change, from being "adulterous" to "irregular." Cardinal Luis Tagle from the Philippines, for example, publicly pronounced from the speaker's table in the Holy See Press Hall on October 14, 2014 that using words like "adultery" to describe the sin was "not helpful." The question left unanswered was: To whom exactly was the term unhelpful?

But the day before had proven even more tumultuous and significant. An exchange took place between Italian archbishop Bruno Forte and me in the Holy See Press Hall. The point of contention was a three-paragraph section of the Midterm Relatio (a half-time working document summing up events, thoughts, and arguments up to that point in the Synod discussions).

The problem was the beginning of paragraph 50, which stated: "Homosexuals have gifts and qualities to offer to the Christian community." Using that as the reasoning, the remainder of the paragraph and the next two went on to establish a framework for "acceptance" of openly professed homosexuals into the very lifeblood of the Church.

It needs to be noted and stressed here that it was not speaking of Catholic men and women who suffer from same-sex attraction and strive through cooperation with grace through the sacraments to remain faithful to the Church's teaching and live a life of chastity, but rather of baptized Catholics who live a life in total contradiction to their baptisms in their support for and living out of a homosexual lifestyle.

When the time arrived for questions to the bishop spokesmen, I directed my query specifically to Abp. Forte and asked if the Synod Fathers were proposing the idea that those with homosexual orientations possess a different set of positive attributes to be used at the service of the Church that heterosexuals do not possess, and if so, could the archbishop please inform the assembled media specifically what those attributes are.

It was later revealed that it was precisely Abp. Forte himself who had written the three troubling paragraphs, so when he answered the question I put to him, it was the proverbial "horse's mouth" that was answering.

Perhaps aware he had been caught and exposed in front of hundreds of international journalists with cameras rolling and pens and keyboards transcribing, Forte laughingly passed over the rich theological context of the question and said, "It is not easy to answer such an ontological question," and then added, "I guess that what I want to express is that we must respect the dignity of every person."

But the genie was out of the bottle. What had been exposed was the agenda of the Synod: to use the red herring of Holy Communion for divorced and remarried Catholics to try and establish the legitimacy of homosexuality and homosexual unions. The case was summed up brilliantly by Cdl. George Pell of Sydney, Australia, who said, "Communion for the divorced and remarried is . . . a stalking horse. They want wider changes—recognition of civil unions, recognition of homosexual unions."

Pell was perhaps the most vocal and outspoken critic of all the prelates, saying publicly at various times that the Synod had been "hijacked" and the process "manipulated" so these aberrant views could be put forward. He was followed very closely by Cdl. Raymond Burke, who agreed in various interviews that the Synod had been manipulated and that the Midterm Relatio had been produced with almost no inclusion of magisterial teachings, Scripture, or anything even closely related to traditional Catholic understanding.

Various other prelates went public with their concerns about the phrase "irregular unions" as applied to the divorced and remarried as well as homosexual relationships. I had an encounter immediately after the release of the Relatio with Holy See spokesman Fr. Thomas Rosica. He asked me if I saw "nothing, not one good, not one human positive in any of these irregular unions. Nothing?"

I promptly answered, "No, Father—not if they go to Hell."

Father Rosica drew back and said, "Michael, the Church doesn't teach that they go to Hell."

Another journalist standing nearby interrupted the exchange with his own unrelated question, and that was the end of that—but not without much of an agenda being exposed.

By the following day, the "irregular union" clergy had their much sought-after headlines. All over the world, secular media types were informing seven billion humans that the Catholic Church was changing its teachings about homosexuality and divorce and remarriage. It was only the presence of independent, faithful Catholic media that was able to counter the argument secular culture was so happy to hear.

As the 2015 Synod got underway, the more progressive crowd came out with guns blazing, picking up right where they left off in 2014. Their aggression caught many by surprise. There was nothing subtle in their approach.

On the opening day of the Synod, Cdl. Lorenzo Baldisseri read the rules and procedures from the much fought-over *Instrumentum Laboris*, the working document that served as a guide for bishops' discussions in the Synod Hall. From the time of its release in late spring, it immediately raised questions, not to mention blood pressure. For example, it was savaged by faithful Catholics for not being really all that Catholic. It was extraordinarily light on Sacred Scripture as well as on magisterial documents. Many said—with good cause—it read more like a sociological analysis of current cultural trends than anything coming from the Church.

A group of cardinals even wrote a private letter to the Pope and gave it to him immediately before the Synod, offering their concerns about the *Instrumentum* and the fact that it was not sufficiently Catholic, as well as expressing concerns over synodal procedures they thought would stifle debate. Near the end of the letter they warned that this type of approach looked as though it were the path followed by main-line Protestant communities, which had spelled their undoing. In the end, their concerns were brushed aside, and inside reports emerged that Pope Francis was angry at the polite backlash.

Also in the opening day, Cdl. Peter Erdő of Hungary read a brilliantly prepared statement reinforcing traditional Catholic teaching with regard to sexual morality and the family. The next day, Canadian arch-bishop Paul André Durocher politely brushed it aside in the Holy See press briefing, saying, "I see Cardinal Erdő's presentation as an impor-tant piece, but it is *one piece* as we move forward trying to listen to the voice, the spirit, leading us forward in the task which is ours."

It is precisely the phrase "the task which is ours" that had and has so many faithful Catholics concerned.

Chapter 7

BORROWING FROM THE CULTURE:
Father Theodore Hesburgh

The changes that had occurred in society were so vast and expansive, not to mention successful from the point of view of evil, that the Catholic revolutionaries borrowed heavily from the secular culture (known in theological terms as "the world").

If we go back to the issue of birth control, we would have to find ourselves on the campus of the University of Notre Dame under the leadership of Fr. Theodore Hesburgh, a dangerous man if there ever was one in terms of undermining the Faith. He used the popular causes of the day, such as the Civil Rights movement, to advance his own image as "new priest"—the socially sensitive priest in tune with modern man. (To this day, a large copy of a newspaper picture showing him arm in arm with Martin Luther King, Jr. hangs in the Student Union.) That he was president of the leading Catholic university in the country suggested, as he intended, that the new man, the new humanity was all very *Catholic*.

He used Our Lady's University to remake the face of Catholic education across America while secretly advancing the cause of birth control in exchange for truckloads of money and prestige given him by the Rockefellers. He actively rallied support among the student body for pro-abortion Democrat politicians. I was a sophomore at Notre Dame during the 1980 US presidential race between GOP challenger Ronald Reagan and incumbent Jimmy Carter. That fall, I personally witnessed Hesburgh going into a large number of classes (my economics class was one of them) for over a week making the case that, as Catholics, while we must oppose abortion, there are also other evils that need opposing. It was straight out of the pro-abortion, Democratic Party handbook.

During the next election cycle—between Ronald Reagan and Walter Mondale in 1984—he allowed then New York governor Mario Cuomo to use Notre Dame as the stage for his presentation of the "personally opposed but" abortion policy, which has since become the mantra of hundreds of Catholic Democrats who continue to vote to have children butchered in their mothers' wombs, all under the guise of being good Catholics because they are personally opposed but can't impose their morality on others.

This has all come about as a direct result of Fr. Hesburgh's rejection and distortion of the Catholic faith at Notre Dame. But the firestorm he began would not stay long confined to the South Bend campus. It was his mastermind that crafted the so-called Land O' Lakes Statement in 1967, divorcing Catholic universities and colleges from the Church under the pretense of "academic freedom"—a concept that would later be dismantled by Pope John Paul II in his encyclical *Ex Corde Ecclesiae.*

Atheists and dissidents and heretics like Fr. Richard McBrien soon populated theology departments and philosophy chairs on Catholic campuses around the country, all thanks to the quiet, unassuming priest who strolled across campus routinely, stopping to visit with students—the same students whose souls he jeopardized by denying them the authentic faith.

Hesburgh gave aid and comfort to Chicago's Msgr. Jack Egan, a priest trained personally by Saul Alinsky in the fine art of "community organizing." Egan had been ostracized by his archbishop, Cdl. John Cody, for his community organizing and social justice efforts, so Hesburgh rolled out the red carpet for Egan, who ended up staying at Notre Dame for nearly twenty years. He used his time there to organize a vast national network of politically liberal and theologically dissident priests who were constantly agitating for more social justice, taking the emphasis away from the spiritual and placing it more on the plight of man.

In the summer of 1965, Hesburgh agreed to a series of secret conferences at Notre Dame organized by Planned Parenthood, the chief aim of which was to get the Church to drop its opposition to birth control. Various notable Catholic clergy and intellectuals attended, and at the end they signed an agreement in support of changing the teaching.

The story of Hesburgh at Notre Dame is one of betrayal of the Faith on a monumental scale, and with a diabolic intensity. Eventually Hesburgh retired, but the damage he had done would long survive him. Interesting to note, Hesburgh died remorseful. If he was repentant, however, only God and his confessor knows. Personal eyewitness reports are that during his last year on earth, he would spend a good deal of time crying over the condition of the university he had led for more than three decades. In the two years before his death, homosexuality had been widely embraced by the administration under his successor, Fr. John Jenkins; the administration had agreed to same-sex partner benefits in the health insurance plan; and the leaders at the school had agreed to pay for university employee contraception. The last one is especially poignant since fifty years earlier, it had been Hesburgh who had brokered the secret back-room deal to try and do whatever the Notre Dame community could do to convince Pope Paul VI to change Church teaching on birth control.

During that time period in the 1960s in Rome, the Pontifical Commission on Birth Control, inaugurated by Pope John XXIII to examine the question of population growth and its surrounding ethical questions, had refocused its work to examine only the question of birth control and whether the Church could accept the pill as a morally permissible means to limit the number of children.

Father Hesburgh, using his influence as president of the most famous Catholic university in the world, got the commission to accept one of his own, John T. Noonan, Jr., onto the Commission. The plan was to tip the vote in favor of rejecting Church teaching.

In the end, as Our Blessed Lord promised, the Holy Spirit protected the integrity of the Church, and Pope Paul VI upheld the Church's ages-old teaching in his landmark encyclical *Humanae Vitae*. But it was not for lack of effort on the part of traitorous men like Fr. Hesburgh, who went on to serve as Chairman of the Board of—as might be guessed—the Rockefeller Foundation.

In fact, Hesburgh was so beloved of the liberal academy, at secular as well as Catholic colleges and universities, that he had been awarded more honorary degrees from those universities and colleges than any other person in human history. Go figure—a complete traitor to the Faith warmly embraced and celebrated by the world! "For what will it profit a man, if he gains the whole world and forfeits his life?" (Matt 16:26). Pray for Fr. Hesburgh's soul.

Although his betrayal of the Faith failed to succeed at striking at the teaching of the Church, for that is divinely protected, his treachery and that of many accomplices was successful at destroying the Faith in the souls of many Catholics. From the 1960s onward, whatever was fashionable in the culture was brought into the Church in an effort to make Her more secular and thereby less of a moral voice worth heeding. The revolutionaries were making the Church on the local level so familiar She could simply be discounted.

Suddenly, hit songs from Broadway and motion pictures like *Jesus Christ Superstar* and *Godspell* were echoing around nearly every parish in America and other countries as well. "Day By Day" became a main-stay as the opening hymn Sunday after Sunday. "I Don't Know How to Love Him" was perfect for a Communion song. As folk music with its sappy lyrics about peace and love soared over America as a protest against the Vietnam War, folk groups started appearing on the steps of sanctuaries crooning about peace. One particular favorite was "One Tin Soldier" from the movie *Billy Jack*.

There was no limit to what could be introduced into parishes, whether liturgies or catechesis or schools. Seemingly anything and everything was up for grabs: music, fashion, decoration. If it happened on the outside, it was good enough to let into the inside. Since the early days of the revolution coincided with the hippie culture of Haight-Ashbury (the street intersection in San Francisco where the "Summer of Love" occurred in 1967), the hippie culture was very evident in Catholic parishes. Felt banners with glued construction paper Holy Spirits replaced statues, and Sunday-best attire was pitched for more "earthy" fashions. Hippies danced a lot, as evidenced at Woodstock, so why not bring dance into the Church? Simply label it "liturgical dancing," and you're all set.

As a little addendum, bringing worldly entertainment into the Church was not a one-way street, funnily enough. As the Church dropped many of its own accoutrements—candles, incense, devotions—the world picked them up. Stores opened up in nearly every city special-izing in formerly Catholic stock and trade. In fact, entire industries came into existence.

Every abnormality of the culture found a home in the Church: the hippie culture, radical feminism, homosexuality, birth control, horrid architecture, tasteless art. You name it, there was a group of traitorous Catholics to clear out space in the sanctuary for it. If a statue or two had to be taken to the basement, or the tabernacle had to be shifted from the center to make accommodation, oh well—it was done.

Chapter 8

THE BERNARDIN MACHINE:
Plowing the Faith Under

This revolution accelerated in the 1970s and 80s. By this time, some of the original revolutionaries were coming into their own—men like Cdl. Joseph Bernardin of Chicago, then Abp. Roger Mahony of Los Angeles, and many, many others. These men had been promoted to powerful posts by a largely unaware and naïve Vatican, and from these posts could rain down even more confusion. Satan was spoiled for choice on whom he could use as his next weapon and what his next line of attack should be.

In the 1970s, Bernardin managed to pull the wool over Rome's eyes. As Pope Paul VI neared the end of his life, worn out from the never-ending battle with Modernists, Bernardin managed to secure permission to begin the practice of distributing Holy Communion in the hand. He had followed the lead of equally unfaithful and treacherous Dutch and German bishops and cardinals a decade earlier. Truth be told, he and many of his allied bishops had already introduced the practice, in violation of canon law, in many dioceses long before Rome ever gave consent.

It was Bernardin, again in league with fellow dissident bishops and clerics (many of whom were homosexual), who ramped up the Church's so-called social justice efforts as a diversionary tactic while they set about dismantling the Faith. Their social justice efforts also had the advantage of attracting large sums of US government money in President Lyndon Johnson's war on poverty. But the aim was never so much to help the poor as to change the image of the Church from a divine society founded to save souls to a social help agency committed to love of neighbor—a façade that still remains solidly in place to this day.

It was Bernardin who leveled the distinction between abortion and poverty in what has come to be known as the "seamless garment" approach to life issues. In short, his approach—stemming from a lecture he delivered on December 6, 1983 at Fordham University titled "A Consistent Ethic of Life: An American-Catholic Dialogue"—said Catholics need to stop giving priority to abortion and start viewing all issues that affect human life as one whole broadcloth. (It was the same message delivered by Fr. Hesburgh to student classes in the fall of 1980).

This in effect created the great divide between dissident and unfaithful social justice Catholics and mostly faithful pro-life Catholics. It also provided cover to left-wing Catholic politicians who could now quote the good cardinal in appealing to liberal Catholics to vote for abortion-rights candidates who were at the same time promoting the eradication of poverty. Abortion and poverty have been on the same level ever since, thanks to Cdl. Bernardin. In fact, the battle between the two camps is played out every election year, when the US Conference of Catholic Bishops (USCCB) issues its meaningless voters' guide titled "Faithful Citizenship," a train wreck of a document aimed at proper instruction and guidance, full of nonsensical doublespeak. It is one of Cdl. Bernardin's enduring legacies, along with Holy Communion in the hand.

It was also Bernardin's overemphasis on fighting poverty and the resultant readoption of community organizing efforts that gave a young Barack Hussein Obama his early training and experience, which he would use as a stepping stone to the White House. Obama worked alongside charitable Catholic outfits in Chicago and learned the ropes of how to politically organize a community in favor of the Democrats under the cover of fighting poverty. It was classic Saul Alinsky tactics.

In regards to the dismantling of the Faith, Bernardin was a promoter of the homosexual agenda during his term in office, placing way ahead of his time. He opened one of America's first gay and lesbian departments in the chancery, where various Catholics worked tirelessly to undermine the Church's teaching under the guise of trying to "minister" to Catholics with same-sex attraction. It was a façade, and the entire archdiocese knew it. In fact, it remains a façade to this day. Bernadin's replacement, Cdl. Francis George, was unable to dislodge the department from his own chancery. In private conversations, he revealed to allies that if he were to touch the hornet's nest of homosexual clergy in Chicago, he estimated he would lose more than a third of his priests—not to mention they would bring activity in the archdiocese to a screeching halt.

This state of affairs, which Cdl. George inherited, was advanced under Cdl. Bernardin. A little-known fact about the cardinal who essentially ran the show in America during his reign from Chicago is that, when he died, he left word in his final instructions that the Chicago Gay Men's Chorus sing at his wake. His wishes were carried out.

During Obama's commencement speech at Notre Dame in May 2009, with Fr. Hesburgh in attendance, Obama publicly paid homage to the memory of the now-dead Bernardin for launching him on his path. He craftily made the whole thing sound resoundingly Catholic, and he was greeted with wild applause from the faculty and students Hesburgh had devoted his life into forming to be inauthentic Catholics. To add insult to injury, the vast majority of the Notre Dame Board of Trustees and Board of Fellows were all well-heeled Chicago campaign activists for Obama.

The triumvirate of Hesburgh, Bernardin, and Obama represented the face of the new Catholicism in the United States: concerned for the poor and immigrants, willing to dialogue about common ground on contentious issues like abortion, and conceding that truth in a pluralistic society is a difficult concept to nail down.

A Protestant-Catholic Church

Cardinal Bernardin is emblematic of everything that went wrong in the Church in the United States from the 1960s on. Worth noting is that the problems that beset the Church in the United States during the reign of Bernardin did not begin with him. The ground had been prepared for quite some time by lackluster leaders like Cdl. Richard Cushing of Boston, who deliberately ducked a public battle with Planned Parenthood over the issue of contraception. Many other issues came together as well to weave a complex tapestry of warning signs as far back as the 1930s that all was not well with Catholicism in the United States.

Despite outward appearances and even suggestions by some that America of the 1950s—complete with Ven. Abp. Fulton Sheen's astonishing success on network television—was ready to embrace the Catholic faith, there was a revolution already quietly operating against the Faith on the part of numerous clergy. It was largely confined to more academic and intellectual circles at the time, almost entirely out of view of the average Catholic in the pew. The upheaval of the 1960s merely allowed the revolutionaries to come out from hiding and exploit the social chaos to advance their own agenda: a takeover of the Church.

The takeover would happen on many fronts—not just in the institutions *per se*, but also in Her ordinary members, the laity. The laity were especially vulnerable because they were the foot soldiers, so to speak, the first to encounter evil in the culture. In the 1960s, for example, suddenly friends and neighbors and other family members were using birth control. Not much was said; it just happened. The poorly catechized Catholic, or the Catholic who was just beginning to feel himself a good American, could easily fail to comprehend the great evil descending on him.

The question of being a good American while also being a good Catholic was one that had plagued Catholics in America almost from the beginning of their minority presence in the country. Most had come over as immigrants and were consigned to the lower rungs of the socio-economic scale. Over a few generations some had managed to climb the ladder and ascend to places of prominence, even notoriety. The Kennedys serve as a prime example.

But the question of whether it was possible to be both a good Catholic and a good American still persisted, especially after World War II, when many minority Catholics admirably fought the Nazi and Japanese empires alongside their majority Protestant countrymen. In fact, the most decorated soldier of the Second World War was Audie Murphy, a Catholic.

Following the war, as America nestled comfortably into the 1950s, the question was given greater latitude. Many Protestants were willing to take a second look at their papist countrymen and this whole Catholic business. So, too, various Catholics were also trying to reconcile the two spheres. One such man was a Jesuit priest, Fr. John Courtney

Murray. He was even featured on the December 12, 1960 cover of *TIME* magazine for his work in this very area.

He presented the idea that Catholics need to understand the unique situation posed to the Faith by the uniqueness of America. Unlike most other nations, America holds no specific creed and promotes no particular religion. It's the ideal pluralistic society. Recall, however, that when Murray was exploring the issue, America was still knitted together by a common moral code, a morality that had derived from Catholicism (whether American Protestants knew it or not). So in the moral arena in the 1950s, there was the reality of common ground. Divorce, remarriage, contraception, abortion, cohabitation, adultery, homosexuality—none of these had yet been enshrined as rights in law and accepted by the common man. (It is stunning to step back and realize that in living memory of many reading this book, all of these errors were roundly condemned for the evils they were; yet in just one generation, by the 1970s, they had become accepted wholesale as actual *goods* by the same nation. The speed with which evil advances is staggering.)

Father Murray became something of an icon to many young seminarians (recall he was on the cover of *TIME*). There was optimism in the air those days among Catholics in America. Bishop Sheen was dominating the airwaves, the churches were packed, vocations were brimming over, notable converts were coming to the Faith, Hollywood was making praiseworthy films lauding Catholicism, and on and on. Catholics were enjoying the post-war boom like the rest of the country and beginning to feel very American. This was in sharp contrast to just twenty years earlier, when Catholics were despised and discriminated against and made to feel like second-class citizens.

It was difficult to be in a country as a religious minority when you were constantly ridiculed. The cultural put-downs were a major reason the University of Notre Dame football team attracted such a huge following. The fan base consisted of persecuted Catholics in the major urban centers of 1920s and 1930s America. The team traveled to and played where the fan base lived, and the happy coincidence arose that those urban centers were also home to the large newspapers of the day. Always anxious for a good story, they were happy to feed the legend of Notre Dame football.

The mystique continued to grow and attracted even more Catholics who felt crushed underfoot. Their attitude was, simply put, *you may hate us for six days a week, but on Saturday, we're going to kick your Protestant asses up and down that football field.* And, of course, they did. Notre Dame football provided a haven for minority Catholics and stood out as a shining star amidst a sea of prejudice and discrimination. It gave downtrodden Catholics something to rally around and lifted up their spirits. Even as far back as the 1920s they even called themselves the Fightin' Irish. Catholics could walk down the street with their heads held a little higher on Sunday mornings after Knute Rockne and the boys in the 1920s, or Frank Leahy and his lads in the 1940s, had laid waste to some other bastion of Protestant imperialism.

By the 1950s, Protestants began warming up, if not to the Catholic religion, then at least to their Catholic countrymen. Father Murray detected an opening and proceeded down the philosophical road of trying to fit in more, getting a much sought-after place at the table. In order to become accepted as full-fledged Americans, with all the rights and privileges that implies, Catholics would have to tone down the religion stuff a bit. This was, after all, a pluralistic society, willing to live by the code that one religion could not claim superiority, moral or theological, over any other.

Murray never denied the superiority of the Catholic faith, but he did come dangerously close to hinting that Catholic identity might have to be surrendered or covered over so as not to offend others in the public square. So the question arose within the Church in the United States: Are you an American Catholic, or are you a Catholic American? For many, desperate to feel fully accepted by their majority Protestant countrymen, the answer, sadly, was: *I'm an American Catholic.* This attitude became the default as the country moved into the 1960s—and it would reap catastrophic consequences.

In fact, the attitude was so alarming that the Vatican actually silenced John Courtney Murray and forbade him from further writing or talking about his "Americanist" notions. And yet, oddly enough, Murray and his ideas would be resurrected just ten years later in Rome itself, at the Second Vatican Council—and in a more glorified fashion. Murray's approach to the world was the basis for the Vatican II document *Dignitatis Humanae*, and it became a major point of exploitation for the revolutionaries in the Church. *Dignitatis Humanae* was even labeled the "American" document. While it would be incorrect to assign the effects of *Dignitatis Humanae* to Fr. Murray, there is no doubt that, almost immediately, it was used to stealthily introduce to the laity the heresy of indifferentism—the notion that all religions are essentially the same, and they are each a path to Heaven and ultimately to God.

It was an idea that became an unofficial way of doing business in the American Church. Before the 1960s, it had been the Catholic Church in America. From the 1960s on and up to the present day, it has been the American Catholic Church. Whether or not he intended it, much of this falls on the celebrated Fr. John Courtney Murray and his rush to have the Church blend into the larger society. Today, the idea that all religions are in their essence mainly the same, separate but equal paths to God, is sacrosanct among average Catholics. It is an orthodoxy that may never be challenged publicly and certainly never by a priest or bishop.

Protestantism is a heresy, regardless of how nice and friendly individual Protestant neighbors, friends, and family members may be. Nothing has changed since the days of the so-called Protestant Reformation (as previously noted, more correctly termed the Protestant Revolt). All or most of the sacraments are denied; the Marian dogmas are rejected; the authority of the Church is discarded; the ministerial priesthood is dismissed; the Catholic interpretation of Scripture is scoffed at (despite the historical reality that it was the Catholic Church that compiled the canon of Scripture and gave it to the world); the papacy is attacked (although a given individual who is Pope may be treated a little more gently than in past centuries).

Protestants have a considerably harder time attaining salvation than do faithful Catholics because they are lacking access to the abundant graces given by Our Blessed Lord to His Mystical Bride. They do not receive the Body and Blood of Jesus Christ. They have no access to absolution for their sins. Many of their baptisms are invalid. They reject the Mother of God, or at a minimum, pay her no attention at all. And this list is just for starters.

Jesus Christ founded one Church and only one Church, and He established it to fight evil in this life and lead people to Heaven. And all salvation flows from His Holy Church. Outside the Church there is no salvation, and in Heaven, there will not be a cacophony of religions. Heaven is most definitely *not* a pluralistic society! If you are in Heaven, then you are joined to the Church Triumphant—the *Catholic* Church Triumphant, for there is no other "Church."

But in the American Church, Protestantism is no longer viewed, understood, or spoken of as a heresy (it's not nice to talk like that). No, the new heresy has been to speak of Protestantism as a heresy. It is considered in bad form to speak directly in this regard about other religions. We are, after all, a pluralistic culture, and room must be allowed for all kinds of faiths and religions—or so they say.

Other religions are false—period. No matter how sincere their adherents may be, they are sincerely in error and sincerely mistaken. Protestantism is a heresy, just as Arianism was and hosts of other "isms" were and are heretical. But in America from the 1960s on, a new approach to heresy was adopted by a clergy and episcopate caught up in a wave of excitement over finally getting that highly valued seat at the table. Perhaps without realizing it, American Catholics traded away their faith to become more American.

The bargain had been fashioned by enemies of Christ within the Church who were able to influence their fellow naïve Churchmen, clerics, and laity to go along with the plan. The first philosophical hurdle necessary to be cleared had been cleared. Catholic identity began to erode. The rush was on to produce the Protestantism-friendly American Catholic Church.

And this is key: The enemies of Christ in the Church desired to destroy the Faith, the teachings, but not the apparatus and working operations of the Church. They needed the buildings, the institutions, the entire workings of the institutional Church, the universities, chanceries, parishes, hospitals, charitable foundations, houses of formation, seminaries, all of it, to bring about an end to Catholicism. In short, they needed the Church structures to destroy the life of the Church. And that meant, eventually, the episcopate would have to be compromised.

When Pope St. Pius X was made bishop in 1844, his mother was unsurprisingly enthused and effusive in her congratulatory maternal praise. And while humoring his mother, he offered her the only realistic answer a man could give having been appointed bishop. He said, "Mama, do you realize what it means to be a bishop—to have in my care the salvation of so many souls? Think of the responsibility! Pray for me, Mama. For if I neglect my duty, I shall lose my soul."

Chapter 9

AMERICAN BISHOPS FOR AN AMERICAN CHURCH:
Four Types

A Protestantism-friendly American Catholic Church needs Protestantism-friendly American Catholic bishops. These bishops, for various reasons depending on the individual bishop, would have to remain blind as bats to the danger that Protestantism poses to Catholicism. They would have to be of a certain kind, one of four types: deceitful and treacherous; incompetent and weak; ignorant and unintelligent; or ambitious and inoffensive, and therefore willing to turn a blind eye to dangers so as not to rock the boat, so as to be seen as a peaceable man worthy of promotion.

Regardless of which of the four categories an individual bishop may fall into, they all share one thing in common: They do not possess sufficient supernatural faith.

For a bishop to be friendly to the Protestant heresy and its destructive force in all its varying forms means he does not have sufficient faith in the Real Presence. For even though the Protestant heresy has broken down into many thousands of warring denominations, each squabbling with the others, their common enemy, that against which they all unite, is the Catholic dogma of the Real Presence of Jesus Christ—Body, Blood, Soul, and Divinity—really, truly, and substantially present under the appearance of bread and wine.

As Servant of God Fr. John Hardon pointed out on numerous occasions, this one teaching unites them all in their rejection of the One True Faith established by the Son of God, precisely as it united all those former disciples at Capernaum who got up and walked away when Our Lord taught this most sublime of all teachings—and precisely as it set Judas against Christ.

How a bishop treats or allows the sacramental Lord to be treated tells a Catholic all he needs to know about the degree of supernatural faith possessed by a successor of the Apostles, and therefore, his degree of intimacy with Our Blessed Lord, from which falls all his other views and actions. If a bishop fails to protect the Faith or the faithful, allows them to be confused, leaves them wondering about many of his actions, commits acts of omission or commission against the Faith, it may always be traced directly back to his insufficient or total lack of faith in the Real Presence.

Type One: The Deceitful, Treacherous Bishop

Judas immediately springs to mind as the exemplar. And quite a few bishops exist who are his successors in spirit. Judas betrayed Our Blessed Lord and is in Hell for it (despite whatever asinine pseudo-intellectual arguments Bp. Robert Barron's favorite theologian Hans Urs von Balthasar thinks). Our Blessed Lord Himself says a number of jarring things about Judas: "It would have been better for that man if he had not been born" (Matt. xxvi : 24), a statement that makes the whole case open and shut. But He also calls him the son of perdition—not exactly a hope-filled comment in terms of Judas' eternal destination. And, of course, Our Lord calls Judas a devil when Judas refuses to believe Our Lord's eucharistic Bread of Life testimony in Capernaum.

So no Catholic worth his weight in grace should ever be amazed that a bishop could be guided by Satan. If Judas Iscariot, who walked and talked with Jesus in the flesh, who performed miracles in Jesus' name, who knew Him so intimately here on earth, could betray Him and give himself over entirely to Satan, then any bishop on earth is capable of doing the same—and many have. Treacherous bishops should never be a cause for a loss of faith. If anything, the fact that they have been present in the Church from the beginning and the Church is still here should be a validation that the Holy Catholic Church *is* the Church established by Almighty God and protected by the Holy Spirit. What man-made institution could survive for 2,000 years with such traitors always appearing on the scene?

Now for a bishop—or anyone, for that matter—to give himself over to Satan doesn't require attending a Black Mass or signing a contract in front of the local gang of devil worshippers. All it requires is being in a state of mortal sin, for if a person is in a state of unrepented mortal sin, he is cut off from the Blessed Trinity, and he has killed the supernatural life within him (mortal sin = *morte* = "death"). At such a moment, he has no recourse to Heaven and is owned by the diabolical. (As Fr. Hardon insisted, a soul in a state of mortal sin is a tool of the devil.) His only hope before dying is to make a full and complete confession in true contrition and humility and perform whatever penance is assigned him to be restored to a state of grace. If he has not done this before dying, he goes to Hell. This is true of any soul, but bears special examination in the case of a wicked bishop.

No one should express any shock over the reality—*the reality*, mind you—that some bishops actively work against Our Blessed Lord and His Holy Catholic Church. Whatever their individual life stories may be, however they came to such a state, the reality is plain: They are enemies of Christ (again, recall Judas). And a man raised to the level of bishop who denies Christ in his heart is not just a tool of Satan, but a fortress of wickedness, a rampart of evil.

And do not be deceived that the only way for such a denial of Christ to be accomplished is through some secret pact exchanging signatures in blood—certainly not. The surest way for a bishop to deny Christ is to deny His teachings, for unlike the laity, the bishop's primary role is to teach the flock. To fail in this single regard is sufficient for a bishop to fall into the clutches of Satan and be damned for eternity. When a man who is a bishop actively refuses to teach the truth of Our Blessed Lord, he is denying Christ personally. As Our Lord ascended to Heaven, as His marked feet lifted from this earth, the last words to fall from His sacred lips to His Apostles were: "Go therefore and make disciples of all nations, baptizing them in the name of the Father and of the Son and of the Holy Spirit" (Matt. xxviii : 19).

Imagine at that point one of the Apostles refusing to do so, and in fact preaching something opposite. He would have immediately joined Judas. Fortunately for us, that did not occur at that point, but it has many times since and still does. If there is one thing faithful Catholics must avoid, it is this ridiculous notion that a bishop is beyond critique. Now that will immediately rankle any bishop reading this, but it is true. A decision a bishop makes, depending on the circumstances, is certainly worthy of consideration, and to whatever degree disagreement may be expressed, it should be. Canon law even provides for this, as does the history of the Church; St. Thomas Aquinas is, in fact, explicit about it.

When a bishop says or does something injurious to the Faith, directly contradicting Church teaching, then it needs to be said quite plainly that he is in opposition to Our Blessed Lord. For example, in the run-up to the Extraordinary Synod of Bishops on the Family and the New Evangelization in Rome in October 2014, various bishops around the world flatly stated that divorced and remarried Catholics should be admitted to Holy Communion. Various others chimed in that the same should be extended to Catholics who are actively homosexual.

There is a two-fold issue here: first, that a successor of the Apostles thinks in this manner, and second, that he voices it so as to agitate for it. Such men belong to the devil. Adultery and sodomy are not open for discussion as possible states of existence when approaching the altar to receive the Body and Blood of Our Blessed Lord. These bishops are modern-day Judases, because like Judas, they do not believe the Eucharist is in fact Jesus Christ Himself. Therefore, the condemnation that fell from the mouth of Our Lord Himself against Judas is equally fitting for them: "Did I not choose you, the twelve, and one of you is a devil?" (John vi: 70).

It is worth noting that Jesus did not refer to His former followers who deserted Him in Capernaum after the Bread of Life discourse as "devils." He reserved that term specifically for a member of the apostolic band. That is because being so closely associated with Our Lord, his fall from grace was much more pronounced and, therefore, his descent into the lower realms—in spirit at that moment and in body shortly thereafter—so disfigured him interiorly that when Our Blessed Lord looked at him, all he could see was one given over to the Father of Lies, who has "no truth in him" (John viii: 44).

It is immaterial whether Judas also did some nice things, smiled at little children, helped someone with this task or that; interiorly, he was a devil. And as the Holy Spirit reveals to us in the Acts of the Apostles, Judas went "to his own place" (Acts i: 25). He was a devil because he denied a teaching of Christ as one of Christ's inner circle— His Apostles. So, too, any man who is a successor of the Apostles who denies a teaching of Christ is a devil, and nothing should be spared to reveal this reality.

And for those who will retort to this analysis by claiming that Jesus called Peter "Satan," the two cases are not in the least comparable. Our Lord calls Peter "Satan" because of a specific circumstance—namely, Peter tried to dissuade Our Lord from the Cross. It is clear from His words He does not mean Peter *is* Satan, merely that in this circumstance, he is being used *by* Satan to be a temptation away from the Cross.

It is precisely because Our Lord calls Judas *a* devil and not *the* devil that we know the total corruption of Judas. Peter was not *transformed* by evil. He merely fell prey to its influence owing to his unfaithfulness and ignorance in understanding and believing what Our Lord had said, albeit through human emotional attachment—he didn't want Jesus to suffer.

Judas, on the other hand, did not just fall prey to evil in a moment of weakness, but was actually transformed by it. He became devilish, so much so that it's what Our Lord saw when He looked at Judas—a devil—so he branded him as such: "one of you is a devil."

And even though they were not his intimates, He reserved the same quality of branding for His contemporary religious leaders, calling them children of the devil. "You are of your father the devil, and your will is to do your father's desires" (John viii: 44). And what specific actions does He upbraid them for, the Pharisees? Failing to recognize the Truth standing right in front of them. They deny the Truth; moreover, they plot to kill it, to turn the people's minds against it. This is why they are forever laying traps for Him in public, trying to trip Him up so they can denounce Him to the crowds.

A son bears a resemblance to his father. That is a fact of nature. So, too, is it a fact of supernature. When Our Lord said to the Pharisees that Satan was a murderer from the beginning and that he had no truth in him, He was saying the same of them, for a son bears the image of his father. And as such, since their father was the devil, they did their father's will. They did his will in the order of the supernatural.

They would have recalled the words of God to the serpent in the Garden: "I will put enmity between you and the woman, and between your seed and her seed" (Gen. iii: 15). Now, millennia later, the offspring of the serpent were being revealed in public, unmasked before the crowds for their hatred toward the Truth, for being in opposition to the offspring of the Woman.

79

How does this not apply to a wicked bishop in precisely the same manner it did to the Pharisees and to Judas? In one respect, it would apply even more gravely. Neither the Pharisees nor Judas had received the fullness of favor bestowed by the sacraments of initiation or Holy Orders. It is even filthier in the soul of a man consecrated to the episcopate to be a son of Satan than it was for the Pharisees and Judas. Recall that as Jesus stood bound before Pontius Pilate, He said that "he who delivered me to you has the greater sin" (John xix : 11). Who handed Our Lord over to Pontius Pilate other than the named sons of Satan, the one collective of Judas and the Pharisees?

If this is how Our Lord spoke of the Pharisees and Judas—the leaders and would-be leaders of His day—with such scorn and contempt, using the language of damnation, what does He see, what reaction does He have when He peers into the soul of an unfaithful bishop who denies Him in His sacred teachings? He beholds the filth of all the ages; He gazes on the soul of a man consecrated, set aside for a specific mission to be used to lead souls to Him, and instead sees the heart of a traitor.

And in keeping with their resemblance to Judas their brother, since they are of the same father, these wicked bishops betray their Master with a kiss, because "their heart is destruction, their throat is an open sepulchre" (Ps. v : 9). A bishop such as this poses a real threat to the Faith because he is not just a tool of the diabolical but an ally. Depending on the degree of influence he wields, such a man could cause untold damage—and many have.

What set Judas on the irreversible path to damnation was his lack of faith in the eucharistic word of Our Lord. And it was irreversible because he lacked the necessary ingredient of faith. Our Lord Himself says that "he who does not believe is condemned already" (John iii : 18). Judas lacked supernatural faith, and would never acquire it— and so was already condemned. He was like his father, a liar and a murderer, from the beginning. He lied about his true motives when the expensive oil was used to anoint Our Lord, pretending to be concerned about the poor—as many bishops do today.

And he was not only an active participant in the murder of Our Blessed Lord, he actually set the entire plan in motion. He was indeed the son of his father, each being a liar and a murderer. And so it is with any bishop who forsakes supernatural faith in his life as bishop. He does not believe, and is already condemned. Such a man is a liar by his very presence in the robes of the Apostles. And such a man is a murderer because, like Judas, he actively participates in the killing of Our Lord by destroying His life in the souls of those under his charge. God forbid that such a man die unrepentant of such evil; the horrors his soul will suffer are too terrifying to contemplate—but a bishop *should* contemplate them, and daily.

Type Two: The Incompetent, Weak Bishop

Cowardly would be an apt description of such a man. And unlike the treacherous bishop, the cowardly bishop *may* be personally orthodox; he may accept the teachings of the Church in his own intellect, but he lacks the courage necessary to do battle to advance and promote those teachings across the board. A weak bishop cannot stand the sight of blood.

In spiritual warfare, blood is going to be spilled. That fact must simply be accepted. The question is not *if*, but *whose*—the blood of the sheep or the blood of the evil one? A cowardly bishop cannot stand the sight of blood because he is ill equipped for war. He lacks conviction, surety, foresight, manliness, and the quality most important in a leader: the power to resist being disliked. He cares too much for human respect.

Again for emphasis, a man may be a good man, possessing various qualities such as kindness, gentleness, sympathy for neighbor, etc. But with all these qualities, he may still be a *weak* man. A good man is not necessarily a good leader. An effective leader is both good *and* strong.

Many bishops in the United States today and for the past two or three generations have been and are good men, but weak. They have not shown the necessary fortitude to confront the Protestant heresy in various manifestations in their own dioceses. Out of fear of being disliked, for example, they have not confronted and defeated the forces—meaning the dissidents and poorly catechized lay people who run religious education programs, be they on a diocesan-wide level or a small CCD class at the parish.

Bear in mind, the primary role of the bishop is to teach, and since he cannot personally teach every person in his diocese, he delegates his authority to others. It is absolutely incumbent on him to ensure that how his authority is being used is correct. He does not get to take a pass and just walk away from his duties. He routinely needs to investigate and ensure that those who are teaching the Faith (school teachers, religious education teachers in parishes, etc.) understand it, believe it, and live it. Failing any of those three, the person must not be allowed to exercise the authority of the bishop by teaching.

The bishop needs to ensure his priests are hiring Catholics who are competent to pass on the Faith, who have the ability to articulate the truths of Jesus Christ because they live those truths and have the natural talent to communicate those truths. This is a sacred duty, and it all redounds to the bishop—his immortal soul is at stake. He can no more brook poor instruction being given than a doctor can brook poison being administered into his patient's IV. Yet we know from mountains of evidence—rather, mountains of *proof*—that the Faith has not and is not being communicated properly to students, whether they are Catholic school students, CCD students, RCIA candidates, or religious education students. The bishops have simply ignored their most important duty, and they will have to answer to Almighty God for it.

A story is told of a group of American bishops dining one evening with Pope John Paul II. They said to him, "Holiness, it appears to us that most Catholics today will go to Heaven because they are so ignorant of the Faith." The Holy Father immediately responded, "They *may* go to Heaven, but for allowing them to be so ignorant, you will go to Hell."

So what would cause a man who may be relatively orthodox in private to disregard his most important duty? The answer lies within the man—his lack of fortitude (one of the seven gifts of the Holy Spirit). If the treacherous bishop lacks supernatural faith, the weak man lacks supernatural hope. He does not trust that God will see him through the difficult task that lies ahead of him. He must go to war with the irreligious religion instructors in his diocese, and he knows, consciously or unconsciously, that this will be a messy affair. On this score, he is without a doubt correct. To go to war now, after decades of malformation of the Faith in so many religious instructors, will absolutely be war. But it must be done.

So unwilling, so unprepared in his own constitution, in his own bones for war is he that he allows himself to be convinced—either by his own ruminations or by people around him, or both—that a more delicate, more finessed, more *nuanced* approach is the better course. He is happy to entertain such pablum because he does not want to be disliked; he does not want to have his time occupied with defending himself against the certain recriminations that will come his way. He does not want to incur the wrath of his clergy, many who are responsible for the miserable state of affairs he must now oversee.

Like all weak men in whatever walk of life, he is self-centered, thinking of his personal loss if he goes to war. A selfish man is an insufficient man to walk in the footsteps of the Apostles. He looks down the road only a few feet, sees the carnage that lies ahead, and shrinks from it because he correctly intuits that the blood to be spilled will be his own. Yet this is why his robes are red—to remind him of his consecration to martyrdom. He is consecrated, put to the task of holiness, for the sake of others, not for himself (recall the earlier section on authentic masculinity). He is to spend himself entirely—reputation, skills, time, energies—to get his people to Heaven. If he was not willing to accept this crucifixion, then he should never have accepted the role.

And this is where he is sorely lacking in the supernatural virtue of trust. Unlike the treacherous bishop who fails utterly because he possesses no supernatural faith, the weak bishop fails because he has no trust that God will be his surety. Our Blessed Lord never deserts those who try their *best* to do His will—and a person's best includes a realistic and sober view of the current crisis and all that needs to be done to save souls *now*, not down the road twenty years from now. What can be done now, in the present moment, *must* be done. Weak men are especially prone to rationalizing and procrastination. But Our Blessed Lord *never* made up excuses, overplayed the prudence card, or procrastinated. Unfortunately, too many of His bishops do.

Weak men are always gathering opinions, forever consulting, becoming frozen by analysis paralysis, all in an unconscious effort either to permanently forestall a firm decision and course of action or to take the path of least resistance, offending the least number of people, which inevitably is the one guaranteed to do nothing in bringing about a solution.

They lack boldness in their very bones because they lack trust in their heart—because they lack supernatural hope in their souls. This was the precise fault of Peter as he stepped out of the boat and onto the water when Our Lord beckoned him. He had faith, for he called to Our Lord and asked Him to command him to leave the boat and walk to him. After Our Lord pulled the sinking Peter from the waves, He said to him, "O man of little faith, why did you doubt?" (Matt. xiv : 31). And herein lies the deep mystery of the interrelation between the supernatural virtues of faith and hope. As one loses hope, *i.e.*, confidence, one begins to lose faith correspondingly.

Peter had faith enough to step out of the boat. He had faith enough to begin the trek through the wind and the waves to Our Lord, but he took account of the wind and the waves—meaning his faith diminished because he did not possess sufficient confidence that the wind and waves could be ignored in the face of Our Lord's miraculous presence. He lost hope, and resultantly his faith was immediately injured. This is the great danger posed to bishops who are weak because of their own personal predilections, be they a desire to please everyone, which stems from a selfish and pride-filled ego to be liked, or any other human fault left unconquered.

A bishop who lacks trust in Almighty God, who is without sufficient storehouses of supernatural hope, will in time come to suffer a decrease in supernatural faith. It is a spiritual certainty. And a bishop who dies lacking supernatural faith will be damned, because without supernatural faith, he will fall into mortal sin. This is exactly what Our Blessed Lord meant when He warned most ominously that whoever does not believe is already condemned.

The danger most prevalent for the man who is good yet weak is that these two aspects cannot endure together forever. One will ultimately triumph because their roots are opposed to each other. Goodness is rooted in the supernatural virtues of faith, hope, and charity. Weakness is rooted in pride. A tree cannot have its roots planted in two opposing soils; the nutrients from the good soil or the toxins from the bad soil will eventually overcome its opposition, and the tree will thrive, or it will die.

When supernatural faith is greatly diminished or lost, which happens when supernatural hope is on the decline, it is supernatural charity that is killed off in the aftermath. A bishop loses true charity for his sheep. Charity, recall, is rooted and exhibited in sacrifice.

The stupid supplanting of the word "love" for charity has brought with it a host of problems. The word "love" in its popular use has lost almost all relation to the notion of sacrifice, meaning the placing of the needs of one's neighbor over one's own needs—in short, a lack of selfishness. The common use of the word "love" today carries with it more a meaning of strongly *like*, as in "I love pizza," "I love my sports teams," "I love you." It is all related to the tastes of the lover rather than to the good of the beloved. As such, it is not genuine love.

It is all related to personal likes and dislikes, often expressed through romantic sentimentalism and even lust. But one thing is certain: It is not true charity. The object of highest concern, of chief and primary concern, is in actual fact self.

True charity is something completely different, not just in magnitude but also in kind. And it is only possible to achieve as one excels in a life of holiness, meaning *all* of the supernatural virtues, since they alone are directed solely to God, Who is holiness. When a bishop fails in the area of supernatural hope, it is a sufficient enough chink in his armor for the devil to get in and despoil him.

Remember at the Last Supper the ravenousness with which Satan approached Our Lord and demanded that he hand over the Apostles, so "that he might sift [them] like wheat" (Luke xxii : 31). Satan knows that if he is able to get to the Apostles, the whole structure will come tumbling down because Our Lord made them key.

No heresy worth its heat in flames ever began from the laity. True enough, many eventually spread like hellfire through the laity, but they all began among the ordained classes, notably bishops, either directly or because they did not do enough to oppose it. This is a most revealing facet of the interior life of the Church. It demonstrates the complete totality involved in being Catholic; you are either all in—"You, therefore, must be perfect, as your heavenly Father is perfect" (Matt. v : 48) (or, as is the case with most of us, must be greatly desirous of perfection and striving after it)—or you are all out and subject to the wind and the waves that will result in your drowning. You are either alive or dead, or speeding on your way to one or the other. There is no in between—no stalling, no time for meetings and consultations and analysis. A bishop either steps out in complete and total trust as a demonstration of possessing the supernatural virtue of hope, or he diddles and fidgets and dithers around while his sheep are slaughtered.

There is no such thing as a good yet weak bishop. Such a man is merely on the path to becoming either all weak or all good. The one inclining to weakness and hesitation will be lost. The one inclining to goodness will soon bring about a restoration of the Faith in those under his care—and whichever result will be evident to everyone, for such is the nature of holiness, with its attendant supernatural virtues.

The weak bishop will speak often of prudence and prudential judgments; this is a great warning sign of weakness. Prudence is portrayed in ecclesiastical circles as a virtue whereby a bishop gets to take no action, or forestall action for such a duration that when finally adopted it has little or no effect. Prudence does, of course, entail exercising judgment as to the best course of action, but it does not mean refusing to address a crisis situation, or downplaying such a situation.

Note that once the clergy sex abuse lawsuits and judgments began piling up and soaring into the billions of dollars, and dioceses started filing for bankruptcy protection, the American hierarchy wasted no time in trying to combat the situation. There was no polling of information, no studies or commissions assembled to see if something should be done. The reason is because the impact of decades of inaction were being felt in the immediate here and now.

Could not the same be said of the consequences of failing to take action in the spiritual realm? Are not souls at this very moment being consigned to Hell for all eternity for dying in a state of mortal sin? Why is there no "Dallas Charter" over this even more grave issue? (The "Dallas Charter," formally known as the "Charter for the Protection of Children and Young People," was drawn up in 2002 as a result of the meeting of US bishops called to address the homosexual priest sex abuse scandal.)

Too often today, said Cdl. Marc Ouellet when he became prefect of the Congregation for Bishops in 2010, a typical bishop will stop and weigh *all* the political ramifications of preaching the Gospel before doing so.

He will take account of the wind and the waves, for example, and he will sink into the waters and drown.

Prudence is the most overused and misapplied of the virtues by members of the episcopate, urged on by their staffs. Their misuse of it has turned large numbers of them into CEOs and bureaucrats who consider it their first duty to preserve the establishment or the status quo. They concern themselves with finances and investments and image, and they do so precisely because their previous actions have brought them to this point—their actions and those of their equally inept predecessors who sat atop the crumbling infrastructure and did nothing to address the root cause.

The cause of the crisis is a lack of faith, not finances. Finances are the symptom. As fewer and fewer Catholics remain Catholic, fewer and fewer pledge their lives, fortunes, children, offerings, and energies to the Church, and resultantly, the Church shrinks. This results in parish closings, Church property sell-offs (oftentimes in violation of canon law), dwindling vocations, smaller collection basket offerings. It is all of a piece, all so intertwined, so interrelated, that when one area is weak, the disease spreads to all other areas.

It is the Faith that needs shoring up, reinforcement, not the diocesan balance sheet. But behold, most bishops lack sufficient trust, supernatural hope that if they keep their eyes fixed on nothing but Christ, He will prevent them from being overcome by the wind and the waves. So they turn to their own devices, which will always be insufficient to overcome the power of the Enemy. A man, no matter who he is, will never defeat a demon without supernatural grace.

Until a bishop prays for and receives supernatural hope so that his faith increases, he will never experience the freedom of ignoring the wind and the waves. A bishop must stand up today and denounce the evil that has infected the Church. He must take ownership and responsibility for his part in it, and he must set a new course and ensure that all under him who exercise his authority are equally on board.

He must denounce failed catechism programs in his diocese that teach a watered-down faith, and denounce catechists who either do not practice what they preach or do not preach correct dogma. He must travel to each parish and denounce the evil of contraception and sodomy and the debilitating effects of sexual immorality on the family. He must put his neck on the line, aware that it might very well be chopped off—but he must trust that having been summoned out of the boat, he will under divine orders continue walking across the water ignoring the wind and the waves. It does not matter how drenched he gets or how tossed about; his duty is to just keep walking, keeping his vision fixed on Jesus—no more, no less.

Such a man will earn his enemies. There will be calls for his removal. Media reports will libel him, and many will stand up and leave. In fact, a stampede out of the parishes should be anticipated. All of these events and others precisely *are* the wind and the waves, and they must be dealt with. When the wind blew water into Peter's eyes, he had to keep walking as he wiped them—but he had to keep walking. The violence that will come about in response to a hope-filled bishop is Satan fanning the flames against him because he is aware the man has Christ with him.

Such a man knows the score; he understands the stakes exactly as the diabolical does. He matches the intensity of the demon stride for stride because such a bishop has Our Blessed Lord with him, for it is the Lord of Hosts Who does battle in the end. We only *engage* the demon, wake him up, rouse him; it is Christ Who commands him and defeats him.

A bishop needs to be a man saturated with supernatural hope, trust that God will win the day for him, no matter the odds, no matter the needs. What material needs is Our Lord incapable of providing? He knows the Church exists in material reality, and He will never cease to provide whatever is needed for that material reality. Supernatural hope is the strongest ally for a bishop fighting heresy.

Type Three: The Ignorant, Unintelligent Bishop

A bishop who is ignorant of today's crisis of faith is bound for Hell. The degree of self-absorption it would take for a bishop to be truly ignorant of the peril his flock is in would be so staggering as to render him already judged and condemned. There is no degree of ineptitude or lack of intelligence that could possibly be offered before the judgment throne of Jesus Christ to excuse a bishop who would simply plead ignorance or lack of understanding.

Ignorance in such a case would always involve some high degree of *willful* ignorance, meaning he simply does not want to deal with the crisis. He may feel he is lacking sufficient intelligence or instincts to confront it. It may be the case that a certain acting despair has set in, that he is powerless to attack any aspect of the situation for fear of worsening it; so his recourse is simply to go below deck, batten down the hatches, and wait to be transferred to another diocese or for the storm to pass. He is not allowed to do either, and his immortal soul, his personal salvation, depends on it.

The ignorant bishop fears the earthly more than he fears Hell, so he is happy to allow the Protestantism-inspired heresy that all men are saved (or we have a reasonable hope that all men are saved) to freely roam about his diocese and among his priests, who just as gleefully transmit it to a willing laity. His willful ignorance has supplanted his need for holy fear. He does not sufficiently fear his own damnation, and as such, he is incapable of fearing for the damnation of his flock. He has cast from his thought any fear of his own soul's being damned. He is therefore the most unintelligent of all bishops because, in the face of monumental piles, mountains of evidence to the contrary, he determinedly sets out on a course destined for failure. He pretends there is no crisis, or minimizes it by saying to himself, "There have always been crises in the Church."

A monumental fool if there ever was one, he lacks sufficient intelligence or will to grasp the reality and truth that crises come in different degrees and types. Bishop Athanasius Schneider recently commented in the summer of 2014 that the crisis now engulfing the Church is one of the four greatest in her 2,000-year history. This is no ordinary or non-existent crisis. It is global in scope and death-dealing in its severity, and its origins are owing to the ignorant and unintelligent bishop.

As we have previously explored, the heart of the current crisis is centered in the Protestant heresy, a heresy that boils down to the concept that man is his own self-determining being, that he determines what is right and wrong, what is theologically sound, what is meant by this or that passage of Scripture, and so forth. This heresy has spread so far and wide that a vast majority of the Church has already been lost to it. In the long view of human history, as earth's closing thunders are heard, it will be plainly seen that the forebear of the Modernist heresy, so aptly called by Pope St. Pius X "the synthesis of all heresies," will be seen to have been the heresy of Protestantism. What wickedness come to fruition in our own time does not have its seeds in that sixteenth-century evil?

An intelligent man would have long since realized that this means the loss over the centuries of hundreds of millions, if not billions, of souls from the One True Faith established by the Son of God. And *that* almost certainly means the loss of countless souls from their intended ends. Cut off from the Faith, they are left to battle Hell without the assistance of sustained supernatural grace, and no such man can overcome a demon.

This sort of bishop is a bishop in denial of reality, and such a man is a spectacle to behold. One asks oneself when encountering this man, this specimen of high ignorance, how he gets through a day. He will sail into a parish for confirmations, for example, completely unaware that the young men are goofing off on their cell phones, or that the young women are dressed as ladies of the night in training, and that for a huge number of parents, this is their first visit to a Catholic Church since their aunt Margaret died sixteen years earlier. Yet to the ignorant bishop, none of this is visible. To the unintelligent bishop, he sees before him a bunch of Catholics neatly dressed and ready for the parties that will happen back at the houses.

He is evidently ignorant of such things because he makes no mention of them. He is speaking, and they are paying no attention. And he as the bishop returns the favor. They are not listening to him, and he is not listening to them. And he pays that fact no attention. It is, at the end of the day, a gathering of the unintelligible: A few dozen or so fourteen-year-olds and their faithless parents fill up a church having no real understanding of why they are there, beyond some perfunctory family or ethnic custom. The bishop arrives, apparently also unaware of why he is there—which is to initiate the next generation of Catholics fully into the Faith. But they don't know the Faith, and he acts as though they do. The whole gathering is a gigantic exercise in hypocrisy on the part of every member of the ordained class.

These young people know next to nothing about the Faith, yet here stands a representative of the parish commending them to the bishop as young people who have closely examined and studied the Faith and are now ready to assume the mantle of Catholics confirmed in the Faith. The parish representative knows that's not true—and so does the bishop. If the parents knew anything of the Faith, they would know it's all a show, too, but they actually *are* ignorant of the Faith, albeit willfully.

And then comes the moment of His Excellency's homily. He pulls out some standard polite laugh line and some pleasantries to share with the crowd. He asks some rhetorical questions of the young people gathered before him. He makes some infinitely forgettable remarks, lays hands on them—and sends them into a world where most of them will be devoured by Satan. He will not talk to them about the reality of being a full-fledged Catholic because, frighteningly, he does not know it himself. Accordingly, his comments must remain polite and sophisticated-sounding, ethereal, but totally unconnected to reality— which is why they are forgettable, as most platitudes are.

He will not speak to them of the great need in their lives of a holy fear (one of the seven gifts they are about to receive) because he himself does not possess it. He will not underscore the reality, the object of that holy fear is a fear of the loss of their immortal souls. He will utter not a syllable of what Our Lord said about persevering to the end and begging the Divine Majesty for just that grace. He will not know how to communicate the truths of the Faith because he has made himself willfully blind to them. Such a man is on the road to Hell, and his pains will be increased accordingly as he steps into eternity, where he shall come face to face with these souls he stood in front of and did not afford the full light of truth. They, too, will be damned, and he will have had a share in it.

While they sat before him in this life and paid him no attention because he said nothing worthy of attention, they most definitely will pay him attention in the fires of Hell as they rip and tear at him, curse him, and vomit forth fire on him for not having told them what he should have told them, and thus, perhaps, having prevented their own arrival in the pits of Hell. And all of this, to his great eternal torture and shame, could have been avoided had he merely opened his eyes and looked on the reality of those entrusted to his care by Our Blessed Lord and His Holy Mother.

The one enduring legacy of the ignorant bishop, of which other bad bishops have a share, is the denial of Hell, or the effective denial of it. They never preach on it because they do not really believe, in their heart of hearts, that what God said is true. They deliberately close their eyes, in a disgraceful display of willful ignorance, to the aspect of divine revelation that reveals that human souls go to Hell, that Heaven is achieved through great rigor and sacrifice. They will not accept, cannot accept, the truth that Hell is the default condition for humanity. It is Hell that we must be saved from, and salvation is only earned or merited on our parts by working out our own salvation "with fear and trembling" (Phil. ii : 12), to quote an earlier bishop.

How is it that they do not grasp the concept of the word "fear"? Denial of Hell does not quench the fires. Saint Paul makes it clear beyond clarity that each one of us is not saved until we are judged as saved, of having so merited salvation by our deeds, our total response to the love of our Heavenly Father, demonstrated by our obedience to the commandments of His Divine Son. Without such a life lived, Hell is the destiny.

We are in this world for one goal and one goal only: to achieve Heaven. It is the only measure of success there is. Merit Heaven and your life has been a success, regardless of whatever failures you experienced during your earthly life. Be damned, and your life has been a failure, regardless of what heights you rose to or successes you enjoyed on earth. But the ignorant bishops do not want to hear this. They have committed their lives to a completely different vision of things, and for them to now reverse course and admit publicly that they have been living in open opposition to the truth of the Catholic Church in failing to preach the truth—this would simply be too much for them to do. They are psychologically ill-equipped to do this on their own. Their transformation will require, will demand, an infusion of grace.

So they continue to stoke the fires of their own destinies as they stand in front of crowds and exchange polite, empty greetings. They refuse to acknowledge the reality of unfaithful clergy on their watch whom they let prowl about the faithful devouring them like "ravenous wolves" in sheep's clothing (Matt. vii : 15). On the surface such men appear to be peaceful and are always portraying a picture of placidity and calm. But the peace they offer is a false peace, for there cannot be peace of soul without the soul's clinging to truth and unity. These men offer neither. They are like the false prophets of the Old Testament who attempted to argue down the likes of Jeremiah and

Isaiah, accusing them of rabble-rousing and sowing discord among the Chosen People.

The ignorant, unintelligent bishop is always babbling on about joy without the slightest concept of what he is talking about. He and his compatriots have conflated the notion of true Christian joy with outward displays of emotion and emotional outbursts, fostering the idea that unless a person is walking around giggling and backslapping in a state approaching immaturity, then he is not truly joyful.

Joy is not rooted in the emotions. It is rooted in the intellect, in the knowledge that one has been graced to know and live by the truth, which is pleasing to Almighty God, and consequently are attaining their salvation. They are working out their salvation "with fear and trembling" (Phil. ii : 12), and this is the cause of joy for them. Such a person possesses the supernatural virtues of faith, hope, and charity and lives in a state of gratitude for his many blessings.

Accordingly, because he is charitable, his chief concern after his own soul is that of his neighbor's. He does not want to be damned, nor does he want his neighbor to be damned. So he confronts evil he sees in his neighbor's life, as a bishop *should* be doing. And there is much evil to be confronted among his fellow Catholics. This is why chief on the list of the seven spiritual works of mercy is admonishing the sinner and instructing the ignorant. To engage in the works of mercy, as is evidenced by their very title, *is* charity. This point needs extreme emphasis. To help a sinner off the road to perdition is not charitable— *it is charity*, just as God is not loving but *love* itself. A person in possession of the supernatural virtues *becomes* those virtues, is absorbed into them, and is a model of them. Charity demands, therefore, such an overflowing of concern for neighbor, friend, family member, concern for their eternal destiny, that the evil in their life that will almost assuredly send them to Hell must be challenged.

The continuing mystery of the ignorant bishop is that he would be the first to suggest such a course of action in the case of some earthbound malady. If a member of the faithful, for example, approached him about an alcoholic family member, or a very dear friend suffering from a psychological illness such as depression, he would offer the correct advice and say the person must face reality about his condition, because he is certainly harming himself and will eventually harm others. But when it comes to applying the same principles to the spiritual welfare of those that Heaven has entrusted to his care, the willfully ignorant bishop will shove his head in the sand and say nothing.

The unintelligent, ignorant bishop will make inane comments like "we must accept a person *where he is*," without the slightest reference to Catholic truth, which is to then move him beyond that point. He never finishes the thought, because to finish the thought would cause war to break out in his diocese, and he would rather sit atop a false peace.

Sure, it is absolutely correct to accept a young man in the middle of a hellish struggle over his same-sex attraction. Any other reaction would be unChristlike. In fact, to not accept such a young man would be evil. But *merely* to accept him and allow him to remain spiritually unchallenged is even more evil than not to accept him at all. To plant the idea in his mind and give it outward approval that acting on his condition is a moral good is a plan of action directly from the Father of Lies. Such a bishop who knows that "gay Masses" or "LGBTQ ministries" are taking place in his diocese and confirming these poor souls in their evil will go to Hell. He prefers love of self, his own false peace, to love of those in his charge. To die in such a state, convinced of having been a good shepherd who kept the peace, who kept "all sides happy," will merit such a man eternal damnation. It is impossible for sin and sanctity to co-exist. To encourage holiness in some while turning a blind eye to evil in others is a complete abdication of the duties of the office of a bishop. Such a man will spend eternity with those he did not try or care to save.

Type Four: The Ambitious, Inoffensive Bishop

Pope Francis set a number of bishops' teeth on edge in the spring of 2014 when he said publicly that bishops should remain in their dioceses and stop jetting around the world because they consider their work in their dioceses a drudgery. He labeled them "airport bishops"—and those bishops who knew he was talking about them didn't like it one bit. It was not the first time the Holy Father went after the career-minded, politically ambitious bishop always seeking after more prestige in ecclesiastical circles. First, such a man wants to be a bishop. Then he wants to be bishop of a larger diocese. Then he wants to be on this committee or that board. Then he wants to be an archbishop of an archdiocese, then a cardinal. Then being a cardinal isn't sufficient, as he wants to be even more self-important.

In order to scale the ladder of Church politics, he must be a consummate politician, steering far away from any persons or causes that might carry with them a possible taint to his ambitions. He is extremely conscious of those with opinion and influence above him, and he desires to be in their company so he can count himself as "having arrived."

So he plays a political game where truth is sacrificed for gain, sometimes convincing himself that once he is in a position of real influence, he will then advance orthodoxy and walk the straight and narrow, becoming an effective general in the Church Militant.

Such a man is a fool. He will have already sacrificed so many principles, so much of himself on the way to these heights, that he will never be able to recapture himself.

Then there are the other ambitious bishops who actually never lie to themselves, never engage in self-deception about one day being able to effect change for the good. In fact, they have no real or lasting concern about "the good." Just as their secular counterparts in the world of business have no real concern for the company or its mission outside of what power or money they may obtain for themselves, doing or promoting "the good" to bishops like these is only a tool to advance themselves and their own ambitions and agendas. They have no lasting connection to authentic goodness. They are, however, at least honest enough to admit this. They are interested in power and influence for themselves, and that is the end of it.

Our Blessed Lord on more than one occasion severely scolded the Apostles for entertaining similar thoughts. Angling for power and greatness and prestige among the apostolic band infuriated the Son of God. It infuriated Him because He knew that such ambitions would be realized only over the corpses of His sheep—for the ambitious man, smelling of the stench of self-importance, has absolutely no regard for the care of the souls in his flock. He is a hireling. He is the exact sort of man Our Blessed Lord spoke of who runs at the first sign of danger to his sheep, more concerned with saving himself than his flock. This man will join his fellow bishops in the pits of Hell, his fellow bishops who lack the supernatural virtues of faith, hope, and charity.

If the treacherous bishop predominantly lacks faith, and the cowardly bishop lacks hope in the first order, and the ignorant bishop chiefly lacks charity, then the ambitious bishop lacks all three in the same measure. This is made clearer and more visible by evidence that the fourth-century priest Arius, after whom the great heresy is named, began his heresy as a result of being denied elevation to the episcopate. He was so ambitious that even after being denied, his ego could not accept the reality, so he acquired earthly influence by denying the divinity of Our Blessed Lord. Fittingly, he died a miserable death and with little doubt is currently in a constant state of being consumed by the fires of Hell.

To what lengths does the ambitious man not go to advance himself? Our Blessed Lord compares this type of man to the worldly, who lord it over their subjects, and He commands His shepherds not to be like this. He brings a child to His sacred embrace and says it is to such as these that the kingdom of Heaven belongs. But the ambitious man has no such understanding. To him, that is all nonsensical piety on which he can wax eloquent if need be. The ambitious bishop is all things to all men. He can stand in front of a somewhat orthodox crowd of Catholics on Monday evening and "speak their language," and on Tuesday after-noon shift gears with aplomb as he meets with and greets Catholics he knows are of a less faithful bent. In his mind, he flatters himself, congratulating himself on his remarkable skill in dealing with people, on his ability to meet people where they are and be a uniter, not a divider. He will even go on record as saying that dividers are injurious to the diocese.

In his ambitious lust, he has mistaken unity with keeping opposing camps separate—and there do exist opposing camps in the Church. This is largely owing to bishops of each stripe, but mostly the ambitious bishop. In order to advance, he needs to be a pleasing figure to all, both orthodox and heterodox. In the current state of confusion and madness that reigns in the Church, a man who is seen as too orthodox or too heterodox enjoys few prospects of advancement. The calculus is really very simple: Why would superiors advance a man who will cause them future grief from Catholics? Better to reward the politi-cian who displays great talent and skill, not to mention fundraising ability, by keeping everyone smiling—everyone, that is, except Our Blessed Lord.

The ambitious bishop is deft at recognizing the reality of opposing camps in his flock. And he is highly skilled in throwing bones to each, to the degree it keeps the divisions smoothed over. He will placate the homosexualists in his clergy, for example, by simply ignoring them—which they correctly assume means they have his permission to continue poisoning the flock—while at the same time smiling and quietly associating with the "pro-life Catholics." He will allow and sometimes even offer the appearance of support for the Traditional Latin Mass crowd, all the while permitting priests in his charge to mislead the faithful in the majority of other parishes in his diocese. Sometimes he will say quotable things to the local media that make it appear he is orthodox, but he'll offer no internal follow-up once the media has reported the story.

The ambitious bishop will set the stage for the continuing immolation of the Faith long after he is gone by appointing priests and laity to the various leadership roles who share his vision of "never rock the boat." Bishops such as these may even secretly congratulate themselves for being so much more orthodox than the previous generation of clerics or lay leaders, but they will have come to understand that challenging the status quo of heterodoxy is a one-way ticket to ecclesiastical Siberia.

The ambitious bishop and his courtiers in the chancery and parishes understand that the vocabulary of the world must be adopted so they all sound very levelheaded; it is the language of the corporate board room mixed with the popular culture. So they speak of "never giving offense," never being "judgmental," exercising "tolerance," always being "charitable"—and they debase the real beauty of what these words stand for by their exploitation of them.

The ambitious bishop has forsaken his duty by dismissing the reality that the Faith by its very nature *is* offensive. There is no way to present the truths of Almighty God to a culture awash in immorality that the culture will not find offensive, because the culture must be challenged and confronted in its sinfulness. But the ambitious trot out such trite phrases as "they aren't ready to hear that yet" or "we have to meet them where they are," or they speak in glowing terms of the few Catholics who still inhabit the pews (but live in opposition to the Faith) by saying, "At least they're coming." They aren't concerned with offering offense as much as with the fallout from their actions (bad publicity and financial loss) from offense having been taken. So the priest, for example, who stands before his congregation and warns of the dangers of Hell for use of contraception will quickly find himself sitting in front of the bishop, whose ambitions may be thwarted by the young Fr. Upstart.

The ambitious bishop ignores the reality that we are absolutely called to make moral judgments, and him most of all—not in some frenzied rush to condemn people to Hell, but to ensure members of his flock do *not* end up going there. So it is a good to call abortion murder, active homosexuality evil, contraception immoral, and so forth. He must stand up and declare with deafening clarity that divorced and remarried Catholics must not approach the altar for Holy Communion, for that would add sacrilege to their adultery.

He must ensure that those on parish councils and those in the legions of "eucharistic ministers" are not practicing birth control, promoting women's ordination, are members of pro-homosexual groups, and the like. It is his duty, his obligation before Almighty God, to do these things because they bear directly on their eternal lives. The bishop must make judgments, and he must follow up on them.

You will find that the ambitious bishop is the most tolerant man around, at least as he styles himself. What he actually is is *permissive*, a far cry from being tolerant. Permissiveness never challenges evil; rather, it accepts it—as the word implies—on a level where evil never has any concerns of being dispatched. Tolerance in regards morality means the *sorrowful* acceptance of a reality that you are working tirelessly to change. It does *not* mean permitting evil because trying to fight it would cause too much disturbance and upset the status quo— meaning, in fact, it would threaten the ambitious bishop's designs for higher office.

The ambitious bishop is actually not as tolerant as he portrays himself, or as he is pleased to allow his underlings to portray him. If anything occurs that threatens his standing or his plans, he deals with it quickly, because at the end of the day, the ambitious bishop possesses a degree of ruthlessness. He will deal with any situation with lightning speed that threatens to undermine his image as the great peacekeeper. This includes cases from across the entire spectrum, from the truth-speaking priest warning his parish of the dangers of immorality, to the priest who is accused of financial impropriety. The calculus is again simple. These cases can immediately become known and talked about and carry with them the potential to present an image of the bishop different from the one he has carefully cultivated. That image is of one always in the logical middle, never being too far to one side or the other. The ambitious bishop is the walking, talking embodiment of "Big Tent Catholicism." And as Our Lord says, he is a hireling.

It is precisely because he promotes the "Big Tent" version of Catholicism that he completely distorts the beautiful notion of charity. He must present and support an incorrect notion of charity because his entire edifice would come tumbling down if he did not. Charity demands that evil be confronted. *God is charity*, and God always confronts and eradicates evil. Evil flees in the face of charity—authentic charity. But confronting evil creates conflict, and this the ambitious bishop cannot brook. There can be no open warfare on his watch, for his image and future ambitions are at stake.

So a false notion of charity must be fostered and allowed to spread. This false notion of charity is very much in keeping with the view of the culture at large of being "nice." In fact, it is directly borrowed from the cultural lexicon. Charity takes on the meaning of simply being polite, sweet, nice, and socially graceful, never saying things that upset people, and certainly never being uncouth enough to say inappropriate things about immorality. After all, not being tolerant makes one judgmental and gives offense. This cultural understanding is so easily adopted by Catholics in the main because they live in the culture. They hear and see this the other six days they are not around the parish, so when they step into the parish and hear the same thing, it all sounds exceedingly familiar to them, and they are very comfortable with it.

This creates an environment for the ambitious bishop that he can capitalize on, for his flock has already largely been brainwashed for him. In short, others have done his dirty work for him. So he completely understands that there is an unconscious acceptance already in place that he can speak to and profit from. He never has to charge his priests with speaking about sexual immorality or Hell or sin because those topics would be seen as judgmental by the brainwashed flock. It is a made-to-order, ready-made windfall for the ambitious bishop because the prevailing social attitude coincides perfectly with his ambitions for self-promotion. Without ever really lifting a finger, he can simply tap into current cultural conditions and win his case. It is the prophet who is the extremist and needs to be sacrificed for the good of the nation. And the ambitious bishop, along with his fellow treacherous, weak, ignorant brother bishops, are just the men to do it.

As a side note, this is not to say that *all* the bishops in the United States fall into one of these four categories of faithlessness. There is a separate category of solid, faithful, holy, truly Catholic bishops who, like all of us, can sometimes err in matters of prudential judgments, but for the faithful bishops, the fount from which their decisions flow is not poisoned like it is with the others. We must pray that Our Blessed Lord blesses His Holy Catholic Church with many more men like this.

It is of utmost importance, having so closely examined the question of failed leadership among US prelates, that we not neglect this singular truth: God Himself has permitted this evil of wicked, lazy, willfully blind, ambitious men to descend on the faithful like wolves. This has not happened serendipitously. It is a punishment from Heaven for the lack of fidelity on the part of the laity. There is shared responsibility between both clergy and laity for the state of affairs in the Church today.

Despite the torrent of evil that engulfed American civilization in the 1960s and forward, good Catholics did not need *shepherds* to stand up; we had it within our power to resist evil in our own lives. We did not need to embrace the culture as we did, no matter how much leaders may have softened us up for such an outcome. Lay Catholics did not abandon their private devotions because the bishops ordered them to. True, the major de-emphasis on prayer and devotion on the part of many priests and bishops could certainly assist the weaker among the faithful to slowly abandon the practices; nonetheless, the laity bear responsibility, to varying degrees, for the current state of affairs in the Church. We have not been faithful. We also, like our leaders, were too often willing to acquiesce to the culture and cave in to a society bidding and tempting us to forsake the truth.

We did not hold fast. We did not ourselves possess the holy fear necessary to pray to our Divine Master for the grace of final perseverance. The only difference between an individual lay Catholic and a bishop running a diocese is that the effect of the bishop's faithlessness has a much greater impact than that of most lay Catholics. The unfaithful bishop will have to give account for his spiritual serial murders, but we individual Catholics will not escape the severity owed us—unless, like the bishops need to, we each—prelate and lay—pray to God for forgiveness, earnestly repent, and set a new course whereby we completely and fully commit ourselves to the restoration of the Faith, each beginning with his own office and station in life.

Whether any bishop repents of his past evil ways does not affect our individual ability to repent and pray for what is needed in our lives for our own salvation. The difference with regard to the bishop is that a much greater responsibility is placed on him to do so, because he can encourage so many more people by his own donning of sackcloth and ashes.

A memorable passage penned by St. John Eudes is worth contemplating here. It is from his work *The Priest: His Dignity and Obligations*, but it applies to bishops even more emphatically.

> The most evident mark of God's anger and the most terrible castigation He can inflict upon the world are manifested when He permits His people to fall into the hands of clerics who are priests more in name than in deed, priests who practice the cruelty of ravening wolves rather than the charity and affection of devoted shepherds. Instead of nourishing those committed to their care, they rend and devour them brutally. Instead of leading their people to God, they drag Christian souls into Hell in their train. Instead of being the salt of the earth and the light of the world, they are its innocuous poison and its murky darkness.

> Saint Gregory the Great says that priests and pastors will stand condemned before God as the murderers of any souls lost through neglect or silence. Elsewhere St. Gregory asserts that nothing more angers God than to see those whom He set aside for the correction of others give bad example by a wicked and depraved life. Instead of preventing offenses against His Majesty, such priests become themselves the first to persecute Him, they lose their zeal for the salvation of souls, and think only of following their own inclinations.

Their affections go no farther than earthly things, they eagerly bask in the empty praises of men, using their sacred ministry to serve their ambitions, they abandon the things of God to devote themselves to the things of the world, and in their saintly calling of holiness, they spend their time in profane and worldly pursuits.

When God permits such things, it is a very positive proof that He is thoroughly angry with His people, and is visiting His most dreadful anger upon them. That is why He cries unceasingly to Christians, "Return, O ye revolting children . . . and I will give you pastors according to my own heart" (Jer. iii : 14–15). Thus, irregularities in the lives of priests constitute a scourge visited upon the people in consequence of sin.

On the other hand, the greatest effect of God's mercy, the most precious grace He bestows upon mankind, is to send worthy priests, men after His own heart, seeking only His glory and the salvation of souls. The greatest blessing that God bestows upon a church, the most signal manifestation of divine grace, is to have a saintly shepherd, be he bishop or priest. This is indeed the grace of graces and the most priceless of all gifts for it includes within itself every other blessing and grace. What is a priest after God's heart? He is an inestimable treasure containing an immensity of good things.

The holy priest is one of the treasures of the Great King, having in his keeping the infinite abundance of God's mercy to enrich worthy souls. He is an inexhaustible fountain of living water, open and accessible to all those who long to come to drink the waters of salvation.

He is a tree of life planted by God in the paradise of the Church, bearing on its branches at all times fruits of everlasting life, freeing from sin and Hell, giving grace and eternal bliss to those who will but eat. Those fruits are the words, instructions, exhortations, prayers, intercession, and example of the life and work of the holy priest.

The priest is a sun cheering the world by his presence and bearing. He brings heavenly blessings into every heart. He dispels the ignorance and darkness of error and radiates on every side bright beams of celestial light. He extinguishes sin and gives life and grace to the multitudes. He imparts new life to the weak, inflames the lukewarm, fires more ardently those who are aglow with the sacred flame of divine love.

He is an angel purifying, illuminating, and perfecting the souls that God has entrusted to him. He is a seraph sent by God to teach men the science of salvation which is concerned only with knowing and loving Almighty God and His Divine Son, Jesus Christ.

The priest is an archangel and a prince of the heavenly militia, waging constant war against the devil who strives to drag countless souls into the depths of Hell.

He studies the needs of his flock in order to exercise the utmost efficiency in supplying their wants. He ferrets out any disorders which may exist among his charges in order to eradicate them; he gives himself unselfishly to the advancement of the glory of God and the salvation of those souls under his direction.

He is the light of those who sit in darkness and in the shadow of death. He is the destroyer of error, schisms, and heresies, the converter of sinners, the sanctifier of the just, the strength of the weak, the consolation of the afflicted, the treasure of the poor. He is the confusion of Hell, the glory of Heaven, the terror of demons, the joy of angels, the ruin of Satan's kingdom, the establishment of Christ's empire, the ornament of the Church, the crown of the Supreme Shepherd.

In a word, the holy priest embodies a world of grace and benediction for the entire Church, but especially for that portion which God has called him to govern and guide. (Ch. 11, "Qualities of a Holy Priest")

Chapter 10

THE FEMINIZED HIERARCHY:
Masculinity Abandoned

The majority of today's bishops were young seminarians when the wave of evil broke over the American culture in the 1960s and 70s. A bishop, for example, who is in his mid-sixties or older was more than likely in seminary and ordained in the late 1960s or early 70s. In other words, they were the first to be impacted by the explosion.

They were set loose as young priests into a Church reeling from all of the societal unrest one could imagine: the Vietnam War protests (many of them consisted of protestors); the widespread rejection by professional Catholics of the Church's teaching on birth control; the Women's Lib movement; the acceptance of abortion on demand; the emergence of the homosexual rights movement; the skyrocketing of divorce rates among Catholic families; the dramatic loss and abandonment of vows by tens of thousands of religious; the rise of a liberal, progressive media, supportive of a liberal, aggressive new politics.

The earth was moving under their feet, reorienting their center of gravity. Add to this that all of these men had experienced the transition to the "New Order" of the Mass from their childhoods. They lived through it. They were the first to receive it and learn the accompanying embarrassing songs composed by former priests who would go on to a life of homosexuality. They saw the old Church dismantled and the new one erected—and they were young priests during this time. Many of them were the first assigned to stand guard over the dismantling of the Faith.

If only they had paid close attention to the words of the Holy Father, who saw coming into sharp focus all that chaos descending on the Church at the same time today's bishops were in their seminary training or being ordained to the priesthood. If only they had listened. In 1968 Pope Paul VI said:

> The Church finds Herself in an hour of anxiety, a disturbed period of self-criticism, or what would even better be called self-demolition [auto-destruction]. It is an interior upheaval, acute and complicated, which nobody expected after the Council. It is almost as if the Church were attacking itself.... It is as if the Church were destroying Herself. (Address to the Lombard Seminary, Rome, December 7, 1968)

The entire world was being turned upside down, and these young future bishops saw it all from the front row. There were two predominant excuses offered for the upheaval in the Church, the auto-demolition that had flooded in from the upheaval of the society: (1) that the Church had to restyle Herself to be more accommodating to Protestants so they would feel less intimidated and convert; and (2) that the Church had to get with the times. The old ways of confrontation and the great walled city were over; the Church had to make Herself more accessible to the world at large. The hostilities had come to an end.

These were the great propaganda lines sweeping through the Church in those days. Those in their fifties, who lagged behind the newly ordained by only ten years or so, saw the initial results of the widespread implementation of all this. They were in middle school and high school in the 1970s just as today's bishops were being ordained priests. The pressure to go along was immense. Pastors began slowly discarding things Catholic. The Catholic identity was being submerged, drowned, as it were, in an ocean of accommodation to the greater culture.

These young priests who would go on twenty to thirty years later to become bishops of the American Church learned their lessons well. The focus had changed from saving souls to managing a bureaucracy dedicated to social justice and reforming the culture—whatever that meant. They did not put the dynamite in place for the destruction; that was done in the 1940s and 50s. They did not light the fuse; that occurred in the 1960s and 70s. But they are witnesses to the explosion that took place when the dynamite went off, and having ascended to the episcopacy in the aftermath, this group has done woefully little to pick up the pieces and restore order. In many cases, they are guilty of having allowed the resulting inferno to continue burning, drawing a multitude of souls into the great firestorm.

They are the first generation of leaders who have had their manhood thoroughly sucked from them by the culture, a culture where the feminine rules supreme and the masculine is debased. They learned this attitude from their instructors in seminary, from the actions of the bishops who ordained them, from their own families who were abandoning the Faith in droves, from the parents of the Catholic school students they supervised, from their own parishioners who lost interest in the practice of their religion, from their fellow clergy who rushed to throw off "the old Church." They absorbed every bit of it, however distasteful or against their better judgments it may have been initially.

They learned how not to be men, how not to stand in opposition to spiritual danger, and learned rather how to be women, to proclaim and repeat such insipid, Protestant theology-inspired phrases like "all are welcome" or "we should not judge," or a host of other spiritually destructive mantras dressed up in high-sounding, well-intentioned, bumper-sticker phrases. They went along with the destruction, in other words. They would have to have played ball or they would not today be bishops. Certainly there are exceptions, but given the politics in the Church and the restructuring and destruction of all that was considered "traditional" that was so forceful in the 1990s, they would not have joined the ranks of the episcopate if they had not at least been collaborators. They learned to lead like women, to accentuate all that is feminine to the virtual exclusion of the masculine.

They folded like a house of cards in the face of altar girls, multiple abuses in the Mass, Holy Communion in the hand, and so forth. They wanted to encourage "inclusiveness" and "tolerance," and to hide their shame or guilt in their complicity in ravaging the Church; they trumpeted the glories of social justice and the need to "help the poor." If you are thinking this sounds like Judas' plan of action, you are right. These men drank in the culture and first ran their parishes accordingly, and later their dioceses—and now they are reaping the rotten fruits of their dismantling of the Faith. They are closing down parishes by the hundreds, "restructuring" their dioceses, working out "new campaigns," and giving those campaigns vaguely "churchy"-sounding names. They hire outside marketing companies and pay them millions of dollars to "rebrand" the Church.

They know in their heart of hearts something is wrong, terribly wrong. The more discerning and honest among them know, too, that they had something to do with this demolition of the Faith, had a major role to play in it. They never mentioned a word about the acceptance of sexual immorality on the part of so many of their congregations. They kept silence and allowed the firestorm to continue sucking in the faithful. And in their early years, they sat somewhat content behind rich storehouses of diocesan wealth and investments. But then came the reality of what their silence in front of evil and their cooperation with it had wrought: the homosexual priest sex abuse scandal.

One by one, these sons of the 1960s were confronted with the consequences of what they had known, even as priests, but to which they had turned a blind eye. As bishops, on their way up the ecclesiastical ladder, they were all certainly aware of this in varying degrees. All that mattered to them was the institution—their precious institution with which they had helped build up and replace the former Church, the same institution to which they owed their careers and mitres. These men have become the living embodiment of the passage from Proverbs: "He who troubles his household will inherit wind" (Prov. xi : 29).

They are currently inheriting the wind. Years of inaction, mixed signals, indecisiveness, "tolerance" of dissidents, horrible catechesis, lack of apostolic zeal, an almost insatiable desire to have the praise of men, an abiding effort to sustain the status quo, a veritable will of iron when it comes to not "rocking the boat," the desire to chase after ecumenism, the casting aside of almost every vestige of Catholic identity—all of this has resulted in a decay of the Faith unprecedented in the annals of Church history. The Faith has survived better in times of sustained persecution than it has under the administration of American bishops over the last thirty years.

Chapter 11

THE MUSTARD SEED:
Unless a Grain of Wheat Falls into the Earth

Only pockets remain of anything that a reasonable person could call Catholic identity. By any and every reasonable indicator, the Church in America is in a state of apostasy, and there are no signs that it's going to change its monumental downward spiral. The fact that three out of four baptized Catholics do not attend Mass, and that one in every ten Americans (35 million) are former Catholics, is proof enough. The Church in the United States has already become what Pope Benedict predicted when he was still a cardinal:

> Maybe we are facing a new and different kind of epoch in the Church's history, where Christianity will again be characterized more by the mustard seed, where it will exist in small, seemingly insignificant groups that nonetheless live an intense struggle against evil and bring good into the world—that let God in. (*Salt of the Earth*, 1997)

Without going over in great detail various polling data and surveys gathered over the past five years, suffice it to say Catholicism is a dying proposition in the United States. A staggering percentage of baptized Catholics between 18–25 surrender the Faith without a fight —which of course portends disaster for the Church in America in the next ten to twenty years. Just as the current crop of bishops who have helped to create the mess is ready to be laid to rest, there may be almost no Catholics left to actually bury them.

There is a massive drop-off in infant baptisms and a meteoric plunge in weddings and First Communions over the past forty years. It is a statistical death spiral. Add to this the rate of conversions to the Faith has fallen off the cliff, down seventy-five percent in the last fifty years. While the rate of conversions was never particularly impressive, what was mediocre at best is now beyond terrible. The possibility of a turnaround is approaching the level of impossibility (in earthly terms, of course).

In summary, the Church in America is contracting in spectacular fashion. Some overview of statistics is helpful in comprehending the precise scale of the destruction.

First, parishes are closing in record numbers. There's been a net loss of 2,000 in twenty years (1990–2010)—a ten percent decline. And since 2010, hundreds more have been closed in major archdioceses (New York, Detroit, Boston) with at least scores more also on the chopping block, slated for closure. And to counter the much-repeated defense from establishment types in the Church bureaucracy, these closings do *not* represent a simple demographic shift, but a real-world shrinking of numbers attending Mass.

Second, priests are advancing in age and dying. For the record, in 1967 there were nearly 60,000 priests in the United States; in 2012 there are approximately 40,000 priests—a thirty-three percent decline. That's a net loss of some 20,000 priests, and the *rate* of loss is picking up steam, as many of the remaining priests are advanced in years. Over the coming decade, the overall number of priests will drop even more than it has up to this point. Shrinking congregations, shrinking parishes, and a shrinking ministerial priesthood cannot be spun to mean anything good in terms of the life of the Church.

Third, religious orders are diminishing in extraordinary fashion. In terms of religious priests (those belonging to orders, such as Jesuits, Dominicans, Franciscans, etc.), in 1967 there were 23,000; in 2012 the number of priests in religious orders had declined to roughly 13,000—a forty-five percent decrease, or a net loss of 10,000. In terms of religious brothers, in 1967 there were 13,000. In 2012 there were just 4,500— a sixty-five percent decrease, or a net loss of 8,500.

The story of the destruction of women religious orders is even more jaw-dropping. In terms of women religious in various orders and communities, in 1964 the orders were booming, with 180,000 sisters. In 2012 the number had gone off the cliff; only 55,000 remained—a seventy percent decrease, or a net loss of 125,000 sisters. And, as with priests, the rate of decline will increase in the coming decade. Many of these women are well advanced in years and will die off within the next decade.

Fourth, diocesan seminaries have emptied out. In 1967, more than 60,000 young men were studying for the diocesan priesthood. But by 2012, that number had plummeted to only 18,000, representing a decrease of almost three quarters. In those forty-plus years, the Church experienced a net loss of 42,000 young men studying for diocesan priesthood, a continuing drop of approximately 1,000 each year.

If there is one small ray of hope, it does appear that perhaps the plummet in seminarians and newly ordained has possibly bottomed out. A handful of dioceses around the United States have reported an uptick in the number of newly ordained, but the numbers are still too inconsistent, and a year or two of slight increases does not a trend make. We should hope that something of a turnaround has begun, and pray for such an event actually to be occurring, but as of 2015, it is still way too early to know anything for certain.

This auto-demolition of the Faith has by no means been confined to the ranks of the religious and ordained. Catholic marriages have taken a nosedive. In 1971 there were nearly 430,000 Catholic marriages. Yet in 2012 there were only 170,000 marriages in the Church in the United States—a sixty percent decline. There is no way this could be viewed other than as a terrible omen of things to come. And for the record, all of these statistics measuring the intensity of the Catholic meltdown are from the US bishops' own data, *The Kennedy Directory*.

Fifth, the number of converts to Catholicism is rapidly declining. In 1960, the Catholic Church in the United States welcomed nearly 150,000 converts to the One True Faith. By 2012, only 75,000 converts came to the Faith—a near-fifty percent drop-off. And such a drop-off is more alarming and disturbing when the overall increase in the American population since 1960 is accounted for. In short, fewer converts are being made from a potential pool of even greater numbers.

Sixth, the number of infant and adult baptisms is in steep decline. In terms of infant baptisms, as recently as just 1997, more than one million babies were baptized into the Catholic faith. In 2012 the number had dropped to just 800,000—a twenty-four percent decline, or a net loss of 250,000 infant baptisms. Clearly the drop in Catholic marriages has begun to have its knock-on effect. And it isn't just the drop in marriages but the reality of how the overwhelming number of Catholics now *view* marriage and sex. More on this later, but for now consider that as contraception and abortion become more and more accepted among Catholics, it only follows that there would be fewer infant baptisms because there are fewer infants. Perhaps more than any other single cause, contraception among Catholics has taken a huge toll in destroying the Church in America.

In terms of adult baptisms, in 1994 there were roughly 80,000, but like every other category, by 2012 only 43,000 adults were baptized into the Faith established by the Son of God for men's salvation. That's a forty-six percent decline representing a net loss of 37,000 adult baptisms.

Seventh, the number of First Communions and confirmations has plummeted. With regard to First Communions, in 2001 we had roughly 900,000. By 2012, that number had dropped to 800,000—a twelve percent decrease, or a net loss of 100,000 in ten years, calculated at 10,000 fewer per year. As to confirmations, in 2004 there were 650,000, but by 2012 we had only 620,000—a five percent decrease, or a net loss of 30,000 confirmations in just ten years.

Eighth, the number of priests, brothers, and sisters teaching has predictably hit rock-bottom. In 1966, Catholic schools had roughly 125,000 priests teaching in them. By 2012, only 1,200 priests could be found heading a class—a ninety-nine percent decline, or a net loss of 123,800 priests teaching. In terms of brothers teaching, 1967 saw roughly 6,000. By 2012, a brother teaching in a classroom was beyond rare—only 698 remained, which represents an eighty-eight percent decline. The Church lost 5,300 teaching brothers. As to sisters teaching in the classroom, in 1964 there were 104,500, but by 2012, the bottom had fallen out: Only 4,000 were left—an unbelievable ninety-six percent decline, or net loss of 100,500.

Again, these numbers aren't fantasy. Every one of them is from the US bishops' official tallies. By every conceivable measure, the Catholic Church in America is in a death spiral. It is now possible, very possible, to envision a United States with no Catholic Church to speak of.

It appears it's far more likely that the Church in the United States will go the way of the Church in the United Kingdom, rather than make some dramatic turnaround. In order for a turnaround to occur, in earthly terms there needs to be something capable of creating a comeback. An analogy from the world of sports might prove instructive.

If your favorite football team is trailing badly at halftime or well into the third quarter, and the opposition just keeps pounding and widening the lead, each fan in his own time eventually comes to face the reality that a comeback isn't possible. The other team runs a better offense, employs a better defense, has better special teams, better athletes, more preparation, more skill—in short, it has every ingredient necessary to secure the win. It might be a knee-jerk reaction initially to hope for a turnover or some other "game-changer." But even on the rare occurrence when your team does recover a fumble or snag an interception, it doesn't "do anything" with the opportunity. The other team rises up and squashes any comeback effort. Such a game, in the vocabulary of sports, is called a blowout—and that is what's happening to the Catholic Church in the United States today.

All the "bad stat" rates are excelling, and all the "good stat" rates are slowing down or even flat-lining, and in some cases declining. It's hard to imagine a bigger catastrophe facing the Church than what will occur in the next ten to fifteen years. Now, some will say, God will step in and save it. First, it *will* take a miracle for this to be overcome. It is not a question of the bus racing toward the cliff; the bus has already gone *off* the cliff. What remains is the fiery explosion down below. Second, it is beyond the sin of presumption to expect that God will simply wave His arm and right the ship, and no Pollyanna approach to the crisis should be tolerated. History has proven time and again that God has allowed various local churches to simply disappear owing to their unfaithfulness. The seven churches of Asia Minor (modern-day Turkey) that Our Blessed Lord addresses in the beginning of the Apocalypse have all vanished.

This current crop of bishops may be the last that will preside over the Church in America, as it is now currently constituted. In the language of computer technology, a reboot may soon be needed, meaning that priests today who will be bishops in the next ten or so years may have to envision an entirely different way of managing affairs in the Church.

In fact, current prelates are already preparing the ground for this, whether they realize it or not. The current parishes, lands, conference centers, religious houses, chanceries, etc. will simply not have enough income to be sustained owing to the rapidly decreasing number of Catholics. In fact, the massive downsizing has already begun.

Besides huge numbers of parish closings, even the large chanceries of yesteryear are now disappearing.

In the archdiocese of Detroit, for example, nearly 40,000 square feet of archdiocesan offices were once spread over two rather sizable office buildings in the downtown area. In 2014, Detroit archbishop Allen Vigneron marched his somewhat ragtag-looking team of officials into a considerably smaller office space of just over 10,000 square feet. The depressing picture of a line of Catholic officials carrying their boxes from the former space, led by the archbishop, was published in the local secular paper. The accompanying article pointed out that the archdiocese was now renting space, whereas before it had owned it.

It would not be unreasonable to anticipate more scenes like this in the near future across Catholic America. Tomorrow's bishops will have to be an ingenious lot in figuring out how to meet the needs of a graying, shrinking number of Catholics who will, by virtue of their age, be less mobile and therefore find it increasingly difficult to attend Mass at a decreasing number of parishes. The geographical footprint of the Church will be a difficult issue to manage as more and more properties will be surrendered to secular buyers to meet expenses. Space will become a severe issue for Church officials. Getting to the "spaces" for Mass might very well prove to be a serious issue for the aging laity.

Pope Benedict, back when he was Cdl. Ratzinger, predicted this several decades ago:

> From the crisis of today the Church of tomorrow will emerge—a Church that has lost much. She will become small and will have to start afresh more or less from the beginning. She will no longer be able to inhabit many of the edifices she built in prosperity. As the number of her adherents diminishes, so will She lose many of Her social privileges. In contrast to an earlier age, She will be seen much more as a voluntary society, entered only by free decision. (*Faith and Future*, 1971)

Where Have All the Children Gone?

What makes a crisis a moment of opportunity as opposed to a defeat is the realization by enough people that things need to change. The ingredients, the causes of the crisis, its root cause needs to be eradicated. If that happens, then a change for the good occurs. If that does not happen, then the enemy wins. And with all the talk of a demographic winter in terms of various national populations aging and shrinking and contracting owing to birth control and abortions, the Catholic population of the United States is on the verge of its own demographic disaster. The reason?

The Catholic population that still has what might be loosely termed an active faith life is not distributed evenly across the demographic chart. It is hugely tilted to the crowd born before 1949 (sixty-five years and older). These make up the largest group at Sunday Mass each week. According to the actuary tables, in ten to fifteen years most of these people will be dead (along with the current bishops in their mid-sixties and over). Approximately two thirds of the active Catholic crowd comes from this demographic group, and there is no indication in *any* other demographic that they're anywhere near being replaced.

It makes sense that as this crowd begins to retire—which they've begun to do—that what will occur is a contraction of the Church in raw numbers (and all of the data includes immigration). Not only is the *rate* of contraction speeding up, but as would be expected ultimately, the raw numbers will soon begin to reflect this as well. One thing is clear: In the next twenty years, at current rates, the Catholic population will more than likely be cut by a quarter to a third from its current levels; and in the next forty years it will be reduced by nearly two thirds from its current levels.

While the current overall US population will also begin to decline or at least flatten out owing to abortion and contraception, it will not decline at as steep a rate as the Catholic population in the same period. This will have the even further adverse effect of shrinking the American Catholic population relative to the total US population. The current ratio is twenty-two percent. Trend lines indicate that in the next fifteen years, Catholics will make up little more than approximately thirteen percent of the population—a drop-off rate approaching fifty percent—something unimaginable just a generation ago.

These current trends for the Church indicate nothing less than a disaster for the Faith *during our lifetimes.*

All of this has accelerated and continues to accelerate on the watch of the current bishops ordained as priests in the 1970s. With rare exceptions here and there, they are leaving an insurmountable problem for the next generation of bishops, a mess that will be impossible to rectify. All of this is owing to a lack of the supernatural virtues, which have been buried under a mountain of radicalized feminism, absorbed by these men in their young ministries. They were taught to cavort with the world instead of fighting against it. They followed their training, and now as the sun begins to set on their careers (for most of them are within just ten years of handing in the required resignation letter), all they have to show for it is a trail of tears and lost souls. They ceased to be the Church Militant and adopted the easier path of the Church of Nice. And now it is too late.

Chapter 12

THE CHURCH OF NICE:
Never Giving Offense

The phrase "Church of Nice" has one simple meaning, yet a multiplicity of applications: It simply means a caving in to the prevailing cultural attitude of never giving offense. Never. To anyone. Ever. So whatever makes people "feel good" is accepted as the way of conducting business, presenting the Faith, the status quo. The focus of the Church of Nice is the people, not God. It is all about emotions to the neglect of the intellect. It is, in the last analysis, a transformation of the faithful into more worldly beings. Pope Francis addressed this great concern in Rome in September 2014:

> We Christians live in the world, fully integrated in the social and cultural reality of our time, and it is right that it is so; however, this carries the risk that we become "worldly," that the salt loses its flavor, as Jesus would say; that is, that the Christian is "watered down," losing the inspiration of newness that comes from the Lord and the Holy Spirit. Instead, they should be the opposite: When the strength of the Gospel remains alive in Christians, they can transform mankind's criteria of judgment, determining values, points of interest, lines of thought, sources of inspiration and models of life. . . .

> It is sad to meet Christians who are watered down, like wine; you cannot tell whether they are Christians or worldly, like watered wine; it is impossible to tell whether it is wine or water. It is sad to meet Christians who are no longer the salt of the earth . . . because they have committed themselves to the spirit of this world, that is, they have become worldly. (Angelus, September 1, 2014)

The Church of Nice is all about the worldly. It has its priorities entirely reversed from authentic Catholicism. It emphasizes the Second Commandment (love of neighbor) over the *greatest* command- ment (love of God). And not only are its priorities backwards, they are also executed poorly. It doesn't understand "love," which is in reality the theological virtue of charity. It confuses love with the idea of politeness and social niceties, never giving offense and being toler- ant and so forth. True love—charity (*caritas*)—is directed to the good of the other, and theologically speaking, to their salvation. It has nothing to do with not giving offense, or not challenging error. True love, char- ity, uses whatever means the circumstances call for to help a person on the road to salvation. Using the best and most appropriate means to enlighten someone on the road to Heaven is the meaning of pru- dence. But all of this is completely misunderstood by Church of Nice congregants, and it has disastrous consequences—meaning people go to Hell.

This wrongheadedness has resulted in, among dozens of things, a dummied-down liturgy, where the relationship most valued is the priest and the congregation. The notion of the Mass as sacrifice is barely given any acknowledgment. The highest, noblest goal a man in the Church of Nice can aspire to is apparently congeniality, a pleas- antness or niceness that accepts every novelty that comes down the road—with the single exception of authentic Catholic identity. It is when the Church of Nice encounters authentic, masculine, muscu- lar Christianity—in a phrase, the Church Militant—that the Church of Nice becomes the Church of Ugly.

As for the thousands of ways the Church of Nice is manifested, they are too numerous to detail. But here are some of the novelties accepted, celebrated, or institutionalized for the sake of being nice:

1. Holy Communion in the hand (never called for by the Church)

2. Altar girls (never called for by the Church)

3. The priest facing the people (never called for by the Church)

4. Gregorian chant, insisted on by Vatican II, dumped in favor of syrupy songs that appeal to people's emotions rather than to their intellects

5. So-called "eucharistic ministers" (never called for by the Church)

6. Protestant music in Mass replacing Catholic sacred music (never called for by the Church)

7. Neglecting the use of Latin in the Mass, in spite of the fact that Vatican II insisted on its use

8. Moving tabernacles away from the center of the parish sanctuary (never called for by the Church)

9. The destruction of Catholic art and architecture

10. The near-total disavowal of the need for the sacrament of confession

11. The near-total absence of promotion of the devotional life

12. Parish youth ministries neglecting and in some cases rejecting Catholic doctrine (because the doctrines don't meet the standard of being "nice")

13. Parish adult religious education neglecting Catholic doctrine (see no. 12)

14. The destruction of Catholic education in parish schools

15. Catholics leading the way on gay "marriage" approval, because disallowing two men to express their love in a sexual manner isn't "nice"; it's far too judgmental

16. The refusal of nearly every US bishop to enforce Canon 915, which mandates denial of Holy Communion to pro-abortion "Catholic" politicians

17. Orthodox seminarians being carefully monitored or not ordained, or whose ordinations are delayed

18. "Gay Masses" in many dioceses with the bishops' knowledge

19. Financial support for pro-abortion and pro-contraception, same-sex marriage groups by the US bishops' anti-poverty program, the Catholic Campaign for Human Development

20. Catholic Relief Services employees' abundant donations to the Obama campaign because he's "nice" and "non-judgmental"

21. Homosexual or homosexual-friendly clergy in numbers greatly exceeding their representation in the overall US population of approximately 1.5–2 percent (Catholic priesthood numbers of homosexual men register at somewhere between 18–54 percent!)

22. Enormous resistance to the Traditional Latin Mass by bishops and priests

23. Non-stop emphasis on "earthly" matters like immigration and gun control

24. The repeated failure to preach against the evil of contraception, now accepted by more than five out of six Catholics

25. Attacks against traditional-minded Catholics by the establishment

26. National Knights of Columbus' refusal to address the issue of pro-abortion, pro-same sex "marriage" politicians in their own ranks

27. Promotion of the anti-Catholic, anti-traditional notion of there being a "reasonable hope" that all men are saved

28. False ecumenism that papers over differences among religions

29. Unwillingness to openly declare the superiority of Catholicism

30. Catholic majorities voting for Obama (twice)

31. Catholic higher education almost totally eradicated, with the exception of a handful of Catholic lay efforts that are struggling because of the decreasing pool of young Catholics interested in the Faith

32. The refusal by the majority of bishops to publicly acknowledge the deep problems, and most especially their causes

33. Dissident priests allowed to keep their positions in parishes

34. Dissidents and heretics being promoted on the Catholic speaking circuit (Fr. Timothy Radcliffe, for example)

35. The collapse of young adult Catholics believing the Faith (less than fifteen percent are active)

36. An ever-shrinking number of faithful Catholics, defined as attending Mass every week

37. A lack of clarification regarding some Vatican II documents

38. The very liberal political leanings of much of the lay leadership (e.g., Obama bumper stickers on cars driven by USCCB staffers and parish leaders all over America)

39. The inability of many bishops to overcome the liberal structures in their own dioceses

40. The lack of official commitment to pro-life Catholic activities (e.g., after forty-plus years of abortion on demand, there is still no national collection on behalf of pro-life efforts, but there are eleven other national collections)

41. The overall "protestantization" of the Church in art, décor, music, style, etc.

42. The substitution of social justice for personal holiness, a favorite of many liberal bishops

43. Widespread acceptance of contraception in the Church, including vast numbers of religious

44. Targeting by liberal chanceries of solid, orthodox priests

45. Massive misapplication of Natural Family Planning, owing to an acceptance of the contraceptive mentality of the culture

46. Lack of preaching or teaching on personal sin

47. Poor seminarian formation

48. Failure to preach the dogma *Extra ecclesiam nulla salus*, or "No salvation outside the Church"

49. Lack of precision regarding Islam's worship of "the same God"

50. Buy-in by the bishops of anthropocentric climate change

51. Failure to decry Americanism and reject a poorly applied idea of religious liberty

52. Allowance of paganism or New Age mysticism in parishes and orders

53. The downplaying of the demonic and the devil

54. Abuse of collegiality in the various bishops' conferences

And that's just for starters. Review that list again and realize that a separate book could be written on every single one of those topics—yet they are all intertwined. It is one gigantic edifice, designed to supplant orthodox Catholicism with a whole new religion whose chief aim is to take over the current structure. That may or may not be the goal of a given individual bishop, but it is the goal of Satan, and he has used and manipulated the treacherous, weak, unintelligent, and ambitious men that have presided over the Church for the past forty or more years. The current crop of bishops is no exception. They consist of the leadership of the Church of Nice, and they foster its growth. They have no understanding of the Church Militant, and as such, they are tools in the hands of the diabolical.

This renders them unable in their current state to fix anything, because they themselves are the instruments by which the evils are being carried out. Pope Adrian VI had a crisis on his hands in the early years following Martin Luther's revolt. He correctly identified and summed up the situation then, which has strong parallels for us now. For if what Bp. Athanasius Schneider has correctly identified as the fourth great crisis in the Church (by way of chronology, not necessarily magnitude) is true, i.e. our current catastrophe, then we can and should be eager to learn from one of the past great crises:

> We frankly acknowledge that God permits this persecution of His Church [the Protestant Revolt] on account of the sins of men, **and especially of prelates** and clergy; of a surety the Lord's arm is not shortened that He cannot save us, but our sins separate us from Him, so that He does not hear. Holy Scripture declares aloud that **the sins of the people are the outcome of the sins of the priesthood**; therefore, as Chrysostom declares, when our Savior wished to cleanse the city of Jerusalem of its sickness, He went first to the Temple to punish the sins of the priests before those of others, like a good physician who heals a disease **at its roots**. (Pope Adrian VI, Letter to the Imperial Diet of Nuremburg, 1522) (emphasis added)

While the sins of bishops of the past may have been concentrated in the search for earthly power and money, the current list would have at its head a search after praise of men, vainglory. This is why so many prelates remain silent and refuse to accuse the culture; they do not want to suffer the rebukes of men. They of course have a million and one excuses to cover their lack of courage, but in the end, they have nowhere to hide. Their track record speaks for itself. And all their efforts and excuses and results have all been gathered together into the Church of Nice, which has a severe problem with ever talking about the Enemy of mankind.

As things came off the rails for the Church following the Second Vatican Council in the late 1960s and early 1970s, Pope Paul VI had no problem calling it like it is.

> We believed that after the Council would come a day of sunshine in the history of the Church. [Here again, we see this odd sentiment during the Council that all was right with the world.] But instead there has come a day of clouds and storms, and of darkness. . . . And how did this come about? We will confide to you the thought that may be, we ourselves admit in free discussion, that may be unfounded, and that is that there has been a power, an adversary power. **Let us call him by his name: the devil.** It is as if from some mysterious crack, no, it is not mysterious, from some crack the smoke of Satan has entered the temple of God. (General Audience, 1972) (emphasis added)

Chapter 13

REASONABLE HOPE THAT ALL MEN ARE SAVED: Not!

The Church of Nice can only exist if the threat of Hell is removed or so extensively downplayed that it has the practical effect of having been removed. The Church of Nice and Hell cannot exist in the same realm; one of them has to go.

The heresy of universalism—that all creation eventually goes to Heaven—has made a comeback in recent years, albeit in a slightly altered form. Universalism is a heresy, condemned explicitly by the Church in repeated times and places. Now the heresy has morphed into a much more palatable one. Instead of directly transgressing Church teaching by declaring as a fact that all men are saved, the latest version simply *suggests* that all men are saved. It does this under the clever phrasing of twentieth-century Swiss theologian Hans Urs von Balthasar with the claim that we have a "reasonable hope" that all men are saved. Notice the switch: from we *know* all men are saved to we have a *reasonable hope* all men are saved.

It is a mere play on words, carrying the same meaning in essence practically applied. It is human nature to give ourselves, the individual, the benefit of the doubt. So it matters little whether the actual heresy that all men are saved permeates the conscious mind, or whether its wicked sister, which claims we have a reasonable hope that all men are saved, does so. Modern man will of course count himself, the individual man we are speaking of here, as being in the category of those saved by a reasonable hope.

It sounds *reasonable*, after all. He isn't a murderous dictator, he thinks to himself. He doesn't blow up buildings, incite jihad, or any such thing that truly wicked men do. He isn't a serial killer or a child molester. He doesn't attend Black Masses, nor is he a devil worshipper. Satan has set the bar so high for a person to consider himself in his true light that the conscience of modern man has been deadened by the overexposure to "great" sin. "I'm no Al Capone," says the modern man living out his sex-fueled, contraceptive life of pornography, excusing his continual engagement in "average" sin while expressing shock and outrage at the occasional "great" sins.

The theologically errant supposition that we have a reasonable hope that all men are saved is a clever deception because it sets up an illusion in the mind of the hearer. The illusion is that the man guilty of "average" sin comes to believe that the only sin is "great" sin—which, of course, he has nothing to do with. He is, therefore, self-absolving, which explains the massive drop-off in the administering of the sacrament of confession. Modern man has no need of confession because he does not commit "great" sin. He tells himself, "I'm not perfect, but God is a loving God and He won't throw the average guy like me into Hell forever." The "reasonable hope" axiom feeds this deceiving line of thought.

So the man of "average" sin imagines he will go to Heaven. The truth is that the difference between the man of "average" sin and the man of "great" sin is *not* that the former goes to Heaven and the latter goes to Hell, but rather that they *each* go to Hell and suffer in a degree proportionate to the sin, average or great.

Again, notice the subtle switch, from we *know* all men are saved to we have a *reasonable hope* all men are saved. One sounds much more reasonable than the other. The reality is that both statements are false because each contradicts the explicit words of Our Blessed Lord in Scripture. Not *everyone* goes to Heaven, and not *nearly everyone* goes to Heaven. It is this one line of thought that has wreaked so much havoc in the Church, and it must be brought to an end because it is the diabolical that has brought it about.

This is his sneak attack, launched against the Church Militant warship —a loss of belief by the individual man about the constant threat of losing his own soul, which brings about a loss of belief in the recognition of sin and its true ugliness in his soul, which brings about a lack of holy fear, which brings about a neglect of prayer for the grace of final perseverance, which brings about an indifference to the Catholic faith, which brings about a lukewarm soul, which brings about that soul's damnation.

Satan has trotted out an old heresy, made it more "hip and cool," and unleashed it on the world at the most opportune time. Society, which is a collection of individual men, has long since abandoned the idea of Hell—at least, certainly the idea that *I* might go to Hell. The feminized God of all mercy and no justice reigns supreme in the mind of contemporary man and has not been combated by the leaders of the Church. No, far from being combated, this error has been *accepted and advanced* by many leaders in many places in the Church. They have not withstood the satanic distortion of God by the one who was first to encounter His divine justice. They have instead set up shop and are selling his wares to those in their care. And this will be to their everlasting shame and torment when the fullness of truth is revealed on the Last Day. Those who will not fight will die in their sin.

And the second great cause for the undoing in the mind of contemporary man of any holy fear is the failure to understand the nature of Heaven. If Hell has been wiped away, Heaven has been "retooled." The contemporary Catholic views Heaven in a similar way as the heresy of Islam does: Heaven is some kind of continuation of this life, just without all the headaches, a place of peace and contentment—which of course it is, but not peace the way the world understands it, as Our Blessed Lord told His Apostles at the Last Supper. The everlasting peace will come as a great reward for battling ferociously in the world, by carrying one's cross, doing penance, loving God above all His creatures. Having thus conquered in the Church Militant the earthly battle, the soul is now admitted into the Church Triumphant. "Well done, good and faithful servant; you have been faithful over a little, I will set you over much; enter into the joy of your master" (Matt. xxv : 21). The peace is a complete resting in God, in the joy that comes from being fully united to God. It is not a continuation of earth's delights and pastimes, which so many liken it to be.

Every soul in Heaven will be Catholic, for the Church Triumphant is the full and final aspect of the Catholic Church. There will be no Lutherans, or Hindus, or Muslims, and so forth in Heaven. It is impossible. To the extent a soul in Heaven submitted to one of these man-invented religions on earth, and to the extent he *may* be saved, he will have long since been purged of his sincerely and invincibly ignorant error in the cleansing fires of the Church Suffering—Purgatory—before being admitted into the Church Triumphant.

The Church Triumphant gathers around the Holy Trinity, honors the Queen, Immaculate Mary, and celebrates with the other saints in glory. Exactly what would an atheist, or a Muslim, or a Hindu, or a Protestant *do* in such a situation? How would they relate? What, for example, would a Baptist say to the Mother of God, His Queen, after having spent his earthly life denying Her Her rightful title? What would constitute the attraction of a Mormon or Jehovah's Witness to the Holy Trinity, people who spent their earthly existence denying and fomenting against the Triune God by trying to turn others from this most sublime truth?

But the indifferentism (the belief that no religion is better than any other but are just different paths to God) spawned by the sin of presumption expands even further by creating the environment of universalism—the hideous notion that all men are saved—or as it's presented more recently, *we have a reasonable hope that all men are saved.* There is absolutely no basis in the preceding 2,000 years of the Church's history for this novelty of the past fifty years.

The proposition that most men are saved is so contradictory to traditional Catholic understanding that when it is laid side by side with that tradition, it doesn't even appear to be the same religion.

First, we should consider that there is almost unanimous agreement among the Fathers, Doctors, and luminary saints of the Church that most people are damned. An assortment of private revelations also speaks in agreement with this. Consider this lengthy list of quotes from Scripture, Fathers and Doctors of the Church, mystics, saints, blesseds, venerables, seers, and popes speaking of the tradition of the Church on the difficulty in attaining final perseverance and the fact that the majority of human beings are damned. It is quite an impressive list:

Matthew vii : 13–14

> "Enter by the narrow gate; for the gate is wide and the way is easy, that leads to destruction, and those who enter by it are many. For the gate is narrow and the way is hard, that leads to life, and those who find it are few."

Mark xx : 16

"For many are called, but few are chosen."

Luke xiii : 23–24

"And someone said to him, 'Lord, will those who are saved be few?' And he said to them, 'Strive to enter by the narrow door; for many, I tell you, will seek to enter and will not be able.'"

1 Corinthians vi : 9–10

"Do you not know that the unrighteous will not inherit the kingdom of God? Do not be deceived; neither the immoral, nor idolaters, nor adulterers, nor homosexuals, nor thieves, nor the greedy, nor drunkards, nor revilers, nor robbers will inherit the kingdom of God."

Galatians v : 19–21

"Now the works of the flesh are plain: immorality, impurity, licentiousness, idolatry, sorcery, enmity, strife, jealousy, anger, selfishness, dissension, party spirit, envy, drunkenness, carousing, and the like. I warn you, as I warned you before, that those who do such things shall not inherit the kingdom of God."

Philippians ii : 12

"[W]ork out your own salvation with fear and trembling."

Hebrews vi : 8

"But if it bears thorns and thistles, it is worthless and near to being cursed; its end is to be burned."

1 Peter iv : 18

"If the righteous man is scarcely saved, where will the impious and sinner appear?"

Ecclesiastes i : 15

> "What is crooked cannot be made straight, and what is lacking cannot be numbered."

Isaiah x : 19

> "The remnant of the trees of his forest will be so few that a child can write them down."

Isaiah xvii : 5–6

> "And it shall be as when the reaper gathers standing grain and his arm harvests the ears, and as when one gleans the ears of grain in the Valley of Reph'aim. Gleanings will be left in it, as when an olive tree is beaten—two or three berries in the top of the highest bough, four or five on the branches of a fruit tree, says the Lord God of Israel."

Isaiah xxiv : 13

> "For thus it shall be in the midst of the earth among the nations, as when an olive tree is beaten, as at the gleaning when the vintage is done."

St. Augustine, Father and Doctor of the Church

> "Not all, nor even a majority, are saved. . . . They are indeed many, if regarded by themselves, but they are few in comparison with the far larger number of those who shall be punished with the devil."

> "It is certain that few are saved."

> "The Apostle commands us to rejoice, but in the Lord, not in the world. For, you see, as Scripture says, whoever wishes to be a friend of this world will be counted as God's enemy. Just as a man cannot serve two masters, so, too, no one can rejoice both in the world and in the Lord."

> "Beyond a doubt the elect are few."

"As a man lives, so shall he die."

"The Lord called the world a 'field' and all the faithful who draw near to him 'wheat.' All through the field, and around the threshing floor, there is both wheat and chaff. But the greater part is chaff; the lesser part is wheat, for which is prepared a barn not a fire. . . . The good also are many, but in comparison with the wicked the good are few. Many are the grains of wheat, but compared with the chaff, the grains are few."

"If you wish to imitate the multitude, then you shall not be among the few who shall enter in by the narrow gate."

St. Thomas Aquinas, Doctor of the Church

"Those who are saved are in the minority."

"Since their eternal happiness, consisting in the vision of God, exceeds the common state of nature, and especially insofar as this is deprived of grace through the corruption of original sin, those who are saved are in the minority. In this especially, however, appears the mercy of God, that He has chosen some for that salvation, from which very many in accordance with the common course and tendency of nature fall short."

"There are a select few who are saved."

St. Alphonsus Maria de Liguori, Doctor of the Church

"Everyone desires to be saved, but the greater part is lost."

"Saint Teresa, as the Roman Rota attests, never fell into any mortal sin; but still Our Lord showed her the place prepared for her in Hell; not because she deserved Hell, but because, had she not risen from the state of lukewarmness in which she lived, she would in the end have lost the grace of God and been damned."

"The saints are few, but we must live with the few if we would be saved with the few. O God, too few indeed they are; yet among those few I wish to be!"

131

"All persons desire to be saved, but the greater part, because they will not adopt the means of being saved, fall into sin and are lost. . . . In fact, the elect are much fewer than the damned, for the reprobate are much more numerous than the elect."

"We owe God a deep regret of gratitude for the purely gratuitous gift of the true faith with which he has favored us. How many are the infidels, heretics, and schismatics who do not enjoy comparable happiness? The earth is full of them, and they are all lost!"

"It is certain that we absolutely require the divine assistance, in order to overcome temptations. . . . Whoever prays obtains this grace; but whoever prays not obtains it not, and is lost. And this is more especially the case with regard to the grace of final perseverance, of dying in the grace of God, which is the grace absolutely necessary for our salvation, and without which we should be lost forever. Saint Augustine says of this grace that God only bestows it on those who pray. And this is the reason why so few are saved, because few indeed are mindful to beg of God this grace of perseverance."

"God, observes a certain author, wishes to be served by his priests with the fervor with which the seraphim serve him in Heaven; otherwise He will withdraw His graces and permit them to sleep in tepidity, and thence to fall, first into the precipice of sin and afterwards into Hell."

"Some will say, 'It is enough for me to be saved.' 'No,' says St. Augustine, 'it is not enough; if you say that it is enough, you will be lost.' He who abuses too much the mercy of God will be abandoned by Him."

"[L]et us bear in mind that unless we are humble we shall not only do no good, but we shall not be saved. 'Unless you . . . become as little children, you shall not enter into the kingdom of Heaven.' In order, then, to enter into the kingdom of Heaven, we must become children, not in age, but in humility. Saint Gregory says that as pride is a sign of reprobation, so humility is a mark of predestination."

"It is certainly a great happiness for some sinners who after a bad life are converted at their death, and are saved; but these cases are very rare: ordinarily he that leads a bad life dies a bad death."

"To obtain salvation we must tremble at the thought of being lost, and tremble not so much at the thought of Hell as of sin, which alone can send us thither. He who dreads sin avoids dangerous occasions, frequently recommends himself to God, and has recourse to the means of keeping himself in the state of grace. He who acts thus will be saved; but for him who lives not in this manner it is morally impossible to be saved."

"The common opinion is that the greater part of adults is lost."

"The greater part of men choose to be damned rather than to love Almighty God."

"The greater number of men still say to God: Lord, we will not serve Thee; we would rather be slaves of the devil and condemned to Hell than be Thy servants. Alas! The greatest number, my Jesus—we may say nearly all—not only do not love Thee, but offend Thee and despise Thee. How many countries there are in which there are scarcely any Catholics, and all the rest either infidels or heretics! And all of them are certainly on the way to being lost."

"What is the number of those who love Thee, O God? How few they are! The elect are much fewer than the damned! Alas! The greater portion of mankind lives in sin unto the devil, and not unto Jesus Christ. O Savior of the world, I thank Thee for having called and permitted us to live in the true Faith, which the Holy Roman Catholic Church teaches. . . . But alas, O my Jesus! How small is the number of those who live in this holy Faith! Oh, God! The greater number of men lie buried in the darkness of infidelity and heresy. Thou hast humbled Thyself to death, to the death of the Cross, for the salvation of men, and these ungrateful men are unwilling even to know Thee. Ah, I pray Thee, O omnipotent God, O sovereign and infinite Good, make all men know and love Thee!"

"We were so fortunate to be born in the bosom of the Roman Church, in Christian and Catholic kingdoms, a grace that has not been granted to the greater part of men, who are born among idolaters, Mohammedans, or heretics. . . . How thankful we ought to be, then, to Jesus Christ for the gift of faith! What would have become of us if we had been born in Asia, in Africa, in America, or in the midst of heretics and schismatics? He who does not believe is lost. He who does not believe shall be condemned. And thus, probably, we also would have been lost."

"All infidels and heretics are surely on the way to being lost. What an obligation we owe God for causing us to be born not only after the coming of Jesus Christ, but also in countries where the true Faith reigns! I thank Thee, O Lord, for this. Woe to me if, after so many transgressions, it had been my fate to live in the midst of infidels or heretics!"

"In the Great Deluge in the days of Noah, nearly all mankind perished, eight persons alone being saved in the Ark. In our days a deluge, not of water but of sins, continually inundates the earth, and out of this deluge very few escape. Scarcely anyone is saved."

St. Benedict Joseph Labre

"I was watching souls going down into the Abyss as thick and fast as snowflakes falling in the winter mist."

"Meditate on the horrors of Hell, which will last for eternity because of one easily committed mortal sin. Try hard to be among the few who are chosen. Think of the eternal flames of Hell, and how few there are that are saved."

"Yes, indeed, many will be damned; few will be saved."

St. Jean Marie Baptiste Vianney, Patron Saint of Parish Priests

"The number of the saved is as few as the number of grapes left after the vine-pickers have passed."

"Shall we all be saved? Shall we go to Heaven? Alas, my children, we do not know at all! But I tremble when I see so many souls lost these days. See, they fall into Hell as leaves fall from the trees at the approach of winter."

"Alas, my friend. We cannot be together in Heaven unless we have begun to live so in this world. Death makes no change in that. As the tree falls, so shall it lie. . . . Jesus Christ said, 'He that does not hear the Church, let him be to thee as a heathen and a publican.' And He also said, 'There shall be one fold and one shepherd,' and He made St. Peter the chief shepherd of His flock. My dear friend, there are not two ways of serving Jesus Christ. There is only one good way, and that is to serve Him as He Himself desires to be served."

"Nothing afflicts the heart of Jesus so much as to see all His sufferings of no avail to so many."

St. Bridget of Sweden

"O Jesus! . . . Remember the sadness that Thou didst experience when, contemplating in the light of Thy divinity the predestination of those who would be saved by the merits of Thy sacred Passion, thou didst see at the same time the great multitude of reprobates who would be damned for their sins, and Thou didst complain bitterly of those hopeless, lost, and unfortunate sinners."

St. Remigius of Rheims

"With the exception of those who die in childhood, most men will be damned."

"Among adults there are few saved because of sins of the flesh."

"Yes, indeed, many will be damned; few will be saved."

St. Francis Xavier

"Ah, how many souls lose Heaven and are cast into Hell!"

St. Frances Xavier Cabrini

"How many among these uncivilized peoples do not yet know God, and are sunk in the darkest idolatry, super-stition, and ignorance! . . . Poor souls! These are they in whom Christ saw, in all the horror of His imminent Pas-sion, the uselessness of His agony for so many souls!"

St. Joseph Cafasso

"Cast a look round the world, just observe the manner of living, of speaking, and you will see immediately whether the evil of sin is known in the world or whether any at-tention is paid to it. Not to speak of those who live de-cidedly irreligious and wicked lives, how few are those who pass for good and who approach the sacraments and are aware of the great evil that sin is, and the great ruin it brings with it. It must necessarily happen that, on ac-count of this certainly culpable ignorance in which most men live, an enormous number will come to be damned, because no sin is pardoned which is not detested, and it is impossible to detest sin properly if it is not known as such."

Pope St. Gregory the Great, Father and Doctor of the Church

"They who are to be saved as saints and wish to be saved as imperfect souls shall not be saved."

"There are many who arrive at the Faith, but few who are led into the heavenly kingdom. Behold how many are gathered here for today's feast day: We fill the church from wall to wall. Yet who knows how few they are who shall be numbered in that chosen company of the elect?"

"The Ark, which in the midst of the Flood was a symbol of the Church, was wide below and narrow above, and, at the summit, measured only a single cubit. . . . It was wide where the animals were, narrow where men lived: For the Holy Church is indeed wide in the number of those who are carnal-minded, narrow in the number of those who are spiritual."

St. Isidore of Seville, Father and Doctor of the Church

"It is as though Jesus said: 'O My Father, I am indeed going to clothe Myself with human flesh, but the greater part of the world will set no value on My Blood!'"

"The greater part of men will set no value on the Blood of Christ, and will go on offending Him."

Bd. Jacinta of Fatima

"So many people are going to die, and almost all of them are going to Hell! So many people falling into Hell!"

St. John of the Cross, Doctor of the Church

"Only a small number of souls achieve perfect love."

"Behold how many there are who are called, and how few who are chosen! And behold, if you have no care for yourself, your perdition is more certain than your amendment, especially since the way that leads to eternal life is so narrow."

St. Jerome, Father and Doctor of the Church

"Many begin well, but there are few who persevere."

"Out of 100,000 sinners who continue in sin until death, scarcely one will be saved."

"So that you will better appreciate the meaning of Our Lord's words, and perceive more clearly how few the elect are, note that Christ did not say that those who walked in the path to Heaven are few in number, but that there were few who found that narrow way. It is as though the Savior intended to say: The path leading to Heaven is so narrow and so rough, so overgrown, so dark and difficult to discern, that there are many who never find it their whole life long. And those who do find it are constantly exposed to the danger of deviating from it, of mistaking their way, and unwittingly wandering away from it, because it is so irregular and overgrown."

St. John Chrysostom, Father and Doctor of the Church

"I do not speak rashly, but as I feel and think. I do not think that many priests are saved, but that those who perish are far more numerous."

"Do you not perceive how many qualities a priest must have that he may be strong in his teaching, patient, and hold fast to the faithful word which is according to doctrine? What care and pains does this require! Moreover, he is answerable for the sins of others. To pass over everything else: If but one soul dies without baptism, does it not entirely endanger his own salvation? For the loss of one soul is so great an evil that it is impossible to express it in words. For if the salvation of that soul was of such value that the Son of God became man and suffered so much, think of how great a punishment must the losing of it bring."

"What do you think? How many of the inhabitants of this city may perhaps be saved? What I am about to tell you is very terrible, yet I will not conceal it from you. Out of this thickly populated city with its thousands of inhabitants not 100 people will be saved. I even doubt whether there will be as many as that!"

St. John Eudes

"Get out of the filth of the horrible torrent of this world, the torrent of thorns that is whirling you into the abyss of eternal perdition. . . . This torrent is the world, which resembles an impetuous torrent, full of garbage and evil odors, making a lot of noise but flowing swiftly past, dragging the majority of men into the pit of perdition."

St. John of Avila, Doctor of the Church

"Take care not to resemble the multitude whose knowledge of God's will only condemns them to more severe punishment."

St. John Neumann

"Notwithstanding assurances that God did not create any man for Hell and that He wishes all men to be saved, it remains equally true that only few will be saved, that only few will go to Heaven, and that the greater part of mankind will be lost forever."

Servant of God Sr. Lucia of Fatima

"Taking into account the behavior of mankind, only a small part of the human race will be saved."

Ven. Maria of Agreda

"The majority of souls appear before the Judgment empty-handed. They did nothing good for eternity."

"Countless hosts have fallen into Hell."

"That those who walk in the way of salvation are the smaller number is due to the vice and depraved habits imbibed in youth and nourished in childhood. By these means Lucifer has hurled into Hell so great a number of souls, and continues thus to hurl them into Hell every day, casting so many nations from abyss to abyss of darkness and errors, such as are contained in the heresies and false sects of the infidels."

St. Philip Neri

"So vast a number of miserable souls perish, and so comparatively few are saved!"

St. Hilary of Poitiers, Father and Doctor of the Church

"How few the elect are may be understood from the multitude being cast out."

St. Justin the Martyr

"The majority of men shall not see God, excepting those who live justly, purified by righteousness and by every other virtue."

St. Louis Marie de Montfort

"The number of the elect is so small, so small, that were we to know how small it is, we would faint away with grief: one here and there, scattered up and down the world!"

"Be one of the small number who find the way to life, and enter by the narrow gate into Heaven. Take care not to follow the majority and the common herd, so many of whom are lost. Do not be deceived; there are only two roads: one that leads to life and is narrow, the other that leads to death and is wide. There is no middle way."

"The number of the elect is so small that were God to assemble them together, He would cry to them, as He did of old, by the mouth of His prophet, 'Gather yourselves together, one by one'—one from this province, one from that kingdom."

St. Leonard of Port Maurice

"A great number of Christians are lost."

"The following narrative from St. Vincent Ferrer relates that an archdeacon in Lyons gave up his charge and retreated into a desert place to do penance, and that he died the same day and hour as St. Bernard. After his death, he appeared to his bishop and said to him, 'Know, Monsignor, that at the very hour I passed away, 33,000 people also died. Out of this number, Bernard and myself went up to Heaven without delay, three went to Purgatory, and all the others fell into Hell.'"

"Our chronicles relate an even more dreadful happening. One of our brothers, well known for his doctrine and holiness, was preaching in Germany. He represented the ugliness of the sin of impurity so forcefully that a woman fell dead of sorrow in front of everyone. Then, coming back to life, she said, 'When I was presented before the Tribunal of God, 60,000 people arrived at the same time from all parts of the world; out of that number, three were saved by going to Purgatory, and all the rest were damned.'"

"Look higher still, and see the prelates of the Holy Church, pastors who have the charge of souls. Is the number of those who are saved among them greater than the number of those who are damned? Listen to Cantimpre; he will relate an event to you, and you may draw the conclusions. There was a synod being held in Paris, and a great number of prelates and pastors who had the charge of souls were in attendance; the king and princes also came to add luster to that assembly by their presence. A famous preacher was invited to preach. While he was preparing his sermon, a horrible demon appeared to him and said, 'Lay your books aside. If you want to give a sermon that will be useful to these princes and prelates, content yourself with telling them on our part, We the princes of darkness thank you, princes, prelates, and pastors of souls, that due to your negligence, the greater number of the faithful are damned; also, we are saving a reward for you for this favor, when you shall be with us in Hell.'"

St. Basil the Great, Father and Doctor of the Church

"I exhort you, therefore, not to faint in your afflictions, but to be revived by God's love, and to add daily to your zeal, knowing that in you ought to be preserved that remnant of true religion which the Lord will find when He comes on the earth. Even if bishops are driven from their churches, be not dismayed. If traitors have arisen from among the very clergy themselves, let not this undermine your confidence in God. We are saved not by names, but by mind and purpose, and genuine love toward our Creator. Bethink you how in the attack against our Lord, high priests and scribes and elders devised the plot, and how few of the people were found really receiving the word. Remember that it is not the multitude who are being saved, but the elect of God. Be not then affrighted at the great multitude of the people who are carried hither and thither by winds like the waters of the sea. If but one be saved, like Lot at Sodom, he ought to abide in right judgment, keeping his hope in Christ unshaken, for the Lord will not forsake His holy ones. Salute all the brethren in Christ from me. Pray earnestly for my miserable soul."

St. Anselm, Doctor of the Church

"It is impossible to be saved if we turn away from thee, O Mary."

"If you want to be certain of being in the number of the elect, strive to be one of the few, not one of the many. And if you would be quite sure of your salvation, strive to be among the fewest of the few; that is to say, do not follow the great majority of mankind, but follow those who enter upon the narrow way, who renounce the world, who give themselves to prayer, and who never relax their efforts by day or night, so that they may attain everlasting blessedness."

Ven. Louis de Granada

"A greater number is lost through false confidence than through excessive fear."

Pope St. Pius X

"Oh, Jesus, Divine Redeemer of souls, behold how great is the multitude of those who still sleep in the darkness of error! Reckon up the number of those who stray to the edge of the precipice. Consider the throngs of the poor, the hungry, the ignorant, and the feeble who groan in their abandoned condition."

St. Vincent Ferrer

"Many religious go straight to Hell because they do not keep their vows!"

St. Bede the Venerable, Father and Doctor of the Church

"Christ's flock is called 'little' (Luke xii : 32) in comparison with the greater number of the reprobates."

"Nor should we think that it is enough for salvation that we are no worse off than the mass of the careless and indifferent, or that in our faith we are, like so many others, uninstructed."

St. Robert Bellarmine, Doctor of the Church

"It is granted to few to recognize the true Church amid the darkness of so many schisms and heresies, and to fewer still so to love the truth which they have seen as to fly to its embrace."

St. Teresa of Avila, Doctor of the Church

"Bad confessions damn the majority of Christians."

"I had the greatest sorrow for the many souls that condemned themselves to Hell, especially those Lutherans. . . . I saw souls falling into Hell like snowflakes."

St. Anthony Mary Claret

"A multitude of souls fall into the depths of Hell, and it is of the faith that all who die in mortal sin are condemned for ever and ever. According to statistics, approximately 80,000 persons die every day. How many of these will die in mortal sin, and how many will be condemned! For as their lives have been, so also will be their end."

St. Peter Julian Eymard

"Ah! How very small is the kingdom of Jesus Christ! So many nations have never had the Faith!"

St. Vincent de Paul

"Ah! A great many persons live constantly in the state of damnation!"

St. Maria Faustina Kowalska

"One day, I saw two roads. One was broad, covered with sand and flowers, full of joy, music and all sorts of pleasures. People walked along it, dancing and enjoying themselves. They reached the end of the road without realizing it. And at the end of the road there was a horrible precipice, that is, the abyss of Hell. The souls fell blindly into it; as they walked, so they fell. And their numbers were so great that it was impossible to count them. And I saw the other road, or rather, a path, for it was narrow and strewn with thorns and rocks; and the people who walked along it had tears in their eyes, and all kinds of suffering befell them. Some fell down upon the rocks, but stood up immediately and went on. At the end of the road there was a magnificent garden filled with all sorts of happiness, and all these souls entered there. At the very first instant they forgot all their sufferings."

St. Francis of Assisi

"Fear and honor, praise and bless, thank and adore the Lord God Almighty, in Trinity and Unity, Father, Son, and Holy Spirit, Creator of all things. Do not put off any longer confessing all your sins, for death will soon come. Give and it will be given you; forgive and you will be forgiven. . . . Blessed are they who die repentant, for they shall go to the Kingdom of Heaven! But woe to those who are not converted, for these children of the devil will go with their father into everlasting fire. Be watchful, therefore. Shun evil, and persevere in well-doing until the end."

St. Robert Southwell

"The path to Heaven is narrow, rough, and full of wearisome and trying ascents, nor can it be trodden without great toil; and therefore wrong is their way, gross their error, and assured their ruin who, after the testimony of so many thousands of saints, will not learn where to settle their footing. Oh how much are the worldlings deceived that rejoice in the time of weeping, and make their place of imprisonment a palace of pleasure; that consider the examples of the saints as follies, and their end as dishonorable; that think to go to Heaven by the wide way that leadeth only to perdition!"

St. John Climacus

"Live with the few if you want to reign with the few."

St. Veronica Giuliani

"The number of the damned is incalculable."

St. Leo of Patara

"I see around me a multitude of those who, blindly persevering in error, despise the true God; but I am a Christian nevertheless, and I follow the instruction of the Apostles. If this deserves chastisement, reward it; for I am determined to suffer every torture rather than become the slave of the devil. Others may do as they please since they are . . . reckless of the future life, which is to be obtained only by sufferings. Scripture tells us that 'narrow is the way that leads to life' . . . because it is one of affliction and of persecutions suffered for the sake of justice; but it is wide enough for those who walk upon it, because their faith and the hope of an eternal reward make it so for them. . . . On the contrary, the road of vice is in reality narrow, and it leads to an eternal precipice."

Saint Arsenius

"Brethren, the just man shall scarcely be saved. What, then, will become of the sinner?"

Blessed Anna Maria Taigi

"The greater number of Christians today are damned. The destiny of those dying on one day is that very few—not as many as ten—went straight to Heaven; many remained in Purgatory; and those cast into Hell were as numerous as snowflakes in mid-winter."

Blessed Angela of Foligno

"They who are enlightened to walk in the way of perfection, and through lukewarmness wish to tread the ordinary path, shall be abandoned."

Blessed James of Voragine

"One day, St. Macarius found a skull and asked it whose head it had been. 'A pagan's!' it replied. 'And where is your soul?' he asked. 'In Hell!' came the reply. Macarius then asked the skull if its place was very deep in Hell. 'As far down as the earth is lower than Heaven!' 'And are there any other souls lodged even lower?' 'Yes! The souls of the Jews!' 'And even lower than the Jews?' 'Yes! The souls of bad Christians who were redeemed with the Blood of Christ and held their privilege so cheaply!'"

Blessed Sebastian Valfre

"I fear that Last Day, that day of tribulation and anguish, of calamity and misery, of mist and darkness, that Day on which, if the just have reason to fear, how much more should I: an impious, wretched, and ungrateful sinner!"

146

This is but a small sampling from the centuries of Catholic tradition. Notice not only the names of popes, saints, Fathers, and Doctors on the list, but the various countries and centuries from which they all come as well. It is farcical to even suggest that a modern-day opinion like "we have a reasonable hope that all men are saved" can be squared with Catholic tradition. It cannot!

And, of course, there are the words from Our Blessed Lord Himself when He says: "Enter by the narrow gate; for the gate is wide and the way is easy, that leads to destruction, and those who enter by it are many. For the gate is narrow and the way is hard, that leads to life, and those who find it are few" (Matt. vii : 13–14).

It can and should be called one of the greatest deceptions of our day, this diabolical notion that we have a reasonable hope that all men are saved. That bishops and priests do not decry this most severe error of thought from the highest courts and sanctuaries of the Church will be to their unending torment. They have the blood of souls on their hands and shall never be admitted to the Heavenly Kingdom so stained.

Attending a Catholic funeral Mass these days is more akin to attending a canonization ceremony. The deceased is hailed and praised and fondly remembered, with barely a mention of the state of his soul in eternity other than to declare him in Heaven. Whatever the state of any given dead man's soul, this constant pronouncing that each dead man has been admitted into the Beatific Vision has the deleterious effect on hearers of causing them to assume this will be the case for them as well.

Viewing the typical funeral, it is beyond clear the vast majority haven't been to Mass in years, as evidenced by their inability to say the prayer responses, present the postures proper to Mass, and so forth. This is especially evident now that some of the Mass has undergone word changes in the past couple of years. Whatever distant memories many of the mourners may recall are now incorrect when applied to the current wording.

Yet prelate after prelate after priest after priest continues to keep up this charade that all is well with the soul of the deceased. Now, there is a monumental judgment from Churchmen who keep insisting that we not judge. How do they know the condition of the dead man's soul?

How do they have any insight into what transpired at the judgment throne of Jesus Christ in the case of Uncle Bob?

In an increasing number of funerals, Uncle Bob hadn't been to regular Sunday Mass in years, hadn't been to confession in an even longer time, and had not received Last Rites. It's quite likely Uncle Bob is damned, despite the sweet, reality-denying talk at the funeral Mass. Uncle Bob supported the idea of contraception, even practiced it in his younger married life; he didn't really like the idea of same-sex "marriage," but took a totally hands-off, live-and-let-live approach, even among members of his own family. He would occasionally view pornography, lust after women, entertain thoughts of impurity, but none of this any more than "normal"; he seldom prayed, had a "few too many" from time to time, and did not really give God a thought unless to use His name in vain.

Uncle Bob, as it turns out, was a typical modern Catholic, so how fitting that he be consigned to eternity by a small gathering of other typical modern Catholics who judge their own fitness for eternity against Bob's sinful life, and conclude they will see Bob in Heaven when they die. All of this, of course, takes place with the willful cooperation of the priest, trained in seminary, ordained by the bishop, and instructed to never upset the people. "They aren't ready to hear this now" is the usual caution; too bad for Bob he didn't hear it when he was still breathing. It is too late for Bob—but what about those others who are still breathing?

What do they get to hear? That we have a reasonable hope that all men are saved, thus confirming the demonic notion in their minds that they will one day enjoy Heaven and they don't really need to do anything in advance of their deaths, denying 2,000 years of Church tradition, the words of Scripture, the private revelations of countless saints, the public apparitions of the Queen of Heaven, the words of Our Blessed Lord Himself even. Bob is in Hell, and his relatives and friends mourning him are on their way to join him soon enough. All of this is to be laid at the feet of weak, cowardly, wicked bishops who let these souls plunge into Hell because they will not jeopardize their own standing in the eyes of men. They do not believe, and they have lost their supernatural faith.

Chapter 14

CATHOLIC MORALITY ABANDONED:
The Consequences

In 2011, an impressive team of highly respected Catholic educators and researchers released results from a national survey they conducted of fellow Catholics over the course of years. They asked Catholics to place themselves in one of three categories they felt best described their commitment level to the Church. The categories were: highly committed, moderately committed, and low commitment. Before examining the numbers in depth, let's consider an overview.

In 2011, nineteen percent of Catholics (about one in five) regarded themselves as highly committed; sixty-six percent (two out of three) self-identified as moderately committed; fourteen percent (one out of seven) identified themselves as Catholics with a low level of commitment.

Tellingly, the percentage of Catholics who consider themselves "highly committed" has dropped thirty percent in the past quarter century. In 1987, more than one in four viewed themselves this way. Now it's one in five. In the same time period, the ranks of the self-identified moderate Catholics shot up by fourteen percent. No doubt about it, Catholics are becoming more and more lukewarm and indifferent about the Faith—exactly how Satan wants it. In a very short time, he has drawn much of the flavor out of the salt.

It is only when a deeper examination of the survey results are studied, however, does the very real crisis present itself. The reality of the damage the Church has undergone is breathtaking.

In that group of Catholics who self-identify as "highly committed" (which, according to the polling methodology, means they attend Mass frequently, rate the Church as very important to them personally, and are unlikely to ever leave the Church), which again is one in five Catholics in America—the cream of the crop, so to speak—sixty percent support birth control, nearly a third believe abortion is acceptable, and, most revealing, in a stirring triumph for the Church of Nice and its "no Hell" policy, these self-identified Catholics are convinced they can support these evils, commit these acts, and still go to Heaven. They have no holy fear because the leadership of the Church has either cooperated with it or sat by silently while the message was drummed out of them.

Consider the enormity of the disaster for just a moment. Four out of five Catholics admit they are not really committed to the Faith. That's troublesome enough; but then among the ones who *do* consider themselves highly committed, almost two thirds of them reject the Church's dogmatic teaching on birth control. And, as the saying goes, there's no such thing as just *one* cockroach; where you see one, there will inevitably be others. In the same way, it is the case in the Church that if you jettison one dogma, you'll jettison others.

In this same group of "highly committed" Catholics, half say going to weekly Mass isn't a necessity—which is a rejection of the Third Commandment and a mortal sin. Half of Catholics who consider themselves "highly committed" believe being married in the Church isn't necessary, and divorce and remarriage is acceptable, thus rejecting the Sixth Commandment. Half support women priests, and two thirds say you can disagree with Church teaching and still be a "good" Catholic.

And again, it needs to be stressed, this is all from the very group who self-identify as "highly committed" Catholics, the top twenty percent. This provokes the question: Exactly what is it they imagine themselves actually committed to? Because it isn't authentic Catholicism. They are firm adherents to the "theology" of the Church of Nice. And to further prove the woeful lack of necessary ingredients for a comeback of the Faith, the question needs to be put out there: If these are the beliefs of the majority of the *most* committed, what is going on with the other eighty percent of Catholics?

It needs to be said, because it's true: Before any serious attempt at recatechizing the faithful can be attempted, before any efforts are poured out on behalf of the much-heralded "New Evangelization," the crisis must be viewed soberly and seriously. Less than ten percent of the roughly 70 million Catholics in the United States can be seen as authentically Catholic. The starting point for any efforts to revivify the faith life of so many tens of millions must begin with this brutal truth. Of the 70 million US Catholics, 63 million are really not Catholic at all.

Even if they went to Catholic schools, served as altar boys, made their First Communions, were confirmed, even attended Mass for part of their youths, the evil that was allowed to come into the Church, the evil of not presenting the truth as preached by the Son of God, the evil that was supposed to be guarded against by the clergy, most especially by the bishops, has overtaken the vast majority of Catholics. Their only connection to the Church these days is a quasi-nostalgic cultural one—a memory from their childhoods they have outgrown and from which they've moved on. Their souls are in peril, and almost no one loves them enough—in the *real* sense of the word "love," meaning sacrificial love—to tell them the truth.

So what's the reality on the ground here? In a typical parish Sunday Mass, half the people present disagree with fundamental Catholic teaching—*half*! This means that if you yourselves believe all Church teachings, the odds are that the person sitting next to you doesn't share the same faith—right there in your pew, right next to you, reaching out to grab hold of your hand during the *Our Father*, exhibiting a unity that doesn't exist. The unity of the Faith among Catholics has been shattered.

Sixty percent of American Catholics have succumbed to the culture of death and believe the Church is wrong on abortion. Unsurprisingly, two thirds of this group of Catholics—a majority of the majority— believe the issue of contraception and abortion should be left to the individual's conscience and, as well, over half of them (53%) believe individuals have final say as to whether or not sex outside of marriage is okay, not the Church—the Church established by the Son of God, Who will judge us on our deeds.

When it comes to levels of participation in the sacraments, another startling piece of evidence emerges. Sixty-three percent of self-identified moderate Catholics in the United States disagree with the teaching authority of the Church (the Magisterium) on the necessity of the sacraments—again, the sacraments established personally by Jesus Christ as the normal avenues of grace for our salvation.

To reject the necessity of the sacraments is to reject the authority of Christ; in other words, such a person does not *really* believe in the divinity of Christ. This is the final end of the heresy present in the Church today, as is the case with every heresy.

Since heresy is a rejection of one or more teachings of the Church, then it is a rejection of Christ, for Christ Himself founded and established the Catholic Church. As He said of His Apostles, on whom He personally conferred His authority to preach, forgive sins and represent His Eternal Sacrifice to the Father: "He who hears you hears me, and he who rejects you rejects me, and he who rejects me rejects him who sent me" (Luke 10:16).

All heresy is in its origin, maturation, and finale a rejection of Our Blessed Lord. So it should in no way surprise us that, as the rejection of Christ is increased by heresy, so a rejection of His Mystical Body should also be manifest.

Research reflects that between 2001 and 2012, the number of First Communions declined from 900,000 to fewer than 800,000, a decrease of twelve percent in just one decade, a statistic made all the more disturbing when one remembers that all the while, the raw number of those who self-identify as Catholic is actually increasing, for the time being.

That's a loss of one percent per year. If the raw number of Catholics is increasing each year, then why is the participation rate in the sacraments other than baptism actually declining? Why are twelve percent fewer children being prepared to receive the Body and Blood of Our Lord?

The answer is quite simple. A critical mass has now been achieved whereby the two realities of people baptizing their children but almost totally neglecting any faith life to speak of beyond baptism has now been reached. It is a *fait accompli* that within a generation, the children baptized in the past few years but not raised in the Faith will grow to adulthood, have children of their own, and *not* have them baptized—and this will be the great point at which the raw number of Catholics will actually begin a precipitous, rapid decline. The Church in America has not even scratched the surface in terms of parish closings. By the time this current crop of bishops in the United States are handing in their resignations to Rome, they will have sat atop the most monumental collapse of the Faith since the Protestant Revolt of the sixteenth century.

What was ushered in before them, and nurtured to full maturity by them, is a brand of Catholicism never before heard of or contemplated on this grand a scale—a *Protestant Catholicism*, complete with all the characteristics that define that specific heresy: a rejection of the Real Presence; a sublimation of the ministerial priesthood; an abandonment of acceptance of magisterial authority; an elevation of personal feeling, emotion, opinion, and interpretation of all things in the realm of the sacred; and most importantly, a self-determination with regard to morality and truth, most especially in the arena of sexual morality.

One of the most central beliefs of the Catholic Church, the Real Presence—meaning that Jesus Christ is present, really, truly, and substantially Body, Blood, Soul, and Divinity under the appearance of bread and wine—is believed by only *half* of all Catholics.

When it comes to the issue of weekly Mass attendance and on Holy Days of Obligation, seventy-seven percent believe they can be good Catholics without attending weekly Mass. This single response reveals a huge underlying problem, not among the liberal and Modernist gang in the Church, but among those usually identified as "good" Catholics. They go to Mass, and they don't know what Mass is!

Continuing with the sacraments, the number of confirmations was at a high in 2004, with 645,000 total, and has declined to 618,000. That's a decrease of six percent in ten years. For a Church given the mission to go out to all nations, this is nothing less than an epic failure. Confirmation is a sacrament of commitment. It is a Catholic's way of wedding oneself to the Church of Christ. Now six percent fewer young Catholics make this oath than just one decade ago, and many who do make this oath fail to uphold it.

One of the greatest tragedies in America is the death of marriage. In the US census, the marriage rate from 1970 was 10.6 per thousand. In 2010 the rate had dropped to 6.8 per thousand—a decrease in the overall US marriage rate of thirty-six percent in forty years. By direct comparison, there were 417,000 Catholic weddings in 1970. By 2010, the raw numbers had dropped precipitously to just 180,000—a drop of fifty-seven percent, with Catholics blazing the trail in the United

States in decrease in marriages among those holding to a religious belief system.

So here's the issue: For decades the *official* number of Catholics according to the US Conference of Catholic Bishops has been increasing markedly, but the number of Catholics actually believing and practicing their faith is in steep, steep decline. This is unsustainable. How much longer before this house of cards totally collapses?

Given this reality surrounding Catholic marriage, it should come as no surprise that half of all American Catholics reject the Church's definition of a valid marriage. To wit, fifty-seven percent of American Catholics believe they can be good Catholics without accepting Church teaching on same-sex marriage, and sixty-seven percent of American Catholics (two out of three) believe they can be good Catholics without adhering to the Church's teaching on divorce and remarriage. Whatever these Catholics are, they are not Catholic.

Chapter 15

REVOLUTION:
The War over Catholic Identity

The identity of something or someone is a constitution of characteristics that describes a thing or being. And yet many who do not possess the characteristics of the Catholic identity persist in still claiming to have it. Sixty-one percent of self-identified Catholics in America support the possibility of female Catholic priests. Seventy percent of Catholics in America view the teaching authority of the Vatican as an unimportant aspect of their identity as Catholics. The Catholic population is twenty-two percent of the US population, and though a survey cannot calculate who in that number is true to the Faith, one can certainly estimate who are not.

Since most Catholics don't have any interest in the Faith anymore, they have no idea of the intense battle being waged at this very moment inside the Church. And the few Catholics who still do go to Mass are largely unaware of the battle as well.

In short, the battle is between a revolutionary ideology that took over the power structures of the Church in full force beginning in the 1970s and has held on to that power ever since, and today's counter-revolutionaries—those who want to undo the damage of the revolution and roll back its incredible gains.

These skirmishes are breaking out everywhere, from the contest going on between old radical feminist nuns and orthodox forces in the Vatican to the liturgical wars being fought in various parishes, to the battles over which catechism program to use in a given parish RCIA program. Then there are the never-ending battles over the abuses at Mass, like receiving Holy Communion in the hand, the regular scheduling of *extra*-ordinary ministers of Holy Communion, and so forth.

There is the tug of war between liberal, heterodox cardinals like Walter Kasper and members of the Italian and German bishops' conferences who openly declare that those living in adultery and those practicing sodomy should be allowed to receive Holy Communion versus other cardinals who are calling them out on their heretical statements.

The war has gotten so heated, in fact, that five cardinals, including Cdl. Raymond Burke, former prefect of the Apostolic Signatura, felt the need in advance of the 2014 Synod to publish a book defending the Church's teaching: that those in objective sinful conditions jeopardize their immortal souls by adding to their sins the sin of sacrilege if they receive Holy Communion without being reconciled to the Church. The book came out in October 2014, purposely timed with the Extraordinary Synod on the Family, which took place in Rome in the same month. As previously noted, the Synod produced headlines all over the world with various cardinals and bishops giving or appearing to give their approval to sacrilege; that is at least how the world's secular media saw it and dutifully reported it. And not much in the way of clarity was forthcoming from Vatican officials who likewise appeared to let confusion reign supreme.

There were comments made, interventions given, and interviews offered where various high-profile leaders were quite up front about wanting to drop the vocabulary of "sin," "adultery," and "disordered" to terms less "offensive" and "mean-sounding." In the run-up to the following year's Synod in October 2015, theological dissidents in the Church kept the same arguments cycling through secular media outlets friendly to the cause.

Speeches, conferences, symposia, books, lectures, interviews, and web postings kept the ideas circulating through the secular world that the Church was in the process of putting the finishing touches on plans to change doctrine. While the most liberal among them, like Washington, DC cardinal Donald Wuerl, would continue to emphasize that all that might change is Church discipline and not dogma, he and others know that is a distinction without a difference in the minds of many hearers. The average Catholic would simply accept what he hears on the surface as reported by the secular media—that divorced and remarried Catholics could now receive Holy Communion—and he would go on with his life, unfazed.

What the average Catholic did not know, and most likely did not even care about, is that he was also being prepared to hear something similar with regard to same-sex unions, for that issue is the next one on deck. Once Holy Communion can be administered to one sort of public sinner, then it would be manifestly unfair to deny it to another kind of public sinner.

The entire life of the run-of-the-mill Catholic has been so altered that his Catholicism now means next to nothing. His identity as Catholic doesn't even occur to him. He has been stripped by clerics and a cooperative culture of any reason to see himself as Catholic. And given the state of affairs in the world and the Church, there is no real reason on the surface to see himself as Catholic.

Lights, Cameras, Silence

The revolutionaries have held the high ground for so long on these battles that most Catholics who go to Mass aren't even aware there is a war being waged. That's because the revolutionaries, or those who support the revolution in its various forms, control the organs of communication—all of them, up until recently. They controlled the diocesan newspaper, the parish bulletins, the Catholic periodicals, and so forth. Any place a Catholic turned to for truthful information, the radicals had that base covered.

That was until an upstart nun founded a TV operation called Eternal Word Television Network (EWTN). Launched in 1981, the operation grew steadily in the 1980s largely carried by Mother Angelica's feisty personality. But at the 1993 World Youth Day gathering in Denver, she witnessed a performance of the Stations of the Cross where a woman played the part of Jesus. Something snapped inside of her at that moment. The reality of all she had been witnessing and hearing going on in the Church—the horrible education in high schools and colleges, the immoral lives of many in the clergy, the rank rejection of practically every teaching in the Church by Her leaders—finally hit her full force. In short, the revolution at last came into sharp focus for her in all its Technicolor ugliness. She went on the air to denounce the evils now so commonplace.

I am so tired of you, liberal Church in America. . . . I resent you trying to destroy the Catholicity of the simple and the poor and the elderly by your ways. . . . Your catechisms are so watered down . . . . I don't like your Church. You have nothing to offer. You do nothing but destroy. . . .

You can't stand Catholicity at this height. You have to spoil it . . . . Your whole purpose is to destroy. . . . You've been strong too long. . . . What a destructive force you have been. . . . Don't call *me* rebellious. No. *You're* rebellious. . . . It's time somebody said something about all these tiny little cracks that you have been putting for the last thirty years into the Church. . . .

I'm tired of your theologians who do nothing but divide and separate and destroy. . . . I don't like your kind of religion. I don't like your ways. . . . You have no right to destroy people's faith . . . . We're just tired of you constantly pushing anti-God, anti-Catholic, and pagan ways into the Catholic Church. . . .

Live your life. Live your falsehood. Live your lies. Leave us alone. . . . But don't pour your poison, your venom on all the Church.

That was a turning point for Mother. No longer would she sit back and talk only about Church teachings and how wonderful they were—which, of course, coming from God, they are. No. She had had enough. No more nice little nun. She called out some of the leaders of the revolution, especially Cdl. Roger Mahony of Los Angeles, a major provocateur and promoter of revolution. She stood up and challenged the Church establishment, and she committed all the resources of her cable TV outlet to the endeavor.

No more would she let heresies and revolutionary strains of thought continue without being confronted. She was sick of it, and she made a point of doing all she could to fight it. And she kicked up quite the dust storm and turned over quite a few tables in the process. Bishops hated her. The old revolutionary guard attacked her every way they could. They mocked her for her orthodoxy and slammed her for her piety and forthright proclamation of Church teaching.

Eventually, the establishment won the battle, and Mother had to resign her headship of the network and surrender it to a lay board of trustees and directors. She hung on for a few more years, making occasional appearances on air, but her health deteriorated and the chapter was closed on any professed religious ever truly challenging the establishment Church.

The lay board of directors, which assumed control after Mother resigned, was at first loyal to Mother's spirit. But as time passed, EWTN fell silent about the revolution, eventually choosing to say nothing to upset the bishops, on whom the continued success of the network—not to mention their livelihoods—now depended. It wasn't really a case of preaching heresy or allowing dissent; it was more the case of simply not confronting the evils going on in the Church—a great white-washing or ignoring of the crisis. As things continued on the same trajectory, Dr. Charles Rice, the eminent law professor at Notre Dame, resigned his position on the board of directors. Rice had seen his beloved Notre Dame give way to the world, and he wanted no part of a lackluster response from the TV outfit begun by Mother Angelica. He saw a movement at EWTN he felt betrayed or ignored Mother's original mission.

Cozying up to the bishops gave the new leaders at EWTN access to the establishment and its money channels. They would sign a truce with the revolutionary forces in the Church in exchange for the ability to increase their footprint, their media exposure in the Catholic world. As long as they didn't criticize the bishops, the bishops would appear on their shows, allow them to attend Church events where they could increase their exposure, let their various hosts speak at Church conferences, where they could sell their books. There was nothing, no access that was denied them, as long as they avoided the topic of the evils in the Church, especially among the hierarchy.

In short, as long as EWTN would roll over and mostly play dead on the abuses and other deep problems present in the Church leadership, they could hang around all they wanted. It was a win-win for the bishops and the network. The ones who paid the price and still do, however, are the faithful who tune in and are left totally in the dark about the evils going on in the Church—like the Catholic speakers circuit, regularly populated with clergy and laity offering heresy-riddled ideas for consumption. EWTN will never talk about such issues and ask the crucial question: "How is this happening?"

In the ensuing time since Mother's departure, the network has seized hold of every form of communication possible. It bought up the nearly dead *National Catholic Register* newspaper from the Legionaries of Christ for next to nothing. The Legion was still reeling from the revelations that its head and founder, the late Fr. Marcial Maciel, had been a pederast, a rapist of his own illegitimately conceived sons, and a financial swindler. When news of all this finally broke into the open under Pope Benedict XVI, the Legion became nearly leprous. But in the face of all the accusations, the editorial staff at the *National Catholic Register* kept insisting Fr. Maciel was guilty of nothing and that his enemies were out to ruin him posthumously.

No one was buying it. And in the end, EWTN bought them. The TV network quickly retooled the *Register* and, without saying much about the circumstances, simply gave the newspaper a face lift, cleaned up its website, and re-presented it to the world as a legitimate Catholic news source.

But the network wasn't done acquiring struggling Catholic "news" outfits. Not long after acquiring *National Catholic Register*, EWTN merged *Catholic News Agency* (CNA) into its increasing portfolio, and then in the summer of 2015, bought up Sophia Press to complete the horizontal media monopoly. The establishment-challenging TV outfit started by Mother Angelica had now done an "inside out" move and had actually *become* the establishment.

Aside from the local ordinary, Bp. Robert J. Baker, the only other prelate on the board of directors is Abp. Charles Chaput, whom many point to as the man orchestrating and directing the media grab. The monopoly is so strong and so vast in the shrinking Catholic world that almost any news that gets reported in the Catholic world must first clear muster with the TV-radio-newspaper-Internet monolith— almost any news.

This is a dangerous situation because it almost ensures that any clampdown on bad news is guaranteed. For example, the 2014 Synod train wreck received nowhere near the degree of scrutiny it deserved as heresy and dissent was bandied about in the secular world.

In an earlier demonstration of its clampdown power, EWTN Radio directed coverage of a developing scandal in such a manner as to conceal the information from the public. The case involved a 2010 developing story that had gained steam regarding scandal at the

Catholic Campaign for Human Development, the USCCB's domestic anti-poverty program. A group of enterprising, independent Catholic media not under the control of the establishment organs were releasing damaging reports proving that the CCHD was giving large grants to various Saul Alinsky community-organizing groups—all Democratic Party favorites.

That the CCHD was practically a Democratic Party operation was hardly new. It had been reported as far back as the 1970s, shortly after its creation by then Abp. Joseph Bernardin. It had quickly earned the nickname "the Democratic Party at Prayer." But those reports had been confined to small and somewhat powerless yet faithful Catholic media underdogs like *The Wanderer*. While Catholics in the know had known all about the CCHD for decades, there were too few of such Catholics to really accomplish any kind of change.

Then came the Internet, and the means of communicating information to Catholics suddenly changed. No longer could the establishment dictate what information could be passed along to the rank-and-file Catholics—the few left who still might care. There was suddenly a new kid on the block: the faithful, *independent* Catholic media, beholden to no bishop or institution of the Catholic establishment.

When the independent Catholic media got hold of the CCHD story, it quickly got beyond the ability of the professional Catholic crowd to control. Catholic radio stations all over the country started broadcasting the story to a largely ignorant and sleepy listening base. These stations were locally owned and operated but had a relationship with EWTN.

EWTN had become the big dog of the Catholic media world and was virtually the sole provider of radio programming to these little Mom-and-Pop outlets. They did produce some local content, but in order to keep their FCC government broadcast licenses, they had to be on the air a certain number of hours per week. Programming is expensive to produce day in and day out, so what most of them did was produce a small number of hours of local programming and then rely on a large number of hours of programming produced by EWTN Radio offices. It worked out fine as a business model—nothing to write home about necessarily, but at least they were on the airwaves and pushing out Catholic programs.

This set-up, however, became kind of a blackmail operation, if EWTN chose to operate like that. With the early reports from the independent Catholic media hitting the Internet that the CCHD was granting money to groups that support abortion, contraception, and homosexuality, the little EWTN affiliates began reporting the story as well—and this is where EWTN exercised its growing muscle.

Recall that the CCHD is a program run under the supervision of the USCCB, but largely operated by lay staffers on the day-to-day level. Those staffers had deep ties to the Democratic Party, and many still do. They had a long history of working relationships dating back to the founding mission of the CCHD under Bernardin. In fact, the CCHD was a sort of clearinghouse for any politically liberal, theologically dissident association coming down the pike looking for funding. It was one thing twenty or thirty years earlier to simply ignore stories circulating among a tiny group of faithful Catholics who kept making noise about the CCHD; it was something entirely different when technology had advanced in such a manner that they could no longer prevent the story from breaking out.

So, just as the story of the CCHD grants going to decidedly un-Catholic groups started gaining ground via the Catholic Internet, one morning the little Catholic radio stations got a call, one by one, from EWTN Radio headquarters, informing them that EWTN had gotten a call from the USCCB that this story was to get no play. The threat was a little more than implied that *if* the stations talked about this story, they would lose access to EWTN Radio programming and be left to fend for themselves, which for the vast majority of them would mean a loss of their FCC licenses because they would be unable to replace the many hours of programming provided to them by EWTN.

Such is the power of a media monopoly. A story was initially crushed under threat of financial ruin.

As it turned out, those at the USCCB and their puppets at EWTN, while trying to control the information, had sorely miscalculated the reach of the independent Catholic media. The story continued; local dioceses were being contacted by concerned Catholics wanting to know what was going on. Try as it might, the establishment media monopoly had only been partially successful in trying to kill the story. A number of bishops around the country took the unprecedented step of killing the annual CCHD collection in their dioceses or reassigning the collection to more local needs.

The USCCB and EWTN could not ignore the story forever, especially as it spread, so they began attacking the Catholic journalists reporting the story and trying to paint them as ill-informed, unreliable, discredited, money-hungry muckrakers interested in making a name for themselves by sowing division. This became the way various EWTN affiliates began portraying the reporters. Drive-time Catholic radio personalities in bigger markets started ripping into the reporters trying to discredit the stories by discrediting them, attacking their integrity.

The more intelligent laity, however, saw through the sham and kept up the pressure on the bishops, until at last, the USCCB announced that an internal investigation would be conducted to examine what, if anything, needed to be "fixed" at the CCHD. In a classic example of the fox guarding the hen house, the "review" of the CCHD policies and procedures was conducted by the CCHD itself—and to no one's surprise, little was discovered in need of fixing. A little tinkering here and there, a half-hearted admission that in one or two cases, something has slipped through the cracks, a canned apology and promise that all was fixed that needed to be fixed, and it was off to the races again.

Two years later it was revealed that the new head of the CCHD, Ralph McCloud (who had succeeded Democratic Party fanboy John Carr), had backed Texas state senator Wendy Davis in her bid to defeat a pro-life Texas lawmaker (which she did). McCloud had been her honorary financial chairman and publicly supported her. While the position was honorary, it still carried significance—McCloud was, after all, the head of the grant-writing for the US bishops' anti-poverty program.

Wendy Davis was the Texas state senator who made news in 2013 by filibustering a pro-life bill in the Texas senate that was aimed at shutting down a good number of abortion chambers. Her filibuster succeeded at first, as the clock ran out on that session of the Texas state legislature, but was eventually turned back after Gov. Rick Perry called a special session and the bill was signed into law. Wendy Davis went on to win her seat and, by extension, her ability to kill the pro-life bill, in part owing to her support from the US bishops' CCHD director Ralph McCloud.

When the newly forming Catholic media conglomerate controlled by EWTN (with Abp. Chaput on its board, who isn't the local ordinary) isn't attempting to kill stories with behind-the-scenes threats, or trying to pour cold water on them by attacking the sources, they are resorting to the more tried-and-true way of simply ignoring the story and giving it no play at all. Such was the case with Rick Estridge, Vice President of Overseas Finance at Catholic Relief Services (CRS), the USCCB's international charitable arm. In the spring of 2015, Church-Militant.com received information that Estridge was an avowed homosexual who had civilly married his male partner, and that everyone at CRS headquarters in Baltimore knew about it. On further investigation, the tip proved reliable. Estridge's social media pages were full of pro-homosexual propaganda and attacks against conservative political candidates who opposed the militant homosexual juggernaut.

ChurchMilitant.com teamed up with the Lepanto Institute's Michael Hichborn to do some further investigating. Hichborn was able to surface the civil marriage license between Estridge and his homosexual partner. Armed with confirmation, CRS was contacted by the Lepanto Institute and ChurchMilitant.com before airing the story. CRS refused comment initially. With that, the two outlets published the incriminating story—and once again, the USCCB was faced with another scandal.

This time, however, a number of bishops were privately irate that an open, in-your-face, civilly married homosexual had been allowed to occupy a high-ranking post at CRS. In closed-door meetings, they demanded he be fired immediately. Eventually, Estridge offered his resignation, and sources say he received a handsome pay-off approaching $400,000 as he walked out the door.

During all this back-and-forth in the independent Catholic media, where the story was covered in detail, barely a mention of the story could be found in the EWTN-controlled media monopoly of television, radio, newspaper, and Internet publishing. Despite the anger privately expressed by a number of bishops, major Catholic media organizations felt no need to cover it at all at first, and then eventually only grudgingly.

The same can be said of story after story. The strategy seems to have developed to first ignore the story, then try to discredit the independent Catholic media sources reporting it, then hope it dies, then give it only the slightest, most scant coverage possible so they can't be accused of ignoring it altogether. This was the case when Vatican Press Office spokesman Fr. Thomas Rosica threatened to sue a Canadian Catholic blogger in early 2015. ChurchMilitant.com broke the story, and the Internet lit up, bringing embarrassment to Rosica for his attempted bullying of a faithful Catholic. Rosica was eventually forced to withdraw his threatened lawsuit under pressure from superiors. But while the Catholic Internet and even conservative media sites were posting the story, it was "crickets" at the EWTN-controlled media monopoly of television, radio, newspaper, and Internet publishing. What media outlets like *Breitbart* and others considered newsworthy, the EWTN empire took a pass on. The policy there seems to be: *No need to get the viewers upset.*

Again, what would the faithful Catholic know of the ruminations and scheming of corrupt and wicked Churchmen at the 2014 Extraordinary Synod on the Family, if not for the independent Catholic media, which brought the world's attention to faithless prelates and their attempts to introduce heresy into the proceedings?

The same can be said of New York's Cdl. Timothy Dolan and his shameful support of active homosexuals marching in the 2015 St. Patrick's Day Parade. The group, known as Out@NBCUniversal, would be the first openly gay group to march officially under its own banner in the 250-plus years of the New York St. Patrick's Day Parade. While it's true Dolan did not necessarily have any active role in deciding to invite the gay group to march, he had accepted the honor of being Grand Marshal to lead the parade. He could have publicly stepped down in protest or quietly petitioned behind the scenes, threatening to go public if NBC—which covered the parade—didn't withdraw plans. He chose neither course. In fact, he publicly declared his support for the parade committee's decision and then tried to rationalize his support by saying the homosexual contingent was not actively promoting homosexuality, but merely identifying as having a same-sex orientation. In fact, the cardinal claimed Out@NBCUniversal was promoting nothing contrary to Church teaching.

This was demonstrably false. His justification immediately proved ridiculous by simply looking at the group's Facebook page, where, within several seconds, anyone could see photos and status updates proving their open, proud support for gay marriage—decidedly contrary to Catholic teaching. One begins to wonder to whom Churchmen like Dolan think they are speaking. The times have changed dramatically, and the previous era of being able to lie, or cheat, or claim something to be true that isn't has gone the way of the Dodo Bird. But his attitude could reflect the latent desire to hold on tightly to the time when a lack of transparency and accountability ruled the day.

And while the independent Catholic media was all over the story, for weeks the EWTN-controlled media monopoly of television, radio, newspaper, and Internet publishing paid it only the slightest attention, and never in a manner that would upset His Eminence. The policy of "no need to get the viewers upset" seemed to be in effect once again.

In fact, Catholic bloggers who *did* speak critically of His Eminence suffered the consequences. Monsignor Charles Pope, a well-known and highly respected priest in the archdiocese of Washington, DC (headed by Cdl. Donald Wuerl), wrote a post on his blog (hosted on the archdiocesan website) respectfully questioning Dolan's participation in the St. Patrick's Day Parade. His post gained traction on social media, being shared multiple times by Catholics scandalized by Dolan's behavior.

But within hours, the post was yanked. In fact, the entire archdiocesan website went blank. The next day the website was back to normal, and Msgr. Pope's blog was up and running—only this time it was missing the critical post. ChurchMilitant.com spoke with unimpeachable sources, who confirmed that Msgr. Pope had been ordered by his superior to take down his post, and he—unhappily but out of obedience—did so. What the world thought was a website glitch was actually the archdiocese censoring one of its priests for criticizing a powerful prelate. This example only proves the necessity of an independent Catholic media not beholden to or under the control of the Church hierarchy.

The fact is, the Catholic establishment media will not talk about many things that need to be talked about—for example, Dolan's praise on NBC of homosexual football player and NFL aspirant Michael Sam. When asked what he thought of the first potential player in the NFL to "come out" as gay, Dolan responded, "Bravo! Good for him!" But not a word on Dolan's blunder from the usual suspects at the EWTN-controlled media monopoly of television, radio, newspaper, and Internet publishing. There is no way in Hades that outfit is going to report a negative word about a powerful cardinal who can harm them. In fact, it could be said in some ways they provide cover for him—which calls into question their integrity as a media outfit.

After the passage in 2012 of same-sex marriage in the state of New York, Cdl. Dolan appeared on EWTN with Raymond Arroyo, who pitched him a series of softball questions, neatly allowing Dolan off the hook with regard to any responsibility for the matter at hand. His Eminence got to calmly explain that the lack of any real fight on the part of New York's bishops to try and defeat the bill was owing to the "bad counsel" he and the other bishops had received from "advisors" who had apparently told him gay marriage didn't have a chance of passing. As a result, Dolan said the bishops had decided to ignore the issue. He then jokingly said he was going to go back to the "advisors" and shake them down for answers, asking them to explain why their information was so wrong. Of course, not another word was ever spoken on the matter—not then and not since.

The idea that same-sex marriage didn't have a chance of passing in the state of New York is laughable. While it did require some last-minute arm twisting by Catholic governor Andrew Cuomo of two Catholic lawmakers who were also Knights of Columbus and cast the deciding votes (another story unreported by the Catholic establishment media), it is beyond ridiculous to suggest the law had no real chance of passing, because, as we know, it did in fact pass. Poll after poll at the time had revealed that a majority of the public was either in favor of it, or had no real opposition to it. The governor of the state had campaigned heavily on the issue, making it the main theme of his campaign. How Cdl. Dolan could have sat with a straight face and told EWTN viewers he'd been counseled by advisors that the law didn't have a chance of passing is breathtaking. Even *New York Times* columnist Maureen Dowd wondered aloud from the editorial pages where the New York Catholic bishops' opposition was. She suggested it was owing to the large numbers of homosexuals in the priesthood, which in her estimation had become a haven for gays. Even the secular media—especially the *New York Times*, which has proven to be no friend of the Church—was wondering where Cdl. Dolan and his fellow bishops had been.

One point Raymond Arroyo did not bring up to His Eminence in the softball-question derby was why, on the Sunday following the passage of the law in New York, the cardinal had made no mention in his homily of the historic statewide evil that had just passed in the state legislature, and why later in the press scrum following Mass he actually *apologized* to New York's gays and lesbians for saying anything that might have offended them. Since he never really said anything at all, one is left wondering what exactly he was apologizing for. But to the larger point, given the current set-up, it's impossible for those kinds of questions to be asked of a prelate.

There's something wrong with the whole picture when a "media interview" about a controversial topic that has the potential to make the interviewee look bad is being done by people controlled by the interviewee himself. It's even worse when the entire system is engineered in such a way as to not only allow but actually favor such an outcome. The goal is protection of the status quo of the Church establishment, not to keep the average Catholic informed. In this way, the establishment media is more a propaganda outfit than a news media outlet. And there is nothing wrong with that as long as they tell their viewers, listeners, and readers that what they are getting is *spin*, and not actual news.

They have made a pact with the USCCB that nary a bad word will ever be said, regardless of the fact that Mother Angelica would blast away at such things. By any reasonable measure, the teachings delivered on EWTN are relatively solid. They do seem from time to time to have developed amnesia with regard to tradition in the Church, however— for example, in the area of liturgy. This leaves some of their programming lacking. But the point here is not to enter into a critique of the programming content. The point, rather, is that the evils present in the Church today (for example, that the bishops will barely breathe a word about contraception or the large-scale abandonment of the Faith by so many Catholics) *never* get air time in any meaningful way that analyzes the reasons for the collapse—something directly opposed to the spirit of the nun who founded the network.

Remember, Mother Angelica saw the evil and called it out, repeatedly and with much exuberance. She did what any good Catholic would do in such a situation, and she paid the price for confronting the revolution—which forces us to ask: Why aren't her successors doing the same now? EWTN, after all, doesn't "belong" to them. It was formed by a sweet, caring little nun who was sick of the liberal revolution causing such a dramatic loss of souls. The current leadership has an obligation to remain true to the network's founding principles put in place by Mother Angelica.

They are not obliged to carry the water for the current crop of revolutionaries, who these days don't need to *foment* revolution anymore because they now control the palace. And be certain of this: To keep quiet about the evil makes you an accomplice, regardless of how much good you do or say otherwise.

The current crisis in the Church is owing to the negligence of today's leaders. They have kept silence all these years, afraid to confront the heresy and mutiny in their own ranks. Some of them will venture out from under the rock of silence every now and then and decry the culture of death, but they will do next to nothing about officials in their charge who promote that same culture of death in the Church.

EWTN will never say a word about the reasons for the continued corruption of Catholic education. They will admit the issue, certainly—they must. Even the most indifferent Catholic can see there is a big problem. But they will never get to the heart of the matter and talk about the *cause*. All they offer is discussion about the symptoms, but they are mute when it comes to the diagnosis. They can't talk about the cause—unfaithful, cowardly bishops—because if they do, those bishops will pull the plug on them and cut off access.

So they, along with their little-read blog supporters also trying to curry favor with Church-establishment types, have rationalized that it is better to say some nice things than to tell the whole truth. And they have erred. All they have to do is look to the foundress of their network for what the right thing to do is when confronted with evil. As Mother lies on her deathbed, having helped shed so much light on conditions in the Church, one wonders how the current leadership lives with their consciences that betray the spirit of Mother. Her one fear was that the revolution would get a hold of her network (and it is *her* network). That fear, it turns out, was well founded. She once famously said she would burn her network to the ground before letting liberals (and by extension those who allow liberals to roam free) to get their hands on it. Unfortunately, Mother was unable to follow through on her plans.

This is why any true media outfit *must have total and complete independence* from the Church establishment. There can, of course, be cordial relations, but when it comes to reporting and analyzing problems and evils within the Church, there can be no *quid pro quo* relationship. A truly free press is just that—free—free to report whatever needs to be reported without fear of suffering recriminations from errant or wicked bishops and their establishment machine.

And frankly, good solid leaders, both lay and clerical—those who actually believe the Catholic faith—should welcome such a development, not be fearful and vengeful. Those who should be fearful are those who have something to fear—like being caught in some malfeasance.

In hindsight, take the example of the former archbishop of Milwaukee, Rembert Weakland, a notoriously wicked man. He sat atop the destruction of the Faith in his diocese for twenty-five years while carrying on as an active homosexual in the shadows. He had a torrid affair with a much younger man, even going so far as to write him a series of love letters. The archbishop's evildoing was finally discovered when his young paramour blackmailed him for nearly half a million dollars, which Weakland paid him, after carefully shuffling funds around that were not his. Despite the payment, Weakland's lover eventually outed him anyway.

How can such a man actually believe the Catholic faith in all its splendor? He can't, because he is steeped in a life of mortal sin. He is living in a manner directly opposed to the Faith.

Whispers and rumors of the archbishop's sordid activities were circulating around the archdiocese for quite some time, but he was able to keep a lid on things because he had no accountability, no organization or group to expose his exploits—exploits that turned out to be massively damaging to the souls in his charge. If only there had been a "plugged-in" Catholic free press to be able to follow events and duly report them. A number of other bishops across the United States had their suspicions about Weakland, but what could a good bishop do? Imagine if such a bishop had had a group he could contact and inform so that the word could get out and the evil brought to an end much sooner than it actually was.

As it is, it was the secular media that finally helped bring about the end of Weakland's reign, just as it was the secular media that brought forth the whole homosexual priest sex abuse scandal, despite various bishops' knowledge of that evil. Pope Benedict later publicly acknowledged and thanked the secular media for their reporting. How much sweeter would it have been had the Holy Father been able to thank Catholic media instead?

But owing to the culture of non-accountability among various Church leaders, it was in the end the secular media in 2002 that brought an end to the reign of Cdl. Bernard Law in Boston. Of course, the motives of the secular media can certainly be suspect because Law was labeled a "conservative"; nonetheless, they did the right thing, even if it may have been for the wrong reason. Pope Benedict publicly thanked the secular media for exposing the horrible evil of sex abuse of mostly teenaged boys by mostly homosexual clergy, and also for the perhaps more insidious practice of bishops lying, distorting, and shuffling priests around and generally covering up the heinous crimes. But think how much different things could have been, how much evil could have been prevented, if an independent Catholic media had existed and had been able to approach bishops with the facts.

Not a few people in the Catholic world knew, or had deep suspicions about, what was going on. As far back as the 1980s, small reports here and there had popped up of serially abusive priests, and bishops had dealt with the reports in a most dismissive way. Their actions allowed the sodomite abuse to drag on for decades.

It must also be considered that not a few bishops themselves might have been abusers prior to becoming bishops, not to mention that while other bishops may not have been actively engaged in sexual abuse of minors, they were still actively practicing homosexuals. (Weakland, for example, a practicing homosexual, has never been accused of raping adolescent boys.)

Then there is the additional consideration that some of these leaders, while not active homosexuals, still had same-sex attraction and therefore were sympathetic to all things "gay." There is the further consideration that some bishops, while not having any same-sex attraction, were extremely sympathetic to the homosexual agenda because they had gay family members, or they had deep friendships with fellow clergy (priests or bishops) whom they knew were homosexual.

This is the case with retired auxiliary bishop Thomas Gumbleton of Detroit, who has close family members who are actively homosexual.

The retired bishop is so sympathetic to the cause of homosexuality that his applause and support for sodomy has gotten him banned by a few brother bishops from speaking publicly in their dioceses. Yet Gumbleton served as vice chancellor of the archdiocese of Detroit for a number of decades, helping to run the archdiocese during the 1970s and 80s, when the archdiocesan seminary, St. John's Provincial, was rife with homosexual activity.

The rector of the seminary, Msgr. Kenneth Untener, was a close friend of Gumbleton's and allowed a program of filth to be aired in his seminary and shown to men being formed to be priests. These men were routinely shown pornographic homosexual videos under the guise of "studying" human sexuality so they could better deal with and counsel the laity. According to men who lived through those years in St. John's, the videos resulted in whipping up the sexual passions of many of the young men (who were homosexual themselves), and numerous sexual encounters occurred throughout the night as a result, some seminarians having to go so far as locking their doors to avoid unwanted visitors.

Gumbleton knew all about this. He and Untener were called to Rome to give an explanation of the scandal to the Vatican. The men were able to sufficiently pull the wool over the eyes of the questioners, pleading ignorance, misunderstanding, etc., even going so far as to lay the blame at the feet of a bishop in the western part of Michigan who had the "human sexuality" class going in his seminary. The story worked; Untener was eventually made bishop and went on to wipe out the Faith among Catholics in the diocese of Saginaw, Michigan before dying in 2004.

How was such evil, multiplied across the nation's dioceses in varying degrees and kinds, able to proliferate to such an extent? Simply put: because there is no real accountability for these men. Unless they commit a crime, they have practically *carte blanche* to rule with an iron fist, squashing any opposition wherever it comes up. Unfaithful, sinful, wicked men ruled (and now rule) many of these dioceses, and the faithful have almost no recourse to challenge and expose them.

And it isn't just a case of sexual sin and forsaking their vow of celibacy. There are many ways to be unfaithful; it's just that sexual improprieties garner headlines. Some bishops have been schooled poorly in theology, receiving horrible formation during their seminary years, for example. Pope Benedict XVI, before becoming Pope, touched on this during a speech to seminarians in Germany when he said that the Church was having to weather the storm of poorly formed bishops. Others have a view of the Church more akin to a social help agency than the supernatural society She truly is. They are what might be termed the *social justice* bishops—those supposedly concerned about the corporal works of mercy, yet entirely negligent of the spiritual works of mercy, which should be their first concern.

Such men allow all kinds of wickedness to occur in their dioceses because it flies under the cover of "charity" and "fighting the root cause of poverty." Granted, there are many fine programs in various dioceses to address conditions of human misery, and these should be applauded—but there need not be a corresponding desertion or diminishment of the Faith in order to fight poverty. But that is precisely the case in many quarters in the Church. Various leaders, intent on changing the Faith and downplaying doctrine, instead play up the social justice business. They pit the Greatest Commandment against the Second Greatest Commandment as though they are in contradiction.

Yet none of this gets any major play in the media, because the secular media doesn't care, and the Catholic media for the most part is controlled by the very men engaging in the evil, or those still operating under the old system of no transparency—which, of course, disinclines them to blow the whistle on themselves. The Faith has been destroyed in the West because of unfaithful or cowardly leaders— those who sought after revolution and those too personally weak to resist it. Those who brought about the revolution represent a hodgepodge of homosexual or homosexual-friendly men, ambitious and career-minded men, and those who had financial gain or career prestige in their sight. These men were aided by and able to manipulate weaker men in the episcopate who did not possess the needed backbone to defend the people of God against their wicked brother bishops.

This second group sat back and let the first set the agenda and then execute it, offering practically no resistance—with the notable exception of a stalwart bishop like Fabian Bruskewitz of Lincoln, Nebraska. Weak bishop after weak bishop simply caved in to issue after issue, like reception of Holy Communion in the hand, altar girls, the overabundance of so-called eucharistic ministers (properly termed extraordinary ministers of Holy Communion—the difference is a theological one), and so forth. The Church in the West was refashioned by wicked men and weak men, with sex, money, and power circulating around them like a swarm of bees.

And because there was no independent Catholic press to alert the faithful to the evil going on, it was assumed by many that what was going on was perfectly acceptable. Others suspected or intuited that what was happening was deeply flawed, but had nowhere to explore their suspicions, and ended up simply leaving the Faith. An alternative faith was being established right in the midst of the sanctuary, right under the noses of the faithful, and there was no one to call the bishops to account for their malice or their cowardice. There were the laudable efforts of such groups as Catholics United for the Faith (CUF) and *The Wanderer*, but for the most part, their efforts remained localized and largely incapable of holding back the tide of evil because they did not have access to large numbers of Catholics.

Still, a moment must be taken to extend deep gratitude for their efforts and work, oftentimes done under great duress and persecution from the Church establishment. To their credit, the bishops who worked to squash them recognized that their work, if given greater readership, could severely hamper their own designs to undermine the Faith. It is said you can tell the quality of a man by the list of his enemies. Many prayers should be offered for the few intrepid souls who sounded the alarm early on, despite the personal cost to themselves, as well as the fact that it was not heard by the overwhelming majority of those who needed to hear it.

But as is also said, that was then and this is now. Technology has provided an entirely new means to reach the few remaining faithful, sound the alarm, and turn up the heat. That technology is called the Internet. It has given a voice to the formerly voiceless Catholics who still cling to the Faith in the face of wicked and cowardly bishops.

Chapter 16

THE NEW EVANGELIZATION:
Without the Evangelizing

There is much excitement these days in the Church establishment over an initiative called the "New Evangelization." The phrase comes from Pope St. John Paul II's 1990 encyclical *Redemptoris Missio*, where he addressed in part the catastrophic meltdown of the Faith in Europe especially, but in other parts of the world as well, including the United States. He said:

> Thirdly, there is an intermediate situation, particularly in countries with ancient Christian roots, and occasionally in the younger Churches as well, where entire groups of the baptized have lost a living sense of the Faith, or even no longer consider themselves members of the Church, and live a life far removed from Christ and His Gospel. In this case what is needed is a "new evangelization" or a "re-evangelization." (33)

Owing to human nature's tendency to cling to all things new and improved, the term "New Evangelization" caught on and completely overshadowed the real emphasis of the Holy Father's comments, which was that there needs to be a *re*-evangelization effort. His Holiness' words were not meant to introduce completely new content for evangelization, but rather a brand new effort at evangelizing those fallen-away Catholics who had not received proper instruction in the Faith. He instructed Catholics to find new ways to talk about the Faith, but did not instruct them to change the content in the process. Of course, that judgment is very subjective; nonetheless, the Church of Nice got on board and continues to ride the train.

For example, Cdl. Dolan has used the opportunity to speak about the effort in somewhat immature words, for example, "The New Evangelization is accomplished with a smile, not a frown." A statement structured like that says much. He is also famous for saying "we got a Church that says yes and not no."

There arose two different understandings of the whole effort, depending on which aspect of the effort was considered "new." Many Church of Nice (Church establishment) types were more than happy to place the emphasis on the content as being new. But in keeping with the Pope's own words and emphasis, it was clear that the "new" did not apply to content, but to the overall *effort*, which is why he used the clarifying term "re-evangelization." He meant that a renewed effort must begin to reach out to those Catholics who have been deprived of the authentic Catholic faith in their earlier years.

In the rush to create a greater bureaucracy and yet another department in chanceries across the country, so-called New Evangelization teams began popping up in various dioceses. It became a means to double down on previous efforts, which had in fact been part of the problem in the first place. So an emphasis has been placed on *how* to communicate with people over *what* is actually being communicated. In many aspects, Catholic truth is being sacrificed or minimized to make it more palatable to fallen-away Catholics.

For example, the Alpha "catechetical" series has been introduced into hundreds of parishes across the nation as a way of presenting an "easier" Catholicism. There is nothing in the series that would present to people's minds the reality that the Catholic Church is the only true religion. In fact, the entire series was formulated in England by the Evangelical wing of the Anglican Communion, with the aim of just introducing a generic Jesus to those who know very little about Him historically.

So the question immediately arises: Why is this series being used at all? This is not in keeping with the aims of John Paul. This miseducation is exactly what the Pope was trying to correct, not employ. To get around the non-Catholic aspect of the non-Catholic catechism, various parishes or dioceses tacked on a Catholic supplement to the end of the course to make the course more Catholic, but even that effort ultimately fails. Various priests are on record saying they use the Alpha program and then tack on Catholic material after the Alpha material is completed.

By what is said and by what is left unsaid, the Alpha material presents an understanding of the theology of the Church and the sacraments contrary to the teaching of the Church. For example, Alpha teaches that revelation is solely based on the Bible. As John Paul stressed in his encyclical *Fides et Ratio* ("Faith and Reason"):

> Scripture . . . is not the Church's sole point of reference. The "supreme rule of her faith" derives from the unity which the spirit has created between Sacred Tradition, Sacred Scripture, and the Magisterium of the Church in a reciprocity which means that none of the three can survive without the others. (55)

Likewise, Alpha's understanding of "Church" is reduced to "simply a gathering of Christians who get together to worship God, to hear what God is saying to them, to encourage one another and to make friends. It should be a very exciting place to be!" This is the view of one of the main instructors of Alpha, as quoted in the book *Why Jesus?* by Nicky Gumbel.

Alpha teaches that what is meant by "Catholic Church" is the "universal Church," which is just the sum total all over the world of those who believe in Christ, regardless of their denomination. Alpha is also pretty clear in instructing students that the Catholic Church is just another denomination.

The question arises almost immediately: After sitting through all fifteen hours (sometimes longer) of video presentations of this kind of talk, exactly how could the parish religion team come in and say: "Now let's make this Catholic"? The section on the sacrament of baptism, for example, is woefully incomplete from a Catholic understanding. It speaks nothing of original sin—never even broaches the topic.

The point in all this is that a twisted understanding of the New Evangelization has led to a cure almost as bad as the original disease: bad catechesis. Alpha is not the only bad course around. JustFaith Ministries is another catechetical train wreck touted in various dioceses and parishes. JustFaith offers virtually no theological instruction and confines itself to promoting social justice programs under the banner of "love of neighbor." The title of the program—JustFaith—is remarkably deceiving as well as clever. It sounds as if a person will be instructed in just the Faith, while in reality he's being propagandized into believing that the Faith is about nothing else than social justice.

The can of worms that Pope St. John Paul II opened is simply that the people charged with re-evangelizing the sheep are the very people who caused the problems to begin with. The leaders themselves are oftentimes poorly formed, stretching back to their own seminary training, and now to ask them to form and train those they lost to begin with is proving to be a very difficult proposition. So, perhaps aware of their own shortcomings and lack of knowledge in how to go about this new evangelization, they bring in "experts" and social scientists and pollsters to provide counsel on how to best market the Faith to an uninterested society—especially to Catholics who formerly attended Mass and received the sacraments.

The entire effort promises to fall flat on its face—or more precisely, promises to *continue* to fall flat on its face, because that is exactly what has happened since John Paul first popularized the idea more than twenty-five years ago. There has been nothing that could even begin to resemble a return to the Faith in any of the European countries or in the United States. Consider that just as John Paul was emphasizing the need for evangelizing in 1990, at that point and moving forward, more than ten percent of parishes in the United States have had be closed down. If the bishops are trying to implement a bold initiative, it clearly isn't working.

Even in Cdl. Dolan's strategy of "smile, don't frown," he has sat atop the largest parish closing/restructuring in the Catholic Church's history in the United States. (It's arguable the archdiocese of Boston under Cdl. Sean O'Malley may have seen more closings and mergers, depending on how things are tallied.) What is clear is that whatever is being tried is not working, and twenty-five years is more than sufficient time to experiment with something. In fact, Catholicism used to be the dominant majority faith among those considered Christian. Within the next five years, if current trends hold, it will slip below the fifty-percent mark among all Christian faiths—the first time in the history of the world that the Church will give up its title of being the majority faith among Christians.

It isn't working because the effort lacks any sense of Catholicity. It is organized and implemented by various leaders, both lay and clerical, who have been weaned on the mother's milk of a pluralistic society. They are ill equipped to stand up in the marketplace and say the simple, bold, declarative truth that the Catholic Church is alone necessary for salvation, and it alone is the One True Faith and all others are false religions. If that is not the jumping-off point for evangelizing, then all efforts might as well be packed in. We see again this conflict within the soul of the American Catholic Church and its hierarchy of wanting to appease, not upset, go along, not be thought judgmental. That approach will never succeed because it is at its core antithetical to the heart of the Catholic faith. It is comparable to having a blind man be the national spokesman for an eyeglass company. *Ain't. Gonna'. Work.* What the New Evangelization needs to be is an unapologetic *Catholic* re-evangelization. What does that look like?

Chapter 17

THE PROBLEM OF CATHOLIC IDENTITY:
A Thoroughly Catholic Solution

The crisis in the Church is ultimately one of a loss of Catholic identity. This has been manifested in a loss of supernatural faith among clergy and laity alike. That loss of faith has resulted in myriad problems of abuse in the liturgy, loss of understanding of the sacraments—most especially the Blessed Sacrament—a destruction of Catholic devotional life, the collapse of education, and on and on. In short, Catholics no longer know who we are.

Failing to understand who we are as a people has made the overwhelming majority of Catholics become something else on the inside, and sometimes even on the outside as well. The interior life of Catholics has been gutted and replaced with something else. Many have become protestant, many others atheist or agnostic; some seek a solution to evil in the political arena, while others have become seekers of a solution to the crisis in false apparitions, schismatic groups, and a host of other substitutes. Satan can despoil the members of the Church in many ways.

Therefore, there must be an authentic, genuinely Catholic response, a thoroughly Catholic solution to the crisis in which we now find ourselves. While it must ultimately be implemented by the bishops, it cannot wait for a conversion on their part. Many of them, as noted earlier, have been so poorly formed that they, sadly, are actually part of the problem—as Pope Benedict said in our earlier quote.

No. This solution must begin with the laity first. Just as it was the faithful laity who refused to accept the heresy of the bishops who supported Arianism in the fourth century, so, too, opposition to the Modernist heresy, accepted by so many bishops today, must proceed from the laity, with the aim being that the hierarchy eventually take over and take the lead. Just as no heresy can really begin with the laity, so ultimately no solution can be sustained by the laity. Our Blessed Lord appointed shepherds over the flock, and it is their duty to protect the sheep. But while they are sleeping, the sheep can certainly feel free to make a lot of noise to wake them up.

First Principles and Word Games

Since the goal is to reinstall a genuine Catholic identity in the hearts and minds of Catholics, this means two major areas of operation are required. First, all that is un-Catholic must be demolished, and second, all that is properly Catholic must be advanced. In short, the work of the Modernist heresy must be undone, completely and totally. Not one stone of that edifice of evil must be left standing on another. Just as when an existing building is being refashioned or repurposed there is first the demolition that must happen, so, too, the demolition of the existing heresy must take place to begin to make room for the new construction. After all, what is the New Evangelization—or better stated, the re-evangelization—other than a rebuilding of the Faith? The words of Our Blessed Lord from the crucifix to St. Francis of Assisi in the eleventh century come immediately to mind: "Rebuild My Church."

In spiritual terms these two goals can be accomplished at the same time—the demolition alongside the new construction. As the authentic faith is being reintroduced, it will have the double effect of destroying the heresy alongside it. The forces of darkness at work within the hearts of traitors in the Church have always recognized this truth. As you advance the lie, the truth is buried (albeit temporarily). It is more akin to a set of scales; as you pile objects on one side, the other side is proportionately and directly impacted. So, too, with truth vs. falsehood.

What is actually at work is the principle of non-contradiction—that a thing cannot both be and not be at the same time in the same respect. The same light cannot be both on and off in the same room at the same time. The same soul cannot be both in a state of grace and in a state of mortal sin at the same time. So when truth is advanced, the lie is dissolved. An authentic reestablishment of Catholic identity must proceed from this first guiding principle. This principle immediately strikes at the heart of the Modernist heresy, because the Modernist heresy is built on the philosophical belief (not fact) that there can be opposing "truths" because there is no objective truth.

It is from this relativism, this subjective notion, which objectively denies all objectivity (funny how that works), that such inane slogans appear like "My body, my choice." The entire abortion lie is built on the idea of relativism, which is used as a cover simply to excuse sexual activity.

God has constructed a universe modeled after His own interior life, where there is no contradiction. So it is only to be expected that the universe and all things in it would reflect the Creator. This is why, when it comes to restoring Catholic identity, the blueprint is actually rather simple and straightforward. Catholic teaching is either true or false. This is why it must be expressed with absolute clarity. The past fifty years or so have seen a storm of vagueness let loose on the Church: unclear statements, documents that could be interpreted in a thousand different ways, an unwillingness to simply call a spade a spade. This atmosphere has allowed the Modernist heresy to thrive. Modernists were happy to introduce vague language into various debates, and once the language was adopted, it allowed even further lack of clarity to seize hold to such an extent that various people in the Church use the same vocabulary, but are not talking about the same thing. We can present as the very first, and in many ways, most important example the word "charity."

That's Uncharitable

Catholics seeking to reestablish an authentic Catholic identity must understand how so many different things have been weaved together to form a tapestry opposed to Catholicism. From radical feminism to bad philosophy to the Sexual Revolution to weak men to the destruction of the family, as well as many others, each one of these areas both arises as its own problem born from the others, but then gives life to each of the other problems. It is a continual symbiosis, a cycle that just keeps expanding to engulf more and more souls. So it truly does present itself to the good Catholic as: Where do I begin? The Modernist heresy is so well-knitted together, so complete in having brought together so many different strains of errant thought and combined them into one gigantic leviathan, that it is small wonder Catholic leaders have so easily fallen prey to it. This heresy is truly *much* larger than the sum of its parts. Even when condemning it, Pope St. Pius X recognized the enormity of the issue when he correctly labeled it "the synthesis of all heresies."

> And now, can anybody who takes a survey of the whole system be surprised that We should define it as the synthesis of all heresies? Were one to attempt the task of collecting together all the errors that have been broached against the Faith and to concentrate the sap and substance of them all into one, he could not better succeed than the Modernists have done. (Pope St. Pius X, *Pascendi Dominici Gregis*, 1907)

So to begin to attack the heresy, one must go directly to its heart, the great defense system it has set up so that none of its individual points can be challenged—and that defense system is the perversion of the notion of charity. Every single "little" heresy proposed by the larger system is able to be stealthily introduced into a conversation by appealing to charity, a *false* notion of charity. One of the most clever ruses used by Modernists is the way they immediately cut off all discussion of a topic by charging their opponent with being "uncharitable."

We see this played out in so-called attack politics almost daily. For example, if someone questions the wisdom or prudence of an Obama plan, the person is immediately labeled a "racist" (uncharitable). If someone points out the evil of sodomy, he gets the label "homophobic" (also uncharitable). And if in the realm of the theological, he says divorced and remarried Catholics should not be admitted to Holy Communion, he is immediately labeled "unmerciful"—the worst form of being uncharitable.

The "That's uncharitable" proposition is the impregnable fortress that allows all the other evils to multiply because you cannot call them evil, so the argument stops. These defense shields must be taken down. They must be blown apart at their source, and that means to immediately go on the attack and demonstrate how riddled with error is this line of reasoning. It is, in the end, to show how those accusing you of being uncharitable are *actually themselves* the uncharitable ones.

Until this "charity" defense is disabled, no amount of argument will win the day on the other substantive issues.

How do we disable it? By speaking directly of it as its own issue. So we must begin to define our terms clearly.

> To be charitable is to have authentic love for others, which means to will what is really good for them. And what is really good for any human being? It is that good for which each of us was created, the Supreme Good, Who is God Himself. If I truly love another person, I want for him what I want for myself—true human fulfillment, the achievement of his final end, the realization of his very reason for being. And this is nothing less than beatitude, eternal union with God.

> If a charitable person sometimes acts towards others in ways they would find offensive, it is because he has their genuine welfare at heart. Like the conscientious physician, he knows that it is sometimes necessary to hurt in order to heal. Totally committed as he is to the Truth, it is no concern to him whether or not he is liked. Could not each of us recount, with gratitude, at least one critical turning point experience in our lives, when we were saved from going over the precipice by someone who cared enough for us to offend us? The offense came as a singular blessing, for it was just the kind of shock we needed to awaken us from our moral stupor, make us aware of the disastrous path we were following, and then take the necessary steps to straighten out our crooked ways. ("On Being Charitable," D.Q. McInerny, Ph.D., Professor of Theology at Our Lady of Guadalupe Seminary, FSSP)

What the Modernists have succeeded in doing is creating an environment in cooperation with the issues of weak masculinity, radical feminism, and so forth, that the supreme "virtue" is to never give offense. We see this constantly in our day-to-day culture: If someone is offended (and almost everyone is all the time), everything comes to a screeching halt. All someone has to do is claim to be offended, and a cascade of recriminations and apologies and media reports ensue that totally obscure whatever the issue at hand was, no matter how important it may have been to the national dialogue.

In fact, the national dialogue, as well as the much more important theological dialogue, is controlled and manipulated by ideologues who have the "I'm offended; that's not charitable" defense at the ready and pull it out every single time the truth is too near to being discussed. Notice the close relationship between the charges "I'm offended" and "That's uncharitable." One is expressed in secular terms, the other in more theological terms, but they have the same philosophical principle—namely, the truth may not be discussed because someone will be adversely affected.

The secular Modernists have constructed an edifice where the truth must be seen through the lens of being "nice." And by "nice" is meant never giving offense, always being "open" to new things, always being polite, sociable, non-judgmental. A nice person is totally, completely, universally, and indiscriminately tolerant, meaning he is the epitome of non-judgmentalism. Nothing he says, nothing he does, is such that it would ever give offense. He is a model maestro of inoffensiveness. As Dr. McInerny so wonderfully expresses it,

> He is positively fluent in the sanitized language of Political Correctness. And because the nice person never offends anyone by anything he says or does, he is, not surprisingly, warmly liked and approved by all. Everybody likes the nice person, and he is welcome wherever he goes.

In short, everyone wants the nice person at their parties, and the reason is simple. Everyone has accepted the moral relativism of the day, and the nice person, like them, is a *de facto* subscriber to moral relativism. The problem for the Catholic man or woman seeking to rebuild the Church, however, is this: Being "nice" is not Catholic. It never has been.

Chapter 18

THE CHURCH OF NICE:
Nice vs. Charitable

Being nice has nothing to do with being charitable. In fact, in the contemporary understanding of being nice, the two ideas are polar opposites. Authentic Catholicism must begin to understand this clearly once again. It is perhaps the most essential ingredient to the restoration of a Catholic identity. Catholicism is not "nice." It is as far away from nice as Satan is from Heaven. But Catholicism is charitable because the founder of the Catholic Church, Jesus Christ, Who, being God, *is* charity itself, Himself.

Too many Catholics, prelates, priests, and laity have bought into the Modernist-inspired notion that being nice is being charitable. So when someone is offended as Catholic truth is being laid out, the process immediately ceases—exactly what the diabolical wants. As with everything, the Church looks to model Our Blessed Lord. In everything He ever said and did, He was the exemplar of charity, which of course flows from His Divine nature.

But for a Modernist to use Our Blessed Lord as the example of "nice," he would have to search long and hard, and he'd come up empty-handed. Frequently, Our Lord was anything but nice. Since nice is of Satan, because it creates the environment where truth can be buried, Our Lord was the walking, talking opposite of being nice.

It might be argued that no other man in human history offended so many people. From his Bread of Life discourse recorded in the sixth chapter of St. John's Gospel, to his emphatic repeated denunciations of the Jewish leaders of His day, even to the point of calling them the children of Satan, Jesus Christ was not nice. And we must never forget, He was trying to smash through their defenses so that they would be open to conversion and consequently save their souls. He did not set about trying to be disagreeable or a contrarian. He knew they had closed themselves off to the truth, so in place of speaking in gentler terms (which He did with frequency as well), He brought the sledgehammer. He was not nice with those who rejected the truth. He even made clear to His followers that rejection of truth was the unforgivable sin.

The Pharisees took enormous offense at Him. They made it their work to destroy Him owing to their great offense. Saint Mark even says point blank: "And they took offense at him" (Matt. xiii : 57). That so much of the Catholic world has forgotten this truth is startling. Any Catholic intent on restoring authentic Catholic identity, whether he be a cleric, religious, or lay, must always keep in the front of his mind and be ready to employ as his first weapon this pure reality: Jesus Christ was crucified for not being *nice.*

Thus, the first ingredient in the authentic Catholic life is *not* to be nice.

And to underscore this very point and make things perfectly clear: The Church Militant exists for the sole purpose of battling back the Church of Nice, to move things away from this current state of affairs and attack the gates of Hell. This is the mission, and there is no other.

Chapter 19

THE CHURCH OF NICE:
Satanic

Since being nice is of Satan, it bears laying out with much clarity inspired by charity that the Church of Nice is satanic in its origins and diabolical in its preachings. Since appeal to the principle of noncontradiction is always available and should be encouraged, then motivated by charity and expressed with clarity, it must be plainly put forth: The average Catholic today is in the grip of the Father of Lies, and this is supported by a Church establishment that, having also accepted the lie, likewise finds itself unable to wrest itself from the clutches of the demonic. To be certain, Our Blessed Lord Himself will rescue His Bride, but He will do it in spite of many of Her leaders.

Just as He came to earth to rescue the remnant of His chosen people whom He knew would respond to His Sacred voice, so, too, will He now do the same with His Church. What means He will employ we do not know. What we do know is that He is faithful, and we must make ourselves available to His Holy Will so that if He desires to use us—any of us in any way—we are completely and totally disposed and at the ready.

The Church of Nice is satanic because it opposes the will of Our Blessed Lord. Just as He called the religious leaders of His own day satanic because they opposed the will of His Heavenly Father and did the will of the devil, so we also find a repeat of the same actions today, and therefore the same conclusions are valid. A person does not need to be a devil worshipper or an atheist to do the will of Satan; he needs merely to oppose the will of God. With great sadness and interior horror should the faithful Catholic reel at the warnings of Church Fathers and Doctors that the greater share of bishops go to Hell.

The Church of Nice creates an environment that excuses sin—which God *hates*—by never speaking of it. It adds sacrilege to this by distributing Holy Communion to multitudes in sin without ever telling them of the consequences of their acts. The Church of Nice promotes an environment where Catholic greatness is buried, plowed under, by worship at the altar of false ecumenism, so that no one may be offended, least of all those who subscribe (largely unknowingly) to a heresy. The Church of Nice abhors the truth, but it does it in such a way as to make it appear as though it supports it.

The Church of Nice is satanic because it presents the lie with a touch of truth so it can be easily digested. It presents the lie that no one really goes to Hell, for example (we have a "reasonable hope" that all men are saved), by appealing to the truth of the supreme goodness of God. But it distorts this teaching by perverting the notion of goodness. As it relates to humans and our salvation, the goodness of God needs to be rightly understood for what it is: that He created us for Himself, incarnated and died for us, continues to share His Divine life with us through the sacraments of His Holy Catholic Church, most especially the Blessed Sacrament. Every bit of this is pure grace, the pure goodness of God. We experience His goodness in the here and now, in the ability for any miserable sinner to simply reach out and come to the infinite God and be accepted by Him with sufficient contrition and desire.

The Church of Nice seeks after appeasement and compromise, shrouding itself in accommodation for the common good. It does not separate itself from the world, but rather allies itself in political arenas, saying it must cooperate with the enemies of Christ in order to bring about greater good. It turns a blind eye to the fact that such tolerance is allowed only if the evil is being actively fought against. Having cooperated and rationalized evil, the Church of Nice then ignores the second part and does nothing to bring about a real change. We see this all over the social justice scandals within the CRS and the CCHD. We see it in the unwillingness of bishops and various Church-associated groups, like the national office of the Knights of Columbus, to call out the evils of Catholics who support child murder and sodomy.

The scandal that erupted in the Church in America during the 2004 presidential election campaign between George Bush and Catholic John Kerry was deplorable. A ruckus ensued at the bishops' semiannual meeting that year over the question of whether the bishops should deny John Kerry Holy Communion owing to his unyielding public support of abortion. On the one side were the usual suspects, including current Washington, DC cardinal Donald Wuerl, then bishop of Pittsburgh, and his allies like Bp. Donald Troutman of Erie, who insisted that nothing be done and Kerry be allowed to receive. On the other side, considerably fewer in number, was Abp. Raymond Burke of St. Louis, who defended Canon 915 of the Catholic Code of Canon Law, which clearly states that individuals like John Kerry must be denied reception of Holy Communion.

Unsurprisingly, given the make-up of the American hierarchy, the Church of Nice approach won, and the question was returned to each individual bishop to decide in his diocese as he saw fit. It didn't take much longer for the whole question to be swept under the rug, as Cdl. Dolan would later confess when he said during an interview that the bishops have pretty much "moved on" from the issue—apparently just as the governing body of the Knights of Columbus has equally "moved on" regarding the question of scandal within the ranks of the association.

During the 2012 battle in the New York state legislature, it was two members of the Knights of Columbus who cast the deciding votes in favor of sodomite marriage, which Catholic governor Andrew Cuomo —who hails from a family of traitors to the Faith, given his father's history—signed into law. Not a word was forthcoming from the national office of the Knights of Columbus. In case after case, where members in local councils have publicly supported some intrinsic evil, other members have complained to national headquarters and been shut down in their appeals for the national leadership to step up and do something. This has been going on for years, and when questioned, the national office issues a press release attacking those reporting the stories—but of course never denies the facts of the case because they are, by definition, undeniable.

The Church in America, because of its immigrant history and traditional association with the Democratic Party, has demonstrated no interest in ruffling feathers in the halls of power—despite the fact that owing to its support of child murder, contraception, sterilization, and so forth, the Party has earned the nickname "the Party of Death." Yet organizations with much to profit by remaining "above the fray," like the Knights of Columbus national office, show no interest in making a statement about the support for these intrinsic evils among their very own rank and file. They have adopted a compromise that is spiritually deadly whereby they give much money to pro-life causes while saying nothing about the pro-abortion members in their own councils, who come to meetings on weeknights, and on weekdays go to their political offices or voting booths and vote for legislation and candidates who continue the killing—based on their votes. It is a dire case of spiritual schizophrenia.

All of this is allowed to continue, or rather simply continues, because very few see anything wrong with it. Take, for example, the case of Cdl. Daniel DiNardo of the Houston-Galveston archdiocese, who allowed his co-cathedral in 2013 to be used for the "ordination" of female Methodist "priests." After their "ordinations," those very same female ministers went to their congregations and preached in favor of child slaughter in the womb. Granted, His Eminence can't stop them from preaching to their congregations that evil is good, but he sure as hellfire doesn't have to launch them on their misguided religion's presentation of intrinsic evil as a moral right from the nave of his own cathedral.

That distinction was apparently still lost on the cardinal when, in the last week of 2014, he or his staff allowed Lisa Raquel Benitez to be buried out of the cathedral after she suffered an untimely death. The problem was that Benitez was heavily involved in Planned Parenthood, both as event manager for the Gulf Coast affiliate as well as advocate for Planned Parenthood Young Leaders. She also publicly promoted the Human Rights Campaign, the largest gay rights organization in the nation, which aggressively promotes same-sex marriage. She was a public torchbearer for some of the greatest evils the modern world now holds forth as normal, especially abortion. And on what would have been her forty-seventh birthday, shockingly, a funeral Mass was offered for her in the archdiocese of Houston's co-cathedral of the Sacred Heart in downtown Houston. The funeral was announced in all the usual obituary columns and forums, including the *Houston Chronicle*, which read: "A mass will be held to celebrate Lisa's life . . . ." In fact, her obituary stressed how her undying support for both causes, abortion and sodomy, made her something of a hero in the local pro-death community.

On both these occasions, Cdl. DiNardo's auxiliary bishop George Sheltz told ChurchMilitant.com and our supporters that all of this was perfectly fine with the cardinal; he apparently wants to reach out to people and support ecumenism. But he seems to lack any corresponding desire to reach out to faithful Catholics in his own archdiocese, and casts a wary eye toward them when it comes to their pro-life efforts.

Then there is the case of the Boston cardinal schmoozing with the political elites of the Party of Death such that even his closest allies and even dear friends were left speechless. When Democrat senator Ted Kennedy died in 2009, he was given the send-off normally associated with saints. Presiding over the entire spectacle was none other than Cdl. Sean O'Malley, head of the Boston archdiocese. In years to come, this may seem like just another case of poor judgment or lack of prudence, but at the time, it was anything but. It was a scandal of gigantic proportions.

Ted Kennedy embodied almost more than any other Catholic politician the concept of traitor to the Faith. In an analogy to politics, he made Benedict Arnold look as if he were a hero. Ted Kennedy was a ruthless defender and promoter of abortion, contraception, and nearly every other evil that came down the pike. He so pilloried, defamed, and slandered US Supreme Court nominee Robert Bork (nominated by President Ronald Reagan) that the nominee's name actually became a verb around Washington, DC—as in "You've been Borked," meaning you've had your reputation torn to shreds. In those Senate Judiciary confirmation hearings in 1987, Kennedy ripped into Bork with abandon. He gave his now infamous tirade, which is known in shorthand as "Robert Bork's America." Kennedy, the upstanding Catholic from the well-heeled Kennedy clan, said in part, "Robert Bork's America is a land in which women would be forced into back-alley abortions [and] blacks would sit at segregated lunch counters . . . ."

Kennedy spent decades cultivating his relationships with the architects of the culture of death largely owing to the fact that in the earlier years, they were nearly all Democrats. Kennedy was part of the private meetings with five Jesuits and dissident priest Charles Curran at the Kennedy Compound in Hyannisport, Massachusetts in 1964, where Kennedy and the priests hunkered down to devise a strategy whereby they could vote and politick for abortion on demand and still give the appearance of being Catholic. In those few summers before *Roe v. Wade* became the law of the land, there was still something of a balancing act in which Catholic politicians had to engage the questions of life and sexual morality. Within a few years, however, Kennedy and his kind ensured that all such matters of conscience were quickly wiped off the national landscape. And they were able to do so because the hierarchy of the day abandoned the issue faster than a sinking ship.

In Ted Kennedy's last years in the Senate, Obama was president and had introduced his wicked Obamacare plan, which had the support of the bishops—until the question of the contraception mandate was discovered buried deep within its more than 2,300 pages of rules and regulations. Obama's champion for this in the Senate was none other than Kennedy, who knew full well about the mandates for contraception and abortifacient birth control. Undeterred, he pushed his fellow senators to pass the Obamacare bill.

As he lay on his deathbed, he released a letter to the public begging, cajoling, charging, and pleading with his fellow senators to pass the bill, complete with its murderous language. This was three days before he entered eternity and would face the countless number of young humans whose blood was on his hands. Shortly after he died, a battle cry of sorts went up in the US Senate that the bill should be passed as a show of respect for the "Liberal Lion" of the Senate whose first concern was the poor and downtrodden. With the nostalgic vote behind the bill, it passed, was signed into law by Obama, with a cadre of Catholic traitors to the Faith standing around the signing table—all owing to Kennedy.

In life, Kennedy was a drunken, adulterous, child-killing, lecherous man who, because of his connections, managed to skirt prosecution in the drowning death of a young woman, Mary Jo Kopechne at Chappaquiddick, as he drove her home late one night after a party. His run for president was derailed owing to her death and the eleven-hour gap when he failed to report the incident. From his secret meetings with renegade Catholic clerics to draw up political blueprints to support abortion, to his decades-long votes in favor of child murder, to his politics of personal destruction launched against anyone pro-life, to his deathbed appeal to pass Obamacare with its contraceptive/abortive mandate, there wasn't one thing about Kennedy that even hinted at the possibility that he believed anything of his Catholic faith. And if he did believe it, it wasn't visible by any of his public acts. That's why the funeral Mass orchestrated for him with Cdl. Sean O'Malley's blessing and presence was scandalous.

In addition to having the air of a celebrity event, well attended by only the finest of high society, politician after politician mounted the pulpit to sing the praises of the baby killer, with the cardinal sitting there in choir in full compliance. And if the event itself—a Catholic funeral Mass for a man of such ill repute—wasn't enough, the entire affair was televised, again with the blessing of the cardinal—the entire affair, that is, with one notable exception: Cdl. O'Malley and his staff were clever enough to make sure when it came time for distribution of Holy Communion, the television cameras showed nothing of who approached to receive and were actually given the Body and Blood of Our Blessed Lord. In attendance, naturally, were the most notable traitors to the Catholic faith in the world of politics, and the cardinal and his staffers knew that televised images of this crowd coming up to receive Holy Communion would cause a massive firestorm and howls of protest in the world of faithful Catholics. So the cameras were simply never pointed in that direction. Like so many other bishops (as Cdl. Dolan conveyed in his earlier-mentioned interview), O'Malley had apparently "moved on" from the issue.

And all of this is certainly not confined to the ranks of cardinals. In Chicago, as the successor to Cdl. Francis George was being installed in the spring of 2015, Abp. Blase Cupich generated his own storm of protest when the governor of Illinois was given Holy Communion at Cupich's installation Mass. The problem is that the governor is not Catholic—a fact that's very well known, and should have been well known to the Chicago archdiocesan leadership. An invitation to the Mass was no doubt sent to the governor's office, at which point it should have been diplomatically suggested to the governor that he not come forward to receive Holy Communion owing to certain theological truths about the Blessed Sacrament. No such caution was issued, nor was any explanation given to the scandalized faithful after the sacrilegious event.

In a similar display of failing to show distinctions when they're called for, the archbishop issued a statement that can only be described as galling following the spate of undercover videos from August 2015 onward showing Planned Parenthood profits off the traffic of aborted infants' body parts. The Center for Medical Progress, an organization committed to exposing the evil of Planned Parenthood and the industry of selling baby parts for profit, produced the incriminating videos, which were beyond disturbing and graphic—they were downright macabre. They presented very clear video and audio of Planned Parenthood officials and employees picking over the bloody remains of aborted infants in lab dishes, poking and prodding them, lifting them up with tweezers and making jokes about the sex of the aborted baby and how much money they could get for this sample or that. Numerous leaders of various organizations, as well as corporate leaders, began distancing themselves from Planned Parenthood. Some states voted to defund the baby-killing giant. Calls emerged on Capitol Hill for defunding on a federal level as well. It was a firestorm of well-deserved bad publicity for the wicked, homicidal organization. Even Hillary Clinton said the videos were gruesome. She, of course, backpedaled from that the next day, expressing her undying support for Planned Parenthood; nonetheless, her initial, instinctual comments are now committed to the annals of history. In the face of all this, with an opportunity to strike a blow, a serious blow, on behalf of the unborn and for the pro-life movement and for the truth, Abp. Cupich instead issued a statement so profoundly missing the mark it was beyond belief. In an op-ed in the *Chicago Tribune*, he compared the horrors of the Planned Parenthood exposés with other social concerns:

> We should be no less appalled by the indifference toward the thousands of people who die daily for lack of decent medical care; who are denied rights by a broken immigration system and by racism; who suffer in hunger, joblessness and want; who pay the price of violence in gun-saturated neighborhoods; or who are executed by the state in the name of justice.

Anyone who has known of the archbishop's history would not have been surprised by his indifference to the plight of the unborn. While bishop of Spokane, Washington, he forbade any of his priests from participating in the 40 Days for Life prayer vigils at abortion chambers. He called such actions "unhelpful." Likewise, after having newly arrived in Chicago as archbishop and questioned on MSNBC about whether he would refuse Holy Communion to pro-abortion Catholic politicians (as required by Canon 915), he ducked and said that isn't something that should be decided at the Communion rail. That was a somewhat amusing answer, given the fact that the archbishop and other prelates and clergy who view things the way he does have worked hard to get rid of Communion rails from inside Catholic sanctuaries for many years now. One wonders if such men have any sense of what a Communion rail even is.

The lowlights from these prelates' reigns are but a small sampling of their doings. In the area of the more mundane and less publicized, each one allows an active ministry for homosexuals to be run out of their chancery offices or in numerous parishes, or both. The cover story is that these "ministries" are helping those with same-sex attraction to be faithful Catholics, but the reality is far from that. None of these ministries was formed with anything of the kind intended.

After the Congregation for the Doctrine of the Faith issued a letter in 1986 titled *On the Pastoral Care of Homosexual Persons*, reaffirming Catholic teaching on homosexuality, a number of bishops responded by forbidding the pro-homosexuality group Dignity and its chapters to hold its subversive meetings on Church property. In response, the Dignity chapters simply disbanded, changed their names, and then marched right back into parish halls and continued holding their subversive meetings. The pastors of the parishes said nothing, and the various bishops simply looked the other way so as not to rock the boat.

Dignity is an organization that lobbies for the Church to change its teachings on homosexuality, and now same-sex marriage—a position that has long been welcomed unofficially by various prelates and their pastors owing to their own homosexuality, or their homosexual-friendly policies. The only official Church-approved outreach to people suffering from same-sex attraction is Courage, started by a dedicated priest in the archdiocese of New York under Cdl. Terence Cooke. Its aim is to assist men and women to live a chaste life faithful to the Gospel through frequent reception of the sacraments.

But Dignity holds no such view. Its view is to eradicate the Church's teaching. Yet Dignity survives to this day and continues to have a close association, if unofficial, with Catholic parishes and bishops all over the country. It may have changed its name in some places, but it's still possessed by the same demons.

Why does this all happen? How can these men continue to support the things they do? It all goes back to the earlier point that the goodness of God has been presented in such a distorted fashion that they and their supporters in the pews of the Church of Nice don't seriously believe there are any consequences for preaching, acting, or believing like this. To portray God's goodness as extending *after* death to the poor miserable sinner who wanted nothing to do with God in this life is to pervert the idea of His goodness. Yet this happens a million times over at Catholic funerals, where the dead are spoken of as "being in Heaven," despite their outright opposition to and rejection of the goodness of God during their earthly lives. Priests with this Church of Nice mentality not only cut off prayers for the dead, they also continue poisoning others by perpetrating this diabolical notion that the clock never runs out. The clock most certainly does run out, and as we have seen from the testimony of Catholic tradition, most of whom it runs out on are damned.

The Church of Nice is satanic because it offers a twisted, perverted understanding of God, denies in practice (and in many cases in actual fact) sin, and denies the ultimate consequence of sin: Hell. It may do so in a clever way by positing that the possibility of Hell exists for any person, but then quickly adds that it is difficult to be damned. In so doing, the Church of Nice turns Our Blessed Lord's own words on their ears. The Divine Master Himself said exactly the opposite. He said, "If any man would come after me, let him deny himself and take up his cross and follow me" (Matt. xvi : 24). And again, "Enter by the narrow gate; for the gate is wide and the way is easy, that leads to destruction, and those who enter by it are many" (Matt. vii : 13).

These falsities and lies, which emanate from the Father of Lies, must be confronted at every turn, no matter who speaks them. They must be exposed for exactly what they are—evil—because they turn people away from the destiny Our Blessed Lord intends for them. As Pope St. John Paul II once offered, evil eventually consumes itself, and we see this happening with every passing day in the Church of Nice. Refer back to those startling statistics earlier cited. The Church of Nice is shrinking every day—and that is good. What is, of course, bad about it is that the reason it's shrinking is because many of the souls in it are dying off—and who can doubt that many of them are damned?

The Church of Nice is shrinking and ineffectual because it is luke-warm, made up of lukewarm souls both in the pews and in the sanctu-ary. Everything lukewarm eventually turns cold and rots. There could be no more apt example of the Church of Nice than when Our Lord spoke of salt losing its flavor: "It is no longer good for anything except to be thrown out and trodden under foot by men" (Matt. v : 13). In fact, the lukewarm draws perhaps the sharpest rebuke from Our Blessed Lord in all of Sacred Scripture when, in the Book of the Apocalypse, He declares, "because you are lukewarm, and neither cold nor hot, I will spew you out of my mouth" (Rev. iii : 16). The Church of Nice couldn't be more lukewarm if it tried. Pope St. Pius V in the sixteenth century made the point clearly when he said, "All the evil in the world is due to lukewarm Catholics." If he thought that then, he wouldn't be able to conceive of the current situation.

Chapter 20

THE CHURCH OF NICE:
It Brings Damnation

Every human being has implanted in his heart knowledge of good and evil—the moral law, natural law. But that reality has alongside it the additional reality that we all have fallen human nature and its accompanying concupiscence—the disorder inherited from our first parents that inclines us to sin, makes sin attractive. And so each one of us emerges from the womb readied for spiritual warfare, and we will engage in this until we draw our last breath. These two warring principles within us—the natural law and concupiscence—have been the subject of thousands of pages in theological tomes, summed up as "spiritual combat."

The duty of the Church, Her divine mandate, is to go out into the world and be a reinforcement to every soul, to bring to that soul the liberating reality of Her Own Sacred Presence, the balm of Gilead, to strengthen the soul to cling to the good in her and oppose the bad in her—concupiscence. The obvious goal, the purpose, is for everlasting life, salvation. Through grace, overflowing from the Church and Her sacraments established personally by Our Blessed Lord for this single end, a soul is empowered by clinging to the divine truth to achieve Heaven. The Church brings salvation to such a soul.

But the Church of Nice feeds the concupiscence within the human heart by excusing sin, ignoring it, denying and distorting truths about God. It serves as a reinforcement not for the divine but for the diabolical. And it is able to accomplish this distortion in the soul by a thousand and one means. This creates a thousand and one paths to Hell—or to build on Our Blessed Lord's own warning, a thousand and one *lanes* on the single road to Hell, making it broad indeed, allowing for many, many souls to travel it.

A time-proven favorite strategy of the diabolical is not so much to preach lies, which of course is a favorite, but even more so, simply *not* to let truth be preached. A person can sin by commission (actively doing something) or by omission (doing nothing). Each leads to sin, which is why at Mass we ask to be forgiven of both forms of sin: "in what I have done, and in what I have failed to do." Consider then for a moment how beyond calculation this tactic has been in securing the eternal damnation of so many souls sitting in the pews of the Church of Nice.

The horrible evil of contraception, which will lead to a persecution of the Church (as Dr. Charles Rice predicted in his last book *Contraception and Persecution* before he died in 2015), is almost never mentioned and almost totally neglected in the Church of Nice, as is every other violation of the Sixth and Ninth Commandments. It's telling that in a 2013 interview with David Gregory on NBC News' *Meet The Press*, Cdl. Dolan—when questioned about the Church's teaching on sexual morality—came back with the very revealing response that "in my almost thirty-seven years as a priest, rare would be the times that I preached about those issues."

In the context of the interview, Dolan was trying to say it was the media that was always bringing these issues up, not the Church. His Eminence is dead right, unfortunately. In another interview (Dolan seems to grant plenty of them), he told the *Wall Street Journal* in March 2012 that the US bishops and clergy (and he made a point of including himself in the pool of bishops) had gotten "gun-shy" about preaching the Church's teachings in these areas. Indeed, a person can sin by commission and omission.

The Church of Nice is leading souls to Hell by a double method—and just one is sufficient, but if Satan is anything, he is thorough and detail-oriented. The first method is by distorting the truth. The second is by *not* correcting error. It is devilish in its exactness. Not a stone is left unturned, nothing left to chance by the Father of Lies—and, of course, as Our Blessed Lord said quite plainly, the goal of his lies is murder, the eternal death of those who believe them or will not fight to stop their proliferation. These lies have destroyed Western civilization; they have brought an end to Christendom—Christendom being the social, economic, political, cultural system founded on Christianity. *That* is dead and gone. Christianity—meaning authentic Christianity, meaning the Holy Catholic Apostolic Church founded and secured on St. Peter—of course remains and always will, as Our Lord promised.

But the Catholic souls seeking to reestablish Catholic identity must realize that the enemy you battle, that we battle, is Satan, and the human beings who do his will whom you also fight are his agents and his tools as long as they remain in mortal sin. They are disciples of the Enemy. Just as Our Lord has His disciples, so, too, does the diabolical. And a great many of them are found in the Church of Nice, for there they have camouflage to carry on their deeds in secret. And most troubling—and therefore the point of which to be most aware—is that many of these souls know nothing of their contract with Hell.

Selling Their Souls

A person can slowly drift into danger without realizing it. But for that to happen, he must first have been cut off from his moorings. And this can happen to any one of us at any time. And in the order of spiritual warfare, it is those still moored to the Church with whom the diabolical is *most* concerned. While Satan certainly continues to keep unmoored souls in a state of confusion—to the extent they do not realize their pitiable conditions, lest they hear the voice of Our Lord through the storms of their lives—Satan reserves his most violent attacks for those still anchored to the Church. It is these on whom he focuses the greater share of his attention. And one of his most fruitful attacks has been to allow such souls to think themselves safe because they are moored to the Church. How many clerics have been damned in spite of occupying high offices in the Church? Bringing it down to the common level, how many religious education directors will face hellfire for improperly instructing souls entrusted to their care? How many pastors for allowing it? How many bishops for not assuring to the best of their ability this doesn't occur?

Yet this is commonplace in the Church of Nice; you could even say it is the very marrow in the bones of the Church of Nice. The entire edifice is built on never giving offense or saying anything to point out the horror of sin. And on this point, it needs to be made clear that sin is a horror in the sight of God. He hates sin. And He hates it with a revulsion the finite human mind cannot comprehend on its own. The level of hate, of enmity God has toward sin would make the universe quake if it were translated into a physical phenomenon. This is the great sin of the Church of Nice: to downplay sin and to make serious sin seem so impossible for humans to commit that souls tumble into Hell for lack of understanding. "My people are destroyed for lack of knowledge" (Hos. iv : 6).

Leaders and parishioners in the Church of Nice have sold their souls to the devil for comfort here on earth. The admonition of Pope Benedict comes to mind here: "The world offers you comfort, but you were not made for comfort. You were made for greatness."

In the Old Testament, God tells Ezekiel:

> If I say to the wicked, "You shall surely die," and you give him no warning, nor speak to warn the wicked from his wicked way, in order to save his life, that wicked man shall die in his iniquity; but his blood I will require at your hand. (Ezek. iii : 18)

He makes clear that if the prophet refuses to instruct the wicked, he will have their blood on his hands, but—and here is the frightening part—the wicked will still die in their iniquity. In other words, people do not get let "off the hook" because the leaders did not properly instruct them. The reason is because they still had the moral truth, the natural law implanted in their hearts, and were still bound to its precepts. God provides every soul with sufficient grace to be saved. Having good leaders only assists the person in doing right, which is of course a welcome assistance, but the absence of good leaders owing to wicked leaders does not secure Heaven for the souls in sin. What happens is the people die and are damned, and the leaders die as well, and their pains in Hell are increased owing to the blood on their hands.

This is paralyzing when you stop and consider the enormity of what is being proposed, of what the truth really is: wholesale damnation of the human race. It is almost too terrifying to contemplate, but it must be faced, for this is the only motivation that will sustain the authentic Catholic in his pursuit of reestablishing Catholic identity— love of souls. This is the single most important hallmark of Catholic identity—love of souls, nothing else.

To be a soul who completely and totally identifies himself with the Catholic Church means that soul is in complete union with Christ, since the Church is the mystical body of Christ here on earth. The overarching will of the Divinity in creating, the sole will of Christ, His sole reason for incarnating, accepting the most abject humility, His bowing to the terrors and agony in Gethsemane, the disgraces He endured before the Sanhedrin, the pain He shared with His Immaculate Mother during His passion, the Cross, the nails, the thorns, the whips, the betrayal of Judas, the desertion of His friends, the establishment of His Church, the institution of the sacraments, His willing imprisonment in the Blessed Sacrament—all of it was done out of the single motivation of *love of souls*. Since this is the sole motivation of God, it must be the sole motivation of those who cling to God. Love of souls is the only identity a Catholic needs, because from that single truth everything else flows. All sacrifices, insults, martyrdoms, joys, exhilarations, thoughts, prayers, actions—all of it will be lived out of the love for souls.

There is no greater charity than to strive to save a soul from the Enemy. Saint James concludes his letter thus: "[K]now that whoever brings back a sinner from the error of his way will save his soul from death and will cover a multitude of sins" (Jas. v : 20). What glory we can share in! See how good God is, that He has granted us a share in His fellowship. We little mortals are left speechless before the magnanimity of the Almighty, that He would deign to welcome us into His work of redemption. We must take up this cause and make it our life's work, whatever our circumstances or condition. And the only way to live a life in this fashion, the only way to challenge the Church of Nice, to stare Satan in the face and have him blink, is not only to be committed to the cause of souls as Our Blessed Lord is, but to "be perfect, as your heavenly Father is perfect" (Matt. v : 48). The way to end the crisis in the Church, to stop it dead in its tracks and reverse its diabolical effects, to reestablish authentic Catholic identity, is to be holy.

Chapter 21

A CHOSEN PEOPLE, A HOLY NATION:
Our Manifest Destiny

The diminution of Catholic identity is both owing to and perpetuates an ignorance of our dignity as Catholics. We have forgotten we have a sacred duty because of our noble status. This status has been a pure gift to us from our Heavenly Father, but having been given, we now possess it. We are a chosen people, holy to God, a royal priesthood, His own special possession. This sets us apart from the world. To be holy, in fact, means this very thing: to be set apart.

We are a royal priesthood, a chosen race, a holy nation, a people set apart. And for what precisely are we set apart? To save the world. Recall the words earlier of Pope St. Pius V about all the evil in the world being due to lukewarm Catholics. In that statement is the shining reality that Catholics who are holy, who live their faith with near-reckless abandon, have within our power sustained by the sacraments the ability to save the world. In fact, we have the commission to do this, the Divine Mandate.

Servant of God Fr. John Hardon once said, "Any Catholic who is not about the business of evangelization might never entertain a serious hope for the Beatific Vision." Stop for a moment and weigh the enormity of that proclamation. Without the desire and accompanying action to bring souls to Christ through His Holy Catholic Church, we will be damned. And this is fitting, for our nobility is rooted in the truth poured into us. And it is not given to us for merely our own sanctification and to remain a private affair. It is given to us to give to others.

Saint Francis de Sales poses the troubling thought that the surest way to Hell is to be a channel of grace—yes, a channel of grace. That is because a channel is merely that which something, like water, passes through without actually changing the channel. The channel is nothing more than a conduit. Judas was a channel of grace. Caiaphas was a channel of grace. Pontius Pilate was a channel of grace. Our redemption was secured in part through the fact that these men were channels of grace. But their actions were evil. God can and does bring good effects from evil actions ("O Happy Fault"), but that does not convert the evil choice into something good. The action remains evil in and of itself.

What St. Francis de Sales counsels us to be are *reservoirs*, not channels, of grace. Reservoirs fill up with grace, and then having reached capacity, spill over to others without losing any of the grace themselves. This is our plan of action, to be "full of grace" to whatever our capacity, and spill it over to others. We must recall when it comes to the divinely mandated duty to save souls, the first one we must save is our own. It is, after all, the only one we have full and complete control over. We must protect her, guard her, nourish her, guide her. She is the spouse of Christ, and we must each see her safely home. We must bring her to the gates of the wedding feast of the Lamb, properly attired in her wedding garment given to us at baptism. We must cherish this garment and treasure our soul. She came from the very hand of the Almighty at the moment we were conceived, and we must attend to her as the divine creation she is.

The way to holiness therefore always involves deep, intimate union with Our Blessed Lord through His Holy Catholic Bride. We are guardians of these nuptials; it is our life's calling, in fact. This means a constant and steady life of prayer. Prayer is the only thing that will not change from this life into the next, for the saved, at least. For the damned, what few prayers they may have once said will be turned into curses—everlasting curses against themselves, their companions in the society of the damned, their demonic masters. All that they ever knew, and all those they ever loved on this earth—all that comes to a total end in the eternal realm.

The elect in Heaven will celebrate that the damned are in Hell because it will reflect the justice of God and, therefore, evidence His glory. The damned are getting what they deserve. They could have experienced a different fate; they chose not to. They could have availed themselves of God's grace and mercy; they chose otherwise. As a result, earthly relationships that once existed between those eventually saved and those eventually damned will simply melt away and come to an end. Our Blessed Lord even intimates this when the Pharisees, in an effort to trip Him up, question Him about marriage in the next life. He says that "in the resurrection they neither marry nor are given in marriage" (Matt. xxii : 30). It is why the vows made at a wedding come to an end at death: "until death do us part."

The family relationship in Heaven will be that of Christ and His Bride, the Church Triumphant. All else will disappear. "Behold, I make all things new" (Rev. xxi : 5). Our relationships to one another will be in Christ. How exactly this means we will relate to one another in Heaven is not known. We do know that beholding God in the face will elevate us to a relationship with one another that right now is beyond comprehension. We will know Moses, David, St. Matthew, St. Peter. Our guardian angel, who is invisible to us now, will be totally realized by us then. Saint Michael will be for us a continual vision of the glory of God reflected in the first creature to defy Satan. We will see one another perfected, with none of the imperfections and effects of original sin still present as they are now with each of us. There will be no more tears, no more sadness or death. These are all things of the former world for the elect.

For the damned, these things will be their never-ending companions: the shame and regret symbolized by the worm that never dies always burrowing into them, bringing to mind the horror of their sins and the reality that they could have been saved; the waves of hopelessness and terror that will break on them continually as they live with the reality in the same never-changing eternal moment, frozen in the "now" that their lot has no end. The fire that is never quenched will be their home forever, torture at the hands of demons they'll be locked away with in their own world without end. From the moment these wretched souls came into existence, the demonic powers lusted for them to be under their everlasting control, because these human beings, for a brief moment in the world of time, had the opportunity to behold what they could never behold, to live as the demons never could have lived. This made the demonic powers insane with envy. Their own agonies increase every time a soul ascends to the celestial realm. They have no means to vent their rage except against the souls of those made in the image and likeness of the God they so detest. And for the souls of those humans who bear the mark of baptism, how much more do the demons concentrate their hatred on them! There in their fiery midst is an eternal reminder that some humans are indeed saved from their clutches.

And in a special note to priests and bishops: If the lay baptized receive the full measure of the demonic hatred spewed out toward those souls indelibly marked by the sign of the Cross, how much more intense will their hatred be toward those souls who daily brought God down from Heaven in the Mass to continue the work of salvation in time and space? As St. Teresa of Avila was shown in a vision, the hands of the priests who were damned burned more intensely than all the rest, owing to the oils of their ordination.

And bishops: Take care that you do all in your power to save every soul you can, lest you join wicked Judas, for although on a lesser scale of evil than he committed, you sell Our Blessed Lord for cheap gain and worldly praise each time you shrink back from your office and promote a lie, disguise the truth, or downplay the eternal realities. Your lot will be worst of all because not only did you call down God from Heaven, you multiplied the number of men who would do so as well every time you laid hands on an ordinand. In fact, you need to quake at the very real possibility of horrors that await you, if some of the very men you ordained are leading souls to Heaven while you are in Hell. The demonic rage at the sight of every soul that enters Heaven at the hands of a man you ordained to God will be exacted from you by the infernal powers. There will be no end to the terrors, pains, and tortures that will be inflicted on you for not cooperating with the will of God. You will be, literally, a marked man, and there will never be any hope of escape. All hope will be gone.

While we have it still within our power, we need to not merely try to be holy but rather to *be holy, be perfect.* We must cooperate with grace so we can become a reservoir of it for ourselves and for others.

Three closing points are worth bearing in mind. Grace is God giving us what we do not deserve. Mercy is God not giving us what we do deserve. Justice is God giving us what we do deserve. Pray for, live, and act in such a way that you may receive and cooperate with the grace of God so as to obtain His mercy. His justice is something too terrible to face. God love you.